D1217044

The Best of Debbie Bliss Children's Knits

The Best of Debbie Bliss Children's Knits

More than 60 patterns for fabulous clothes, accessories and toys

EBURY PRESS
LONDON

First published in 1998

1 3 5 7 9 10 8 6 4 2

Text and knitwear designs copyright © Debbie Bliss
1991, 1992 and 1993
Photography copyright © Sandra Lousada
1991, 1992 and 1993

Debbie Bliss has asserted her right to be
identified as the author of this work.

The knitwear designs in this book are copyright and
must not be knitted for resale.

All rights reserved. No part of this publication may be
reproduced, stored in a retrieval system, or transmitted
in any form or by any means, electronic, mechanical,
photocopying, recording or otherwise, without the prior
permission of the copyright owners.

First published in the United Kingdom in 1998
by Ebury Press
Random House, 20 Vauxhall Bridge Road,
London, SW1V 2SA

Random House Australia (Pty) Limited
20 Alfred Street, Milsons Point, Sydney
New South Wales 2061, Australia

Random House New Zealand Limited
18 Poland Road, Glenfield
Auckland 10, New Zealand

Random House South Africa (Pty) Limited
Endulini, 5a Jubilee Road,
Parktown 2193, South Africa

Random House UK Limited Reg. No. 954009

ISBN 0 09 185362 1

Photography by Sandra Lousada
Designed by Jerry Goldie Graphic Design
Styling by Marie Willey

Printed and bound in Italy by New Interlitho Italia S.p.a.
Milan

The material in this book has been previously published
in the following titles:

New Baby Knits
Kids' Knits for Heads, Hands and Toes
Farmyard Knits

Contents

Cardigan and Baby Blanket
SEE PAGE
64

Duck All-in-One

SEE PAGE

66

*Aran Sweater
with Triangle Welt
and Collar*

SEE PAGE
70

Garter Stitch Jacket with Hat and Hens

S E E P A G E
72

*Duck Sweater
and Pants*

SEE PAGE
75

*Bee Cardigan,
Bootees and Hat*
SEE PAGE
77

Striped Sweater with Zig Zag Collar and Bootees

SEE PAGE
78

Fair Isle Cardigan with Beret
SEE PAGE
79

Fair Isle Sweater with Hat
SEE PAGE
81

Farm Animals
Slippers
SEE PAGE
83

Nursery Sweater

SEE PAGE
73

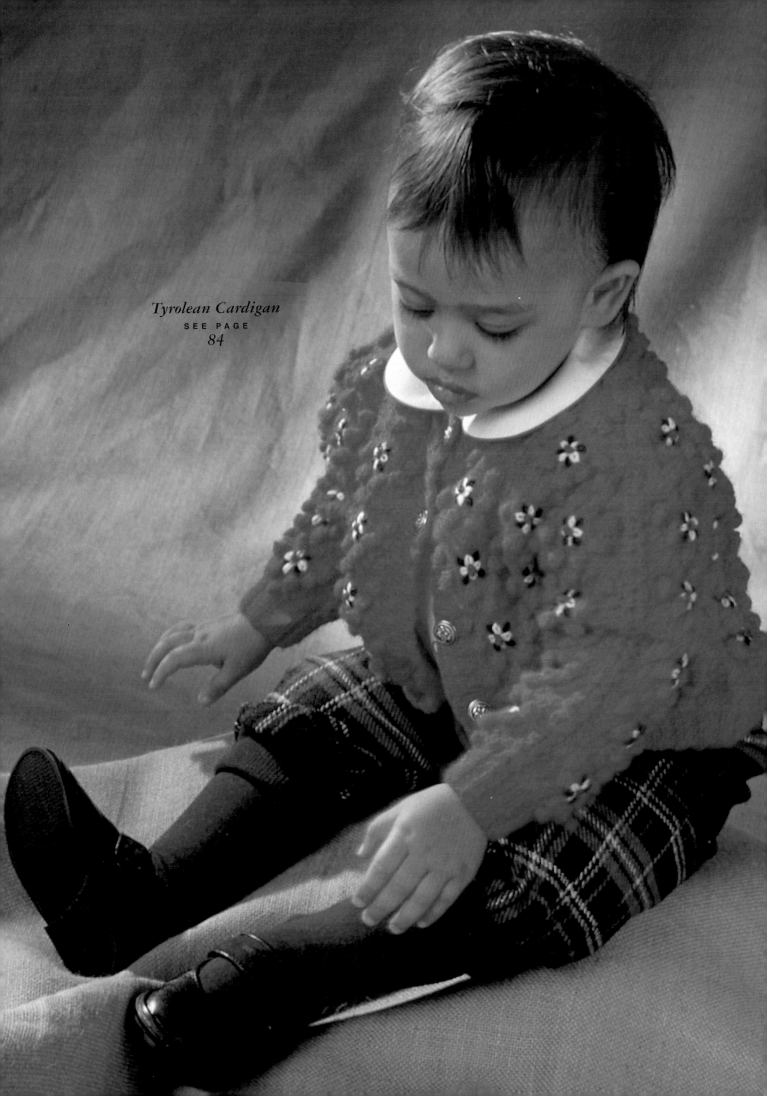

Tyrolean Cardigan
SEE PAGE
84

Scandinavian Cardigan, Hat and Boots

SEE PAGE
85

Long Line Fair Isle
Sweater with Pockets
and Socks
SEE PAGE
87

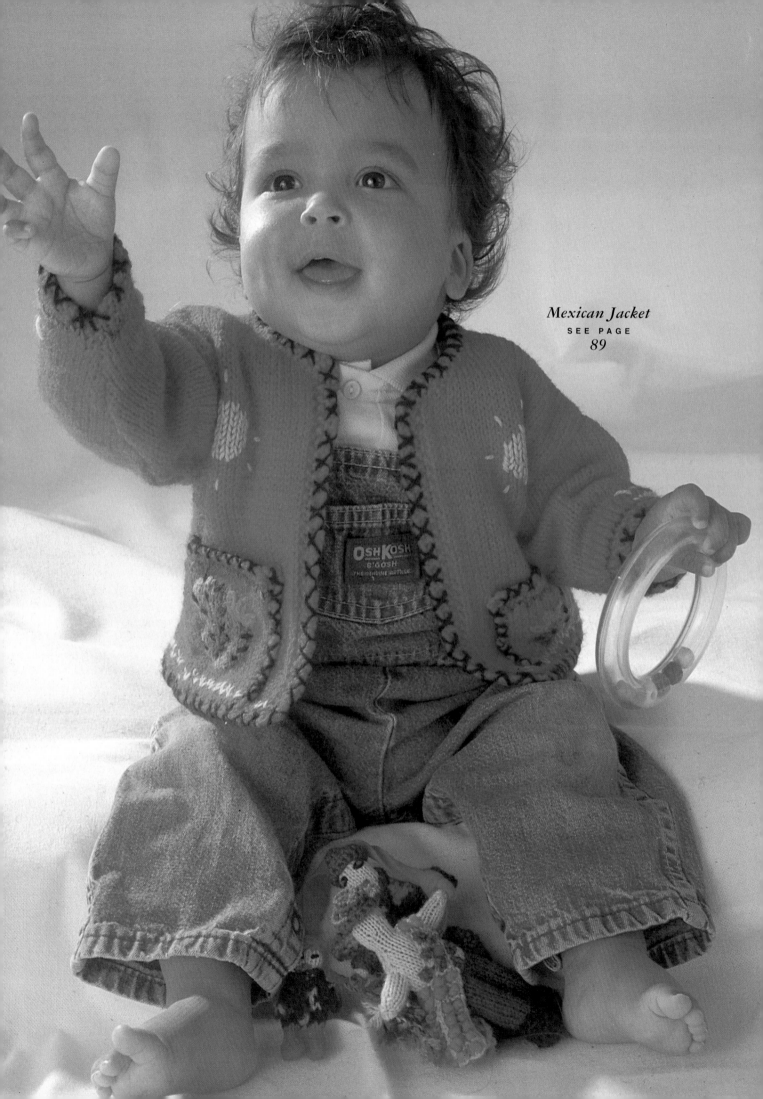

Mexican Jacket
SEE PAGE
89

*Hooded
Fair Isle Jacket*
SEE PAGE
91

*Aran Sweater
with Farmyard
Panel*
SEE PAGE
92

Cotton Smock
SEE PAGE
93

Cable Sweater with Chicken Panel

SEE PAGE
95

Cow Sweater
SEE PAGE
97

Classic Jacket

SEE PAGE
98

Hen and Chick
Cardigan
SEE PAGE
99

Farmyard Picture Book Sweater

SEE PAGE
100

Patchwork Sweater
SEE PAGE
102

Knitted Toys
SEE PAGE
103

Farmyard Jacket

SEE PAGE
107

Duck and Sheep
Fair Isle Cardigan
SEE PAGE
109

Double Moss Stitch and Cable Jacket
SEE PAGE
110

Mexican Sweater
SEE PAGE
111

Wheatsheaf
Sweater
SEE PAGE
113

Aran Sweater Dress
SEE PAGE
115

*Aran Coat
with Large Collar*
SEE PAGE
116

Tunic with Pig Motif
SEE PAGE
118

Navajo Jacket

SEE PAGE
119

*Fisherman's Rib
Cardigan with
Saddle Shoulders*

SEE PAGE
121

*Fisherman's Rib
Sweater with Saddle
Shoulders*

SEE PAGE
122

Hearts and Hens Sweater

SEE PAGE

122

Sampler Sweater
SEE PAGE
124

Milk-Maid Sweater
SEE PAGE
125

Alphabet Sweater
SEE PAGE
126

*Striped
"Wee Willie Winkie"
Hat, Socks and
Teddy Bear*

SEE PAGE
128

Teddy Bear Hood,
Mittens and Bootees
SEE PAGE
129

*Mouse Hat
and Bootees*
SEE PAGE
131

*Multi-coloured Hat
and Socks*
SEE PAGE
132

Crown Hat
SEE PAGE
130

*Nursery Hat
and Shoes*
SEE PAGE
133

Inca Hat and Socks
SEE PAGE
135

Ladybird Hat
and Slippers
SEE PAGE
136

Reindeer Hat, Scarf,
Mittens and Socks
SEE PAGE
137

Jester Hat and Gloves

SEE PAGE

138

*Crochet Bonnet and
Lace-trimmed Hat*

SEE PAGE
139

African Style Hat
SEE PAGE
142

Aran Scarf and
Fingerless Gloves
SEE PAGE
140

Fair Isle Beret and Gloves

SEE PAGE
142

Basic Information

NOTES

Figures for larger sizes are given in ( ) brackets. Where only one figure appears, this applies to all sizes.

Work figures given in [ ] the number of times stated afterwards.

Where 0 appears no stitches or rows are worked for this size.

YARNS

All amounts are based on average requirements and should therefore be regarded as approximate. Addresses for Rowan Yarns are given on page 144. If, however, you cannot find the yarn specified, you can substitute a yarn of similar weight and type. The descriptions of the various Rowan and Jaeger yarns are meant as a guide to the yarn weight and type (i.e. cotton, wool, et cetera). Remember that the description of the yarn weight is only a guide and you should test a yarn first to see if it will achieve the correct tensions (gauge).

The amount of substitute yarn needed is determined by the number of metres (yards) required rather than by the number of grammes (ounces). If you are unsure when choosing a suitable substitute, ask the assistant at your yarn shop to assist you.

Description of Rowan Yarns

Cotton Glace - a lightweight cotton yarn (100% cotton) approx 112m (123yd) per 50g (1¾oz) ball

Designer DK - a double knitting (US worsted) weight yarn (100% pure new wool) approx 115m (125yd) per 50g 1¾oz) ball

Handknit DK Cotton - a medium weight cotton yarn (100% cotton) approx 85m (90yd) per 50g (1¼oz) ball

Rowan 4 ply Cotton - a 4 ply yarn (100% cotton) approx 170m (220yd) per 50g (1¾oz) ball

Magpie Aran - a medium weight yarn (100% pure new wool) approx 150m (164yd) per 100g (3¾oz) hank

Description of Jaeger Yarns

Matchmaker Merino 4 ply - a 4 ply yarn (100% pure new wool) approx 183m (198yd) per 50g (1¾oz) ball

Baby Merino 4 ply - a 4 ply yarn (100% pure new wool) approx 183m (198yd) per 50g (1¼oz) ball

TENSION

Tension is the number of stitches and rows per centimetre (inch) that should be obtained on given needles, yarn and stitch pattern. To check your tension, knit a sample at least 12.5 x 12.5cm (5in) square, using the same yarn, needles and stitch pattern as those to be used for main work. Smooth out the finished sample on a flat surface but do not stretch it. With a ruler, mark out a 10cm (4in) square with pins. Count the number of stitches and rows between pins. If the number of stitches and rows is greater than specified try again using larger needles; if less use smaller needles.

Tension is not as crucial when knitting toys as it would be for other knitted garments. A tighter or looser tension will produce a smaller or larger toy than that shown in the photograph, and a loose tension will produce a more open fabric through which the stuffing will show or come through.

STUFFING

Overstuffing stretches the fabric so that the stuffing shows through and understuffing makes the toy too floppy. Watch out for 'lumps' when stuffing. Tear the edges of each piece of stuffing as you go along so that the edges blend in when inserted.

SAFETY

It is very important that a toy is suitable for the age of the child for whom it is intended. Toys given to children under 3 years of age should not have any added extras such as buttons or eyes which could become loose. Make sure that any toys given to the very young have all limbs and any accessories securely sewn in place. Washable stuffing, which conforms to safety standards, should always be used and yarns should be either 100% wool or 100% cotton.

Abbreviations

alt=alternate
beg=begin(ning)
cont=continue
dec=decreas(e)ing
foll=following
inc=increas(e)ing
k=knit
m1=make one by picking up loop lying between st just worked and next st and work into the back of it
patt=pattern
p=purl
psso=pass slipped stitch over
rem=remain(ing)
rep=repeat
sl=slip
skpo=slip 1, k1, pass slipped st over
st(s)=stitch(es)
st st=stocking stitch
tbl=through back of loop(s)
tog=together
yb=yarn back
yf=yarn forward
yon=yarn over needle
yrn=yarn round needle

Cardigan and Baby Blanket

See Page
6

MEASUREMENTS
Cardigan
To fit age   **4–9 Months**

Actual chest measurement	60	**cm**
	23½	**in**
Length	28	**cm**
	11	**in**
Sleeve seam	18	**cm**
	7	**in**

Baby blanket 54 cm x 69 cm/21¼ in x 27 in

MATERIALS
Cardigan 4x50 g balls of Rowan DK
Handknit Cotton in Cream (MC).
1x50 g ball of same in each of Brown,
Red, Blue and Yellow.
Baby Blanket 7x50 g balls of Rowan DK
Handknit Cotton in Cream (MC).
1x50 g ball of same in each of Brown,
Red, Blue and Yellow.

Pair of 4 mm (No 8/US 5) knitting
needles.
Medium size crochet hook.
4 buttons for Cardigan.

TENSION
20 sts and 28 rows to 10 cm/4 in square
over st st on 4 mm (No 8/US 5) needles.

ABBREVIATIONS
Ch = chain; **dc** = double crochet; **MB** =
make bobble as follows: [K1, P1, K1, P1]
all in next st, turn, P4, turn, K4, turn, [P2
tog] twice, turn, K2 tog; **ss** = slip stitch;
tr = treble.
Also see page 63.

NOTE
Read Charts from right to left on right
side rows and from left to right on wrong
side rows. When working motifs, use
separate lengths of contrast yarns for
each coloured area and twist yarns
together on wrong side when changing
colour to avoid holes.

Cardigan

BACK
With 4 mm (No 8/US 5) needles and MC,
cast on 60 sts. Beg with a K row, work in
st st and patt from Chart 1 until 76th row
of Chart 1 has been worked.
Shape Shoulders
Cont in MC, cast off 10 sts at beg of next
2 rows and 9 sts at beg of foll 2 rows.
Cast off rem 22 sts.

LEFT FRONT
With 4 mm (No 8/US 5) needles and MC,
cast on 29 sts.
Beg with a K row, work in st st and patt
from Chart 1 until 50th row of Chart 1 has
been worked.
Shape Front
Cont working from Chart 1, dec one st at
front edge on next row and every foll 3rd
row until 19 sts rem. Cont straight until
76th row of Chart 1 has been worked.
Shape Shoulder
Cont in MC, cast off 10 sts at beg of next
row. Work 1 row. Cast off rem 9 sts.

RIGHT FRONT
Work as given for Left Front, reversing
shoulder shaping.

SLEEVES
With 4 mm (No 8/US 5) needles and MC,
cast on 30 sts.
Beg with a K row, work in st st and patt
from Chart 1, inc one st at each end of

3rd row and every foll 4th row until there
are 50 sts, working inc sts into patt. Cont
straight until 48th row of Chart 1 has been
worked. Cast off.

TO MAKE UP
Join shoulder seams. Sew on sleeves,
placing centre of sleeves to shoulder
seams. Join side and sleeve seams.
Crochet Edging
With crochet hook, MC, right side facing
and beg at Right Front side seam, work 1
round of dc (the number of dc should be
divisible by 3) along cast on edge of Right
Front, up Right Front, across back neck,
down Left Front, along cast on edge of
Left Front and Back, working 3 dc in
corners, ss in first dc.
Next round [2 tr in same dc as ss, miss 2
dc, ss in next dc] to end, making 4
buttonhole loops along straight edge of
Right Front by working 3 ch, miss 2 dc, ss
in next dc. Fasten off.
Work crochet edging along cast on edge
of sleeves. Sew on buttons.
With Yellow, embroider cockerels' beaks
and with Brown outline sheep with short
straight stitches (see diagram page 65).

Baby Blanket

BOBBLE MOTIF – worked over
19 sts.
1st row (right side) K19.
2nd row P19.

3rd and 4th rows Work 1st and 2nd rows.
5th row K9, MB, K9.
6th row P19.
7th and 8th rows As 1st and 2nd rows.
9th row K6, MB, K5, MB, K6.
10th to 12th rows Work 6th to 8th rows.
13th row K3, MB, K11, MB, K3.
14th to 20th rows Work 6th to 12th rows.
21st row As 5th row.
22nd row P19.

TO MAKE
With 4 mm (No 8/US 5) needles and MC,
cast on 107 sts. K 4 rows.
Work in patt as follows:
1st row (right side) K2MC, K across 1st
row of Chart 2, with MC, K2, work 1st row
of bobble motif, K2, K across 1st row of
Chart 3, with MC, K2, work 1st row of
bobble motif, K2, K across 1st row of
Chart 4, K2MC.
2nd row K2MC, P across 2nd row of
Chart 4, with MC, K2, work 2nd row of
bobble motif, K2, P across 2nd row of
Chart 3, with MC, K2, work 2nd row of
bobble motif, K2, P across 2nd row of
Chart 2, K2MC.
3rd to 22nd rows Rep last 2 rows 10 times
more, but working 3rd to 22nd rows of
Charts and bobble motifs.
23rd to 26th rows With MC, K.
27th row With MC, K2, work 1st row of
bobble motif, K2, K across 1st row of
Chart 5, with MC, K2, work 1st row of
bobble motif, K2, K across 1st row of
Chart 2, with MC, K2, work 1st row of
bobble motif, K2.
28th row With MC, K2, work 2nd row of
bobble motif, K2, P across 2nd row of
Chart 2, with MC, K2, work 2nd row of
bobble motif, K2, P across 2nd row of
Chart 5, with MC, K2, work 2nd row of
bobble motif, K2.
29th to 48th rows Work 3rd to 22nd rows.
49th to 52nd rows With MC, K.
53rd to 78th rows Work 1st to 26th rows,
but working Chart 6 instead of Chart 2,
Chart 7 instead of Chart 3 and Chart 8
instead of Chart 4.
79th to 104th rows Work 27th to 52nd
rows, but working Chart 4 instead of Chart
5 and Chart 3 instead of Chart 2.
105th to 130th rows Work 1st to 26th
rows, but working Chart 9 instead of Chart
3 and Chart 7 instead of Chart 4.
131st to 156th rows Work 27th to 52nd
rows, but working Chart 4 instead of
Chart 2.
157th to 182nd rows Work 1st to 26th
rows, but working Chart 6 instead of Chart
2, Chart 2 instead of Chart 3 and Chart 10
instead of Chart 4.
183rd to 208th rows Work 27th to 52nd
rows, but working Chart 7 instead of Chart
5 and Chart 3 instead of Chart 2.
Cast off.

Work crochet edging around four sides as given for Cardigan. With Yellow, embroider cockerels' beaks and with Brown, outline sheep with short straight stitches (see diagram this page).

CHART 1

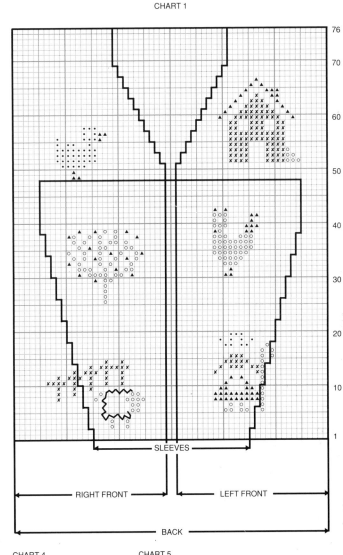

SLEEVES

RIGHT FRONT | LEFT FRONT

BACK

KEY

☐ = Cream   ○ = Brown   ▲ = Red

✗ = Blue   • = Yellow

〜〜〜 = Short straight stitches

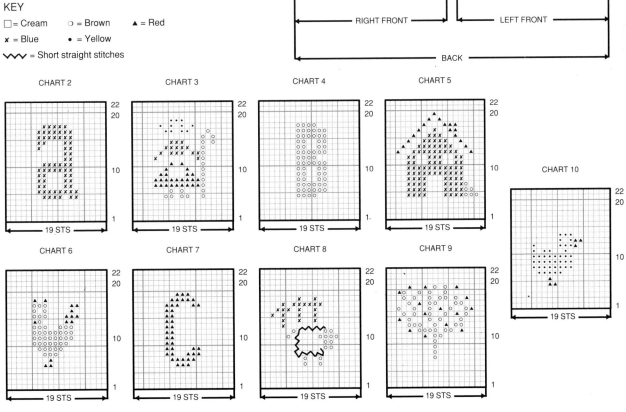

CHART 2   CHART 3   CHART 4   CHART 5

22 20 10 1 — 19 STS

CHART 10

22 20 10 1 — 19 STS

CHART 6   CHART 7   CHART 8   CHART 9

Duck All-in-One

See Page
7

MEASUREMENTS

To fit age	0–3	3–6	6–9	Months
Actual chest measurement	53	56	59	cm
	21	22	23¼	in
Length from beginning	44	48	52	cm
of leg cuff to back neck	17½	19	20½	in
Inside leg seam	9	11	13	cm
	3½	4¼	5	in
Sleeve seam	14	16	18	cm
	5½	6¼	7	in

MATERIALS
6(7:7) 50 g balls of Rowan Designer DK Wool in Cream (MC).
1(2:2) 50 g balls of same in Gold (A).
Oddment of Black for embroidery.
Pair each of 3¼mm (No 10/US 3) and 4 mm (No 8/US 5) knitting needles.
6 buttons. Piece of thin foam.

TENSION
24 sts and 32 rows to 10 cm/4 in square over st st on 4 mm (No 8/US 5) needles.

ABBREVIATIONS
See page 63.

LEFT FOOT
Upper Foot – knitted sideways.
With 4 mm (No 8/US 5) needles and A, cast on 20(21:22) sts.
Beg with a K row, work 10(12:14) rows in st st.
** Make tucks as follows:
1st to 4th rows Work 4 rows in st st.
5th row [K next st tog with corresponding st 4 rows below] to end.
6th row P.
7th row K17(18:19), turn.
8th row and 3 foll alt rows Sl 1, P to end.
9th row K14(15:15), turn.
11th row K11, turn.
13th row K7, turn.
15th row K3, turn.
16th row Sl 1, P to end.
Rep these 16 rows once more, then work 1st to 6th rows again. **
Work a further 38(42:46) rows in st st.
Cast off.
Sole
With right side of work facing, 4 mm (No 8/US 5) needles and A, pick up and K6(7:8) sts along lower (wider) edge of upper foot to centre of first tuck, [pick up and K10 sts to centre of next tuck] twice, pick up and K31(33:35) sts to cast off edge. 57(60:63) sts.
Beg with a P row, work 5 rows in st st.
Next row [K next st tog with corresponding st 5 rows below] to end.
Dec row P0(2:2), [P8(8:6), P2 tog] 3(3:4) times, [P2, P2 tog] 6(7:7) times, P3(0:1). 48(50:52) sts.
Shape Sole
1st row [K8(8:9), K2 tog tbl, K5, K2 tog,
K7(8:8)] twice.
2nd row and 2 foll alt rows P.
3rd row [K8(8:9), K2 tog tbl, K3, K2 tog, K7(8:8)]twice.
5th row [K8(8:9), K2 tog tbl, K1, K2 tog, K7(8:8)] twice.
7th row [K8(8:9), sl 1, K2 tog, psso, K7(8:8)] twice.
Cast off purlwise.

LEFT LEG
*** With right side of work facing, 3¼mm (No 10/US 3) needles and MC, pick up and K43(45:47) sts along top edge of foot.
1st row K1, [P1, K1] to end.
2nd row P1, [K1, P1] to end.
Rep last 2 rows twice more.
Inc row [Rib 1, m1] 5 times, [rib 1, m1, rib 2, m1] to last 5(7:6) sts, [rib 1, m1] 4(5:5) times, rib 1(2:1). 74(77:81) sts.
Change to 4 mm (No 8/US 5) needles.
Beg with a K row, work in st st until Leg measures 9(11:13) cm/3½(4¼:5) in from beg of rib, ending with a P row.
Shape Crotch
Cast off 3 sts at beg of next 2 rows. Dec one st at beg of next 4 rows. 64(67:71) sts. *** Leave these sts on a spare needle.

RIGHT FOOT
Upper Foot – knitted sideways.
With 4 mm (No 8/US 5) needles and A, cast on 20(21:22) sts.
Beg with a K row, work 38(42:46) rows in st st.
Work as for Upper Foot of Left Foot from ** to **.
Work a further 10(12:14) rows in st st.

Cast off.
Sole
With right side of work facing, 4 mm (No 8/US 5) needles and A, pick up and K31(33:35) sts along lower (wider) edge of upper foot to centre of first tuck, [pick up and K10 sts to centre of next tuck] twice, pick up and K6(7:8) sts to cast off edge. 57(60:63) sts.
Beg with a P row, work 5 rows in st st.
Next row [K next st tog with corresponding st 5 rows below] to end.
Dec row P3(0:1), [P2 tog, P2] 6(7:7) times, [P2 tog, P8(8:6)] 3(3:4) times, P0(2:2). 48(50:52) sts.
Shape Sole
1st row [K7(8:8), K2 tog tbl, K5, K2 tog, K8(8:9)] twice.
2nd row and 2 foll alt rows P.
3rd row [K7(8:8), K2 tog tbl, K3, K2 tog, K8(8:9)] twice.
5th row [K7(8:8), K2 tog tbl, K1, K2 tog, K8(8:9)] twice.
7th row [K7(8:8), sl 1, K2 tog, psso, K8(8:9)] twice.
Cast off purlwise.

RIGHT LEG
Work as for Left Leg from *** to ***

MAIN PART
Next row (right side) K across Right Leg sts then Left Leg sts.128(134:142) sts.
Work 13 rows straight.
Shape Front Opening
Cast off 3 sts at beg of next 2 rows. 122(128:136) sts.
Cont straight until work measures 30(33:36) cm/12(13:14¼) in from beg of rib, ending with a P row.
Divide for Right Front
Next row K29(31:33) sts, turn.
Work on this set of sts only. Cont in st st for a further 9(10:11) cm/3½(4:4¼) in, ending at front edge.
Shape Neck
Cast off 3 sts at beg of next row. Dec one st at neck edge on every row until 21(22:23) sts rem. Cont straight until armhole measures 14(15:16) cm/5½(6:6¼) in, ending at armhole edge.
Shape Shoulder
Cast off 10(11:11) sts at beg of next row. Work 1 row. Cast off rem 11(11:12) sts.
Divide for Back
With right side facing, rejoin yarn to rem sts and K64(66:70) sts, turn.
Work on this set of sts only. Cont in st st until Back matches Right Front to shoulder shaping, ending with a P row.
Shape Shoulders
Cast off 10(11:11) sts at beg of next 2 rows and 11(11:12) sts at beg of foll 2 rows. Leave rem 22(22:24) sts on a holder.

Left Front

With right side facing, rejoin yarn to rem sts and K to end. Complete to match Right Front.

SLEEVES

With 3¼-mm (No 10/US 3) needles and MC, cast on 34(36:38) sts.
Work 3 cm/1¼-in in K1, P1 rib.
Inc row Rib 0(1:2), [inc in next st, rib 2] 11 times, inc in next st, rib 0(1:2). 46(48:50) sts.
Change to 4 mm (No 8/US 5) needles.
Beg with a K row, work in st st, inc one st at each end of every 3rd row until there are 66(70:76) sts. Cont straight until Sleeve measures 14(16:18) cm/5½(6¼:7) in from beg, ending with a P row. Cast off.

NECKBAND AND HOOD

Join shoulder seams.
With right side of work facing, 3¼-mm (No 10/US 3) needles and MC, pick up and K 19(20:21) sts up right front neck, K across back neck sts, inc one st at centre, pick up and K19(20:21) sts down left front neck. 61(63:67) sts.
1st row P1, [K1, P1] to end.
2nd row K1, [P1, K1] to end.
Rep last 2 rows twice more.
Inc row Rib 5 and slip these sts onto a safety pin, rib 5(5:4), inc in next st, [rib 9(6:7), inc in next st] 4(6:6) times, rib

5(5:4), slip last 5 sts onto a safety pin. 56(60:64) sts.
Change to 4 mm (No 8/US 5) needles.
Beg with a K row, work in st st for 12(14:16) cm/4¾(5½:6¼) in for hood, ending with a P row.
Shape Top
Next row K37(39:41) sts, K2 tog tbl, turn.
Next row Sl 1, P18, P2 tog, turn.
Next row Sl 1, K18, K2 tog tbl, turn.
Rep last 2 rows until all sts are worked off on either side of centre sts.
Leave rem 20 sts on a holder.

HOOD EDGING

With right side of work facing, 3¼-mm (No 10/US 3) needles and MC, rib across 5 sts from right side of hood, pick up and K 26(29:32) sts up right side of hood, K across centre sts, dec one st, pick up and K 26(29:32) sts down left side of hood, then rib 5 sts from safety pin. 81(87:93) sts. Rib 7 rows. Cast off in rib.

BUTTONHOLE BAND

With right side of work facing, 3¼-mm (No 10/US 3) needles and MC, pick up and K 77(83:89) sts evenly along right side of front opening to top of hood edging.
Work 3 rows in rib as on Neckband.
1st buttonhole row Rib 7(8:9), [cast off 2, rib 10(11:12) sts more] 5 times, cast off 2, rib to end.

2nd buttonhole row Rib to end, casting on 2 sts over those cast off in previous row.
Rib 4 rows. Cast off in rib.

BUTTON BAND

Work to match Buttonhole Band omitting buttonholes.

BEAK (make 2)

With 4 mm (No 8/US 5) needles and A, cast on 18 sts.
Beg with a P row, work in st st, inc one st at each end of 2nd row and 2 foll rows. 24 sts. Work 15 rows straight. Cast off.

TO MAKE UP

Join sole, foot and leg seams, then back crotch seam. Join front crotch and centre seam to front opening. Overlap buttonhole band over button band and catch down at base of opening. Sew in sleeves, placing centre of sleeves to shoulder seams. Join sleeve seams. With right side of beak pieces together, join seam all round beg and ending 3 cm/1¼-in from cast off edges. Turn to right side. Cut a piece of foam to fit beak and place inside. Place top open end of beak over hood edging at centre and bottom end and foam under the edging and slip stitch in place. With Black, embroider eyes. Sew on buttons.

Cow All-in-One

See Page 8

MEASUREMENTS To fit age	0–3	3–6	6–9	Months
Actual chest measurement	53	56	59	cm
	21	22	23¼	in
Length from beginning of leg cuff to centre back neck	44	48	52	cm
	17¼	19	20½	in
Inside leg seam	9	11	13	cm
	3½	4¼	5	in
Sleeve seam	14	16	18	cm
	5½	6¼	7	in

TENSION
22 sts and 44 rows to 10 cm/4 in square over garter st (every row K) on 4 mm (No 8/US 5) needles.

ABBREVIATIONS
See page 63.

NOTE
Read Charts from right to left on right side rows and from left to right on wrong side rows. When working in pattern, use separate small balls of yarn for each coloured area and twist yarns together on wrong side when changing colour to avoid holes.

MATERIALS
5(6:6) 50 g balls of Rowan Designer DK Wool in Cream (MC).
3(3:3) 50 g balls of same in Black (A).
Small amount of same in Brown.
Pair each of 3¼ mm (No 10/US 3) and 4 mm (No 8/US 5) knitting needles.
6 large and 4 small matching buttons.

LEFT FOOT

With 4 mm (No 8/US 5) needles and A, cast on 32(34:36) sts.
1st row and 4 foll alt rows (right side) K.
2nd row [K13(14:15), m1, K1, m1, K2] twice.
4th row [K13(14:15), m1, K3, m1, K2] twice.
6th row [K13(14:15), m1, K5, m1, K2] twice.
8th row [K13(14:15), m1, K7, m1, K2] twice.
10th row [K13(14:15), m1, K9, m1, K2] twice. 52(54:56) sts.
11th to 15th rows K.

16th row K13(14:15), K2 tog tbl, K7, K2 tog, K to end.
17th to 19th rows K.
20th row K13(14:15), K2 tog tbl, K5, K2 tog, K to end.
21st to 23rd rows K.
24th row K13(14:15), K2 tog tbl, K3, K2 tog, K to end.
25th row and 4 foll alt rows K.
26th row K12(13:14), K2 tog, K3, K2 tog tbl, K to end.
28th row K11(12:13), K2 tog, K3, K2 tog tbl, K to end.
30th row K10(11:12), K2 tog, K3, K2 tog tbl, K to end.
32nd row K9(10:11), K2 tog, K3, K2 tog tbl, K to end.
34th row K8(9:10), K2 tog, K3, K2 tog tbl, K to end. 36(38:40) sts.

LEFT LEG

** Change to MC and K 1 row.
Change to 3¼mm (No 10/US 3) needles.
Next row (wrong side) *[K1, P1] twice, [K1, P1] all in next st; rep from * to last 1(3:5) sts, [K1, P1] 0(1:2) times, K1. 43(45:47) sts.
Next row P1, [K1, P1] to end.
Next row K1, [P1, K1] to end.
Work a further 3 rows in rib.
Next row Rib 3(3:2), [m1, rib 1, m1, rib 2] 13(13:14) times, [m1, rib 2] 0(1:1) time, rib 1. 69(72:76) sts.
Change to 4 mm (No 8/US 5) needles. **
Cont in garter st, work 8(16:24) rows.
Place Chart 1 as follows:
Next row (right side) K25(26:28)MC, K across 1st row of Chart 1, K25(27:29)MC.
Next row K25(27:29)MC, K across 2nd row of Chart 1, K25(26:28)MC.
Work a further 10 rows as set.
Place Chart 2 as follows:
Next row K11(12:14)MC, K across 1st row of Chart 2, patt to end.
Next row Patt to last 23(24:26) sts, K across 2nd row of Chart 2, K11(12:14)MC.
Work a further 14 rows as set.
Shape Crotch
Keeping patt correct, cast off 3 sts at beg of next 2 rows. Dec one st at beg of next 4 rows, working sts in MC when Chart 2 has been completed.
Leave rem 59(62:66) sts on a holder.

RIGHT FOOT

With 4 mm (No 8/US 5) needles and A, cast on 32(34:36) sts.
1st row and 4 foll alt rows (right side) K.
2nd row [K2, m1, K1, m1, K13(14:15)] twice.
4th row [K2, m1, K3, m1, K13(14:15)] twice.
6th row [K2, m1, K5, m1, K13(14:15)] twice.
8th row [K2, m1, K7, m1, K13(14:15)] twice.
10th row [K2, m1, K9, m1, K13(14:15)] twice. 52(54:56) sts.
11th to 15th rows K.
16th row K28(29:30), K2 tog tbl, K7, K2 tog, K to end.

17th to 19th rows K.
20th row K28(29:30), K2 tog tbl, K5, K2 tog, K to end.
21st to 23rd rows K.
24th row K28(29:30), K2 tog tbl, K3, K2 tog, K to end.
25th row and 4 foll alt rows K.
26th row K27(28:29), K2 tog, K3, K2 tog tbl, K to end.
28th row K26(27:28), K2 tog, K3, K2 tog tbl, K to end.
30th row K25(26:27), K2 tog, K3, K2 tog tbl, K to end.
32nd row K24(25:26), K2 tog, K3, K2 tog tbl, K to end.
34th row K23(24:25), K2 tog, K3, K2 tog tbl, K to end. 36(38:40) sts.

RIGHT LEG

Work as Left Leg from ** to **. Cont in garter st, work 16(24:32) rows.
Place Chart 3 as follows:
Next row (right side) K14(16:18)MC, K across 1st row of Chart 3, K19(20:22)MC.
Next row K19(20:22)MC, K across 2nd row of Chart 3, K14(16:18)MC.
Work a further 18 rows as set.
Shape Crotch
Cast off 3 sts at beg of next 2 rows. Dec one st at beg of next 4 rows. 59(62:66) sts.

BODY

Next row Patt across Right Leg sts, then Left Leg sts. 118(124:132) sts.
Work a further 13 rows, working sts in MC when Chart 1 has been completed.
Shape Front Opening
Cast off 3 sts at beg of next 2 rows. 112(118:126) sts.
Patt 30(32:34) rows.
Place Chart 4 as follows:
Next row Patt to last 25(27:29) sts, K across 1st row of Chart 4, K5(7:9)MC.
Next row K5(7:9)MC, K across 2nd row of Chart 4, patt to end.
Work a further 18 rows as set.
Place Chart 5 as follows:
Next row Patt 54(56:58), K across 1st row of Chart 5, patt to end.
Next row Patt 34(38:44), K across 2nd row of Chart 5, patt to end.
Cont as set until work measures 30(33:36) cm/11¾(13:14) in from beg of rib, working sts in MC when Chart 3 has been completed and ending with a wrong side row.
Right Front
Next row K26(28:30), turn.
Work on this set of sts only. Cont straight for a further 9(10:11) cm/3¾(4:4½) in, ending with a wrong side row.
Shape Neck
Cast off 3 sts at beg of next row. Dec one st at neck edge on every row until 19(20:21) sts rem. Cont straight until work measures 44(48:52) cm/17¼(19:20⅜) in from beg of rib, ending with a right side row.
Shape Shoulder
Cast off 10(10:11) sts at beg of next row. K 1 row. Cast off rem 9(10:10) sts.
Back
With right side facing, rejoin yarn to rem

sts and patt 60(62:66) sts, turn.
Work on this set of sts only. Cont straight until Back matches Right Front to shoulder shaping, working sts in MC when Chart 5 has been completed and ending with a wrong side row.
Shape Shoulders
Cast off 10(10:11) sts at beg of next 2 rows and 9(10:10) sts at beg of foll 2 rows. Leave rem 22(22:24) sts on a holder.
Left Front
With right side facing, rejoin yarn to rem 26(28:30) sts and patt to end.
Complete to match Right Front, working sts in MC when Chart 4 has been completed and reversing shapings.

RIGHT MITTEN

*** With 4 mm (No 8/US 5) needles and A, cast on 16 sts.
1st row and 2(3:3) foll alt rows (wrong side) K.
2nd row [K1, m1, K6, m1, K1] twice.
4th row [K1, m1, K8, m1, K1] twice.
6th row [K1, m1, K10, m1, K1] twice.
2nd and 3rd sizes only
8th row [K1, m1, K12, m1, K1] twice.
All sizes
K 3 rows.
Next row K1, m1, K12(16:14), [m1, K2] 1(0:1) time, m1, K12(15:14), [m1, K1] 1(0:1) time. 32(34:36) sts.
K25(29:33) rows. Change to MC and K 1 row. ***
Change to 3¼mm (No 10/US 3) needles.
Next row Cast on 8(9:9) sts, K0(0:1), [P1, K1] to last 0(1:0) st, P0(1:0).
Next row K0(1:0), [P1, K1] 8(8:9) times, turn.
Work on this set of sts only. **** Rib 1 row.
1st buttonhole row Rib 3, cast off 1, rib to last 4 sts, cast off 1, rib to end.
2nd buttonhole row Rib 3, cast on 1, rib to last 3 sts, cast on 1, rib 3.
Rib 2 rows. Cast off in rib. ****

RIGHT SLEEVE

With 3¼mm (No 10/US 3) needles and right side facing, rejoin MC yarn to rem sts, cast on 8(8:9) sts, K0(0:1), [P1, K1] to last 0(0:1) st, P0(0:1). 32(34:36) sts.
Rib 4 rows.
Next row (wrong side) Rib 3(3:4), m1, [rib 5(4:3), m1] to last 4(3:5) sts, rib to end. 38(42:46) sts.
Change to 4 mm (No 8/US 5) needles.
Cont in garter st, work 10(14:18) rows, inc one st at each end of 3(3:4) foll 3rd (4th: 4th) rows. 44(48:54) sts.
Place Chart 6 as follows:
Next row K4(6:9)MC, K across 1st row of Chart 6, K15(17:20)MC.
Next row With MC, K twice in first st, K14(16:19), K across 2nd row of Chart 6, with MC, K3(5:8), K twice in last st.
Cont as set until Chart 6 has been completed, **at the same time**, inc one st at each end of every foll 3rd(4th:4th) row until there are 62(66:70) sts, working inc sts in MC.
Cont in MC only until Sleeve measures

14(16:18) cm/5½(6¼:7) in from beg of rib, ending with a wrong side row. Cast off.

LEFT MITTEN

Work as given for Right Mitten from *** to ***.
Change to 3¼mm (No 10/US 3) needles.
Next row P0(1:0), [K1, P1] 8(8:9) times, turn.
Work on this set of sts only.
Next row [K1, P1] to last 0(1:0) st, K0(1:0).
Work as given for Right Mitten from **** to ****.

LEFT SLEEVE

With 3¼mm (No 10/US 3) needles and wrong side facing, rejoin MC yarn to rem sts, cast on 8(9:9) sts, P0(1:1), [K1, P1] to last 0(1:0) st, K0(1:0).

Next row Cast on 8(8:9), P0(1:1), [K1, P1] to last 0(1:1) st, K0(1:1). 32(34:36) sts. Rib 4 rows.
Next row (wrong side) Rib 3(3:4), m1, [rib 5(4:3), m1] to last 4(3:5) sts, rib to end. 38(42:46) sts.
Change to 4 mm (No 8/US 5) needles.
Cont in garter st, work 4(6:10) rows, inc one st at each end of 1(1:2) foll 3rd (4th:4th) rows. 40(44:50) sts.
Place Chart 1 as follows:
Next row K20(22:25)MC, K across 1st row of Chart 1, K1(3:6)MC.
Next row With MC, K twice in first st, K0(2:4), K across 2nd row of Chart 1, with MC, K19(21:24), K twice in last st.
Complete to match Right Sleeve.

NECKBAND

Join shoulder seams.

With 3¼mm (No 10/US 3) needles, MC and right side facing, pick up and K 19(20:21) sts up right front neck, K across 22(22:24) back neck sts, inc one st at centre, pick up and K 19(20:21) sts down left front neck. 61(63:67) sts.
1st row (wrong side) P1, [K1, P1] to end.
2nd row K1, [P1, K1] to end.
Rep last 2 rows twice more.
Next row Rib 5 and slip these sts onto a safety pin, rib 5(5:4), inc in next st, [rib 9(6:7), inc in next st] to last 10(10:9) sts, rib 5(5:4), slip last 5 sts onto a safety pin. 56(60:64) sts.

HOOD

Change to 4 mm (No 8/US 5) needles.
Cont in garter st, work 8(12:16) rows.
Place Chart 7 as follows:
Next row K6(8:10)MC, K across 1st row of

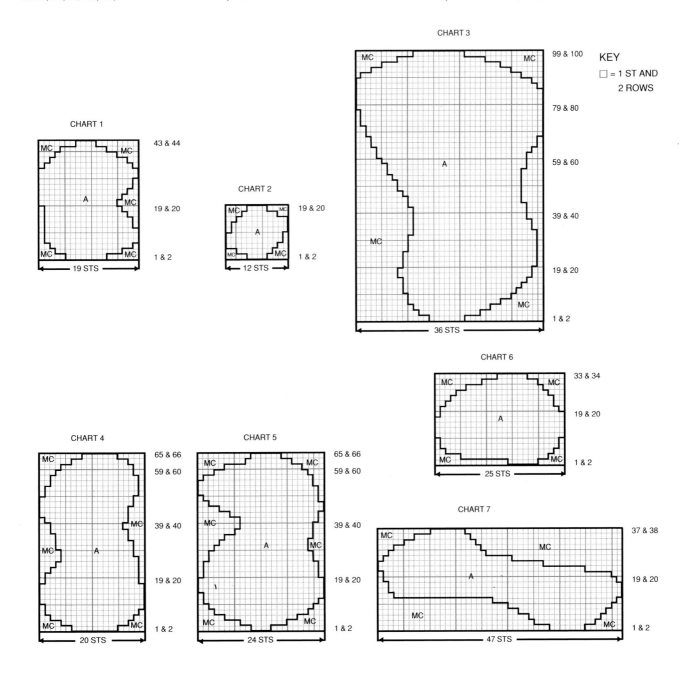

CHART 3

CHART 1

CHART 2

KEY

□ = 1 ST AND
   2 ROWS

CHART 6

CHART 4

CHART 5

CHART 7

Chart 7, K3(5:7)MC.
Next row K3(5:7)MC, K across 2nd row of Chart 7, K6(8:10)MC.
Work a further 36 rows as set. Cont in MC only until work measures 12(14:16) cm/4¾(5½:6¼) in from top of rib, ending with a wrong side row.
Shape Top
Next row K37(39:41), K2 tog, turn.
Next row K19, K2 tog tbl, turn.
Next row K19, K2 tog, turn.
Rep last 2 rows until all sts are worked off at each side of centre sts.
Leave rem 20 sts on a holder.

HOOD EDGING
With 3¼mm (No 10/US 3) needles, MC and right side facing, rib 5 sts from right side of hood safety pin, pick up and K 26(29:32) sts up right side of hood, K across 20 sts on holder, dec one st at centre, pick up and K 26(29:32) sts down left side of hood, rib 5 sts on left side safety pin.

81(87:93) sts.
Rib 7 rows. Cast off in rib.

BUTTONHOLE BAND
With 3¼mm (No 10/US 3) needles, MC and right side facing, pick up and K 77(83:89) sts evenly along right side edge of front opening to top of hood edging. Work 3 rows in rib as given for Neckband.
1st buttonhole row Rib 7(8:9), [cast off 2, rib 10(11:12) sts more] 5 times, cast off 2, rib to end.
2nd buttonhole row Rib to end, casting on 2 sts over those cast off in previous row. Rib 4 rows. Cast off in rib.

BUTTON BAND
Work to match Buttonhole Band omitting buttonholes.

EARS (make 2)
With 4 mm (No 8/US 5) needles and A, cast on 16 sts. Work 4 rows in garter st. Cont in garter st, dec one st at each end

of next row and every foll alt row until 2 sts rem. K2 tog and fasten off.

HORNS (make 2)
With 4 mm (No 8/US 5) needles and Brown, cast on 12 sts. Work 8 rows in garter st. Cont in garter st, dec one st at each end of every row until 2 sts rem. K2 tog and fasten off.

TO MAKE UP
Join foot and leg seams, then back crotch seam. Join front crotch and centre seam to front opening. Lap buttonhole band over button band and catch down to base of opening. Join side seams of mittens, leaving buttonhole band free. Join sleeve seams. Sew in sleeves. Sew on large buttons to button band and small buttons to sleeve cuffs. Fold ears in half at cast on row and catch down. Sew in place. Fold horns in half lengthwise and join seams. Sew in place.

Aran Sweater with Triangle Welt and Collar

See Page 9

MEASUREMENTS

To fit age	1–2	2–3	Yrs
All round at chest	68	73	**cm**
	26¾	28¾	**in**
Length to shoulder	38	43	**cm**
	15	17	**in**
Sleeve seam	20	24	**cm**
	8	9½	**in**

MATERIALS
8 (9) 50g balls of Rowan Designer DK Wool.
1 pair each of 3¼mm (No 10/US 3) and 4 mm (No 8/US 5) knitting needles.
Cable needle.

TENSION
22 sts and 28 rows to 10 cm/4 in over st st on 4 mm (No 8/US 5) needles.

ABBREVIATIONS
Cr 4L = slip next 2 sts onto cable needle and leave at front, P2, then K2 from cable needle
Cr 4R = slip next 2 sts onto cable needle and leave at back, K2, then P2 from cable needle.
CF = slip next 2 sts onto cable needle and leave at front, P1, then K2 from cable needle.
CB = slip next st onto cable needle and leave at back, K2, then P1 from cable needle.
C4B = slip next 2 sts onto cable needle and leave at back, K2, then K2 from cable needle.
C4F = slip next 2 sts onto cable needle and leave at front, K2, then K2 from cable needle.
MK = (Make knot) [K1, P1, K1, P1, K1, P1, K1] all in next st, then with point of left-hand needle, pass 2nd, 3rd, 4th, 5th, 6th and 7th sts over 1st st.
Also see page 63.

PANEL A –worked over 12 sts.
1st row (wrong side) K2, P2, K4, P2, K2.
2nd row P2, K2, P4, K2, P2.
3rd and every foll alt row K the K sts and P the P sts as they appear.
4th row P2, Cr 4L, Cr 4R, P2.
6th row P4, Cr 4L, P4.

8th row P6, CF, P3.
10th row P7, CF, P2.
12th row P3, MK, P4, K2, P2.
14th row P7, CB, P2.
16th row P6, CB, P3.
18th row P4, C4B, P4.
20th row P2, Cr 4R, Cr 4L, P2.

22nd row As 2nd row
24th row As 4th row.
26th row P4, Cr 4R, P4.
28th row P3, CB, P6.
30th row P2, CB, P7.
32nd row P2, K2, P4, MK, P3.
34th row P2, CF, P7.
36th row P3, CF, P6.
38th row P4, C4F, P4.
40th row As 20th row.
These 40 rows form patt.

PANEL B –worked over 10 sts.
1st row (wrong side) K1, P8, K1.
2nd row P1, K8, P1.
3rd and 2 foll alt rows As 1st row.
4th row P1, C4B, C4F, P1.
6th row As 2nd row.
8th row P1, C4F, C4B, P1.
These 8 rows form patt.
PANEL C – worked over 20 sts.
1st row (wrong side) [K3, P2] twice, [P2, K3] twice.
2nd row [P2, CB] twice, [CF, P2] twice.
3rd row and every foll alt row K the K sts and P the P sts as they appear.
4th row P1, [CB, P2] twice, CF, P2, CF, P1.
6th row [CB, P2] twice, pick up loop between sts and [K1, P1, K1] into it, turn, P3, turn, slip 1, K2 tog, psso, P1, then pass the bobble st over this st, P1, CF, P2, CF.
8th row [CF, P2] twice, [P2, CB] twice.

10th row P1, [CF, P2] twice, CB, P2, CB, P1.

12th row [P2, CF] twice, [CB, P2] twice.
These 12 rows form patt.

PANEL D – worked over 12 sts.
1st row (wrong side) K2, P2, K4, P2, K2.
2nd row P2, K2, P4, K2, P2.
3rd row and every foll alt row K the K sts and P the P sts as they appear.
4th row P2, Cr 4L, Cr 4R, P2.
6th row P4, Cr 4R, P4.
8th row P3, CB, P6.
10th row P2, CB, P7.
12th row P2, K2, P4, MK, P3.
14th row P2, CF, P7.
16th row P3, CF, P6.
18th row P4, C4F, P4.
20th row P2, Cr 4R, Cr 4L, P2.
22nd row As 2nd row.
24th row As 4th row.
26th row P4, Cr 4L, P4.
28th row P6, CF, P3.
30th row P7, CF, P2.
32nd row P3, MK, P4, K2, P2.
34th row P7, CB, P2.
36th row P6, CB, P3.
38th row P4, C4B, P4.
40th row As 20th row
These 40 rows form patt.

BACK
With 4 mm (No 8/US 5) needles, cast on 102 (110) sts.
Work in patt as follows:
1st row (wrong side) K1, [P1, K1] 3(5) times, work 1st row of Panel A, *K1, P4, K1, work 1st row of Panel B, K1, P4, K1*, work 1st row of Panel C, rep from * to * once, work 1st row of Panel D, K1, [P1, K1] 3 (5) times.
2nd row P1, [K1, P1], 3 (5) times, work 2nd row of Panel D, *P1, K4, P1, work 2nd row of Panel B, P1, K4, P1*, work 2nd row of Panel C, rep from * to * once, work 2nd row of Panel A, P1, [K1, P1] 3 (5) times.
3rd row P1, [K1, P1] 3 (5) times, work 3rd row of Panel A, *K1, P4, K1, work 3rd row of Panel B, K1, P4, K1*, work 3rd row of Panel C, rep from * to * once, work 3rd row of Panel D, P1, [K1, P1] 3 (5) times.
4th row K1, [P1, K1] 3 (5) times, work 4th row of Panel D, P1, C4B, P1, work 4th row

of Panel B, P1, C4B, P1, work 4th row of Panel C, P1, C4F, P1, work 4th row of Panel B, P1, C4F, P1, work 4th row of Panel A, K1, [P1, K1] 3 (5) times.
These 4 rows set patt. Cont in patt as set, working appropriate rows of Panels until work measures 35 (40) cm/13¾(15¾) in from beg, ending with a wrong side row.
Shape Shoulders
Cast off 16 (17) sts at beg of next 2 rows and 16 (18) sts at beg of foll 2 rows.
Leave rem 38 (40) sts on a holder.

FRONT
Work as given for Back until work measures 29 (34) cm/11½ (13½) in from beg, ending with a wrong side row.
Shape Neck
Next row Patt 39 (42), turn.
Work on this set of sts only.
Dec one st at neck edge on every row until 32 (35) sts rem.
Cont without shaping until work measures same as Back to shoulder shaping, ending at side edge.
Shape Shoulder
Cast off 16 (17) sts at beg of Next row.
Patt 1 row. Cast off rem 16 (18) sts.
With right side facing, slip centre 24 (26) sts onto a holder, rejoin yarn to rem sts and patt to end. Complete to match first side.

SLEEVES
With 3¼mm (No 10/US 3) needles, cast on 40 (44) sts. Work in K1, P1 rib for 3 cm/1¼ in.
Next row Rib 0 (2), [inc in each of next 3 sts, rib 1] to last 0 (2) sts, rib 0 (2). 70 (74) sts. Change to 4 mm (No 8/US 5) needles.
Work in patt as follows:
1st row (wrong side) K1, [P1, K1] 4 (5) times, work 1st row of Panel B, K1, P4, K1, work 1st row of Panel C, K1, P4, K1, work 1st row of Panel B, K1, [P1, K1] 4 (5) times.
2nd row P1, [K1, P1] 4 (5) times, work 2nd row of Panel B, P1, K4, P1, work 2nd row of Panel C, P1, K4, P1, work 2nd row of Panel B, P1, [K1, P1] 4 (5) times.
3rd row P1, [K1, P1] 4 (5) times, work 3rd row of Panel B, K1, P4, K1, work 3rd row of Panel C, K1, P4, K1, work 3rd row of

Panel B, P1, [K1, P1] 4 (5) times.
4th row K1, [P1, K1] 4 (5) times, work 4th row of Panel B, P1, C4B, P1, work 4th row of Panel C, P1, C4F, P1, work 4th row of Panel B, K1, [P1, K1] 4 (5) times.
These 4 rows set patt. Cont in patt as set, working appropriate rows of Panels, **at the same time**, inc one st at each end of next and 2 foll 2nd (3rd) rows, then on every foll 3rd row until there are 94 (102) sts, working inc sts into double moss st (side edge) patt. Cont without shaping until work measures 20 (24) cm/8 (9½) in from beg, ending with a wrong side row. Cast off.

COLLAR
Join right shoulder seam. With 3¼mm (No 10/US 3) needles and right side facing, pick up and K 23 sts down left front neck, K across 24 (26) sts at centre front, dec 4 (2) sts evenly, pick up and K 23 sts up right front neck and K across 38 (40) sts on back neck, dec 6 (2) sts evenly. 98 (108) sts. Work 7 rows in K1, P1 rib, inc one st at centre of last row on 1st size only. 99 (108) sts. K3 rows.
*Next row** (right side) K9, turn. Work on these sts only.
Next row K2 tog tbl, K5, K2 tog.
Next row K3, MK, K3.
Next row K2 tog tbl, K3, K2 tog.
Next row K5.
Next row K2 tog tbl, K1, K2 tog.
Next row K3.
Next row Sl 1, K2 tog, psso. Fasten off.
With right side facing, rejoin yarn to rem sts. Rep from * until all sts are worked off.

WELT EDGINGS
With 3¼mm (No 10/US 3) needles and right side facing, pick up and K 81 (90) sts evenly along cast on edge of Back. K 3 rows. Now work as given for collar from * until all sts are worked off.
Work front edging in same way.

TO MAKE UP
Join left shoulder seam and rib section of collar.
Sew on sleeves, placing centre of sleeves to shoulder seams.
Join side and sleeve seams.

Garter Stitch Jacket with Hat and Hens

See Page
10

MEASUREMENTS To fit age	6–9	9–12	12–18	Months
Actual chest measurement	58	62	65	cm
	22¾	24½	25½	in
Length	28	31	34	cm
	11	12¼	13½	in
Sleeve seam	16	18	20	cm
(with cuff turned back)	6¼	7	8	in

MATERIALS
Jacket
4(5:5) 50 g balls of Rowan Designer DK Wool.
6 buttons.
Hat
1(1:2) 50 g balls of Rowan Designer DK Wool.
Hens
Small amount of DK yarn in Rust or Cream.
Oddment in Black for embroidery.
Oddments of Yellow and Red felt.
Wadding.
Pipe cleaners.
Pair of 4mm (No 8/US 5) knitting needles.

TENSION
22 sts and 44 rows to 10 cm/4 in square over garter st (every row K).

ABBREVIATIONS
See page 63.

BACK
Cast on 64(68:72) sts. Work in garter st until Back measures 26(29:32) cm/10¼(11½:12¾) in from beg.
Shape Neck
*Next 2 rows K26(27:28), sl 1, yf, turn, sl 1, K to end.
Next 2 rows K23(24:25), sl 1, yf, turn, sl 1, K to end.
Next 2 rows K20(21:22), sl 1, yf, turn, sl 1, K to end.
Next row K to end. *
Rep from * to *. K 1 row. Cast off knitwise.

POCKET LININGS (make 2)
Cast on 20(22:22) sts. Work 26(30:30) rows in garter st. Leave these sts on a holder.

LEFT FRONT
Cast on 35(37:39) sts. Work 30(34:34) rows in garter st.
Place Pocket
Next row (wrong side) K9(9:10), cast off next 20(22:22) sts, K to end.
Next row K6(6:7), K across sts of pocket lining, K to end.
Cont in garter st across all sts until Front measures 25(28:31) cm/10(11:12¼) in from beg, ending at side edge.

Shape Neck
Next 2 rows K29(30:31), sl 1, yf, turn, sl 1, K to end.
Next 2 rows K27(28:29), sl 1, yf, turn, sl 1, K to end.
Next 2 rows K25(26:27), sl 1, yf, turn, sl 1, K to end.
Next 2 rows K23(24:25), sl 1, yf, turn, sl 1, K to end.
Next 2 rows K22(23:24), sl 1, yf, turn, sl 1, K to end.
Next 2 rows K21(22:23), sl 1, yf, turn, sl 1, K to end.
Next 2 rows K20(21:22), sl 1, yf, turn, sl 1, K to end.
Next row K to end. **
K 2 rows. Cast off knitwise. Mark front edge to indicate 6 buttons, first one 1 cm/½ in up from cast on edge and last one 1 cm/½ in down from cast off edge.

RIGHT FRONT
Cast on 35(37:39) sts. Work 5 rows in garter st.
1st buttonhole row (right side) K2, cast off 2, K to end.
2nd buttonhole row K to last 2 sts, cast on 2 sts, K2.
Work as given for Left Front to ** making buttonholes at markers and placing pocket as follows:
Next row K6(6:7), cast off next 20(22:22) sts, K to end.
Next row K9(9:10), K across sts of pocket lining, K to end.
K 1 row. Cast off knitwise.

SLEEVES
Cast on 41(43:45) sts. Work 42 rows in garter st. Cont in garter st, inc one st at each end of next row and every foll 6th row until there are 53(57:61) sts. Cont straight until Sleeve measures 21(23:25) cm/8¼(9:10) in from beg. Cast off.

TO MAKE UP
Join shoulder seams. Sew on sleeves, placing centre of sleeves to shoulder seams. Join side and sleeve seams, reversing seams on cuffs. Turn back cuffs. Catch down pocket linings on wrong side. Sew on buttons.

HAT
Cast on 81(89:97) sts. Cont in garter st until work measures 13(15:17) cm/5(6:6¾) in from beg.
Shape Top
Dec row K1, [K2 tog, K6] to end.
K 3 rows.
Dec row K1, [K2 tog, K5] to end.
K 1 row.
Dec row K1, [K2 tog, K4] to end.
Cont in this way, dec 10(11:12) sts as set on every alt row until 21(23:25) sts rem.
K 1 row.
Dec row K1, [K2 tog] to end.
Break off yarn, thread end through rem sts, pull up and secure. Join seam, reversing seam on last 4 cm/1¼ in for brim. Turn back brim.

HENS
Cast on 20 sts. Work in garter st for 9 cm/3½ in. Cast off.
Fold diagonally and join one side to point. Stuff with wadding, then insert folded pipe cleaner in middle of wadding. Cut triangle in Yellow felt for beak and half circle in Red for wattle. Insert them into opening near top point, secure in position. Join opening. Cut 3 triangles along top edge of strip of Red felt for comb. Sew to top of head. With Black, embroider eyes. Form hen into shape.
Make one more in same colour and one in another colour.

Nursery Sweater

See Page
18

MEASUREMENTS

To fit age	18–24	36	Mths
All round at chest	65	76	cm
	25½	30	in
Length to shoulder	36	41	cm
	14	16	in
Sleeve seam	23	25	cm
	9	10	in

MATERIALS

4 (5) 50 g balls of Rowan Designer DK Wool in main colour (M). Small amounts of any DK yarn in 10 contrast colours (see chart for shades).

1 pair each of 3¼mm (No 10/US 3) and 4 mm (No 8/US 5) knitting needles.

TENSION

22 sts and 28 rows to 10 cm/4 in over st st on 4 mm (No 8/US 5) needles.

ABBREVIATIONS

See page 63.

NOTE

Use separate length of yarn for each motif and twist yarns together on wrong side when changing colour to avoid holes. If preferred, small areas of contrast may be Swiss Darned when knitting is complete.

BACK

With 3¼mm (No 10/US 3) needles and M, cast on 70 (82) sts.
Work in K1, P1 rib for 4 cm/1½ in, inc one st at each end of last row. 72 (84) sts.
Change to 4 mm (No 8/US 5) needles.
Beg with a K row and working in st st throughout, work 13th (1st) to 104th row of chart 1, reading K (right side) rows from right to left and P rows from left to right.
Cont in M only.
Shape Shoulders
Cast off 18 (23) sts at beg of next 2 rows.
Leave rem 36 (38) sts on a holder.

FRONT

Work as given for Back until 88th row of chart 1 has been worked.

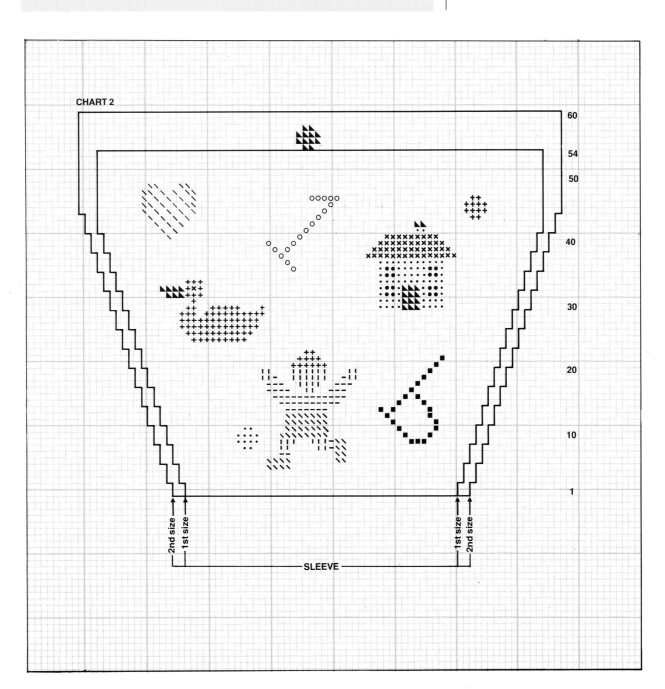

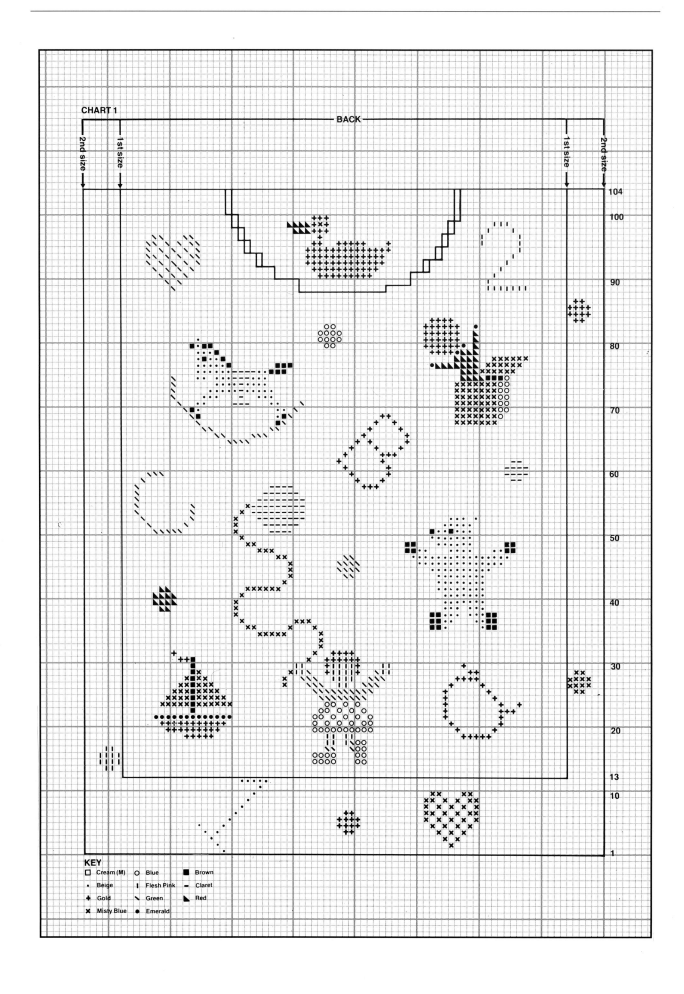

CHART 1

BACK

2nd size
1st size
1st size
2nd size

104
100
90
80
70
60
50
40
30
20
13
10
1

KEY

☐ Cream (M)	○ Blue	■ Brown
• Beige	❘ Flesh Pink	— Claret
✛ Gold	╲ Green	◤ Red
✕ Misty Blue	● Emerald	

Shape Neck
Next row Patt 29 (35), turn.
With right side facing, slip centre 14 sts onto a holder, join yarn to rem sts and patt 2 rows. Complete to match first side.

SLEEVES

With 3¼mm (No 10/US 3) needles and M, cast on 42 (46) sts. Work in K1, P1 rib for 4 cm/1½ in, inc one st at each end of last row. 44 (48) sts.
Change to 4 mm (No 8/US 5) needles.
Beg with a K row and working in st st throughout, work in patt from chart 2, **at the same time,** inc one st at each end of every 3rd row until there are 72 (78) sts.
Cont in patt without shaping until 54th (60th) row of chart 2 has been worked.
With M, cast off.

NECKBAND

Join right shoulder seam.
With 3¼mm (No 10/US 3) needles, M and right side facing, pick up and K 20 (21) sts down left front neck, K across 14 sts at centre front, pick up and K 20 (21) sts up right front neck and K across 36 (38) sts at back neck. 90 (94) sts.
Work 9 rows in K1, P1 rib. Cast off in rib.

TO MAKE UP

Work Swiss Darning if necessary (see diagram page 111).

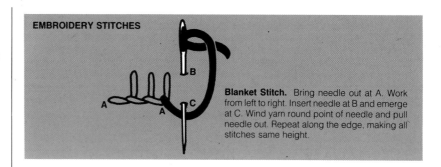

EMBROIDERY STITCHES

Blanket Stitch. Bring needle out at A. Work from left to right. Insert needle at B and emerge at C. Wind yarn round point of needle and pull needle out. Repeat along the edge, making all stitches same height.

Embroider faces and bow in girl's hair.
Join left shoulder and neckband seam.
Sew on sleeves, placing centre of sleeves to shoulder seams.
Join side and sleeve seams.
With Green, work blanket stitch (see diagram) along all ribbed edges.

Duck Sweater and Pants

See Page 11

MEASUREMENTS

To fit age	3–6	6–12	Mths
All round at chest	55	60	cm
	21½	23½	in
Length to shoulder	26	29	cm
	10¼	11½	in
Sleeve seam	14	16	cm
	5½	6¼	in
All round at hips	52	61	cm
	20½	24	in
Length	29	37	cm
	11½	14½	in
Inside leg	8	10	cm
	3	4	in

MATERIALS

Sweater 3 (3) 50 g balls of Rowan 4 ply Cotton in main colour (M).
1 ball of same in first colour (A).

Small amounts of same in second colour (B).
Oddment in third colour (C) for embroidery.
1 pair each of 2¾mm (No 12/US 1) and 3¼mm (No 10/US 3) knitting needles.
2 buttons.
Pants 2 x 50 g balls of Rowan 4 ply Cotton in main colour (M).
1 ball of same in contrast colour (C).
1 pair each of 2¾mm (No 12/US 1), 3 mm (No 11/US 2) and 3¼mm (No 10/US 3) knitting needles.
Length of 1.5 cm/½in wide elastic for waist.

TENSION

28 sts and 36 rows to 10 cm/4 in over st st using 3¼mm (No 10/US 3) needles.

ABBREVIATIONS

See page 63.

NOTE

Use a separate length of yarn for each motif and twist yarns together on wrong side when changing colour to avoid holes.

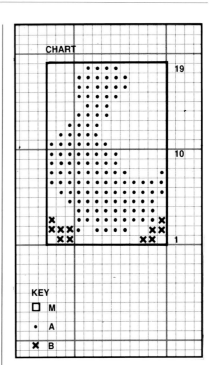

CHART

19
10
1

KEY
☐ M
• A
✕ B

Sweater

BACK

With 2¾mm (No 12/US 1) needles and M, cast on 74 (82) sts.
1st row (right side) K2, [P2, K2] to end.
2nd row P2, [K2, P2] to end.
Rep these 2 rows until work measures 4 cm/1½ in from beg, ending with a wrong side row and inc 3 sts evenly across last row. 77 (85) sts.
Change to 3¼mm (No 10/US 3) needles. Beg with a K row, work 4 rows in st st. Reading K rows from right to left and P rows from left to right, work border patt from chart as follows:
1st row K10 (12) M, [work across 13 sts of 1st row of chart, 9 (11) M] 3 times, 1M.
2nd row P10 (12) M, [work across 13 sts of 2nd row of chart, 9 (11) M] 3 times, 1M.
3rd to 19th rows Rep 1st and 2nd rows 8 times more then work 1st row again but working 3rd to 19th rows of chart.**

Beg with a P row, cont in st st and M only until work measures 26 (29) cm/10¼ (11½) in from beg, ending with a P row.

Shape shoulders

Cast off 13 (14) sts at beg of next 2 rows and 12 (13) sts at beg of foll 2 rows. Leave rem 27 (31) sts on a holder.

FRONT

Work as given for Back to **. Now cont in st st and M only until work measures 18 (19) cm/7 (7½) in from beg, ending with a P row.

Divide for Opening

Next row K35 (39), cast off 7, K to end. Cont on last set of sts only until work measures 23 (25) cm/9 (10) in from beg, ending with a P row.

Shape Neck

Cast off 3 sts at beg of next row. Dec one st at neck edge on every row until 25 (27) sts rem.

Cont without shaping for a few rows until work measures same as Back to shoulder shaping, ending with a K row.

Shape Shoulder

Cast off 13 (14) sts at beg of next row. Work 1 row. Cast off rem 12 (13) sts. With wrong side facing, rejoin yarn to rem sts and P to end. Complete to match first side, reversing all shaping.

SLEEVES

With 2¾ mm (No 12/US 1) needles and M, cast on 34 (38) sts.

Work 3 cm/1¼ in in rib as given for Back welt, ending with a wrong side row and inc 6 sts evenly across last row. 40(44) sts. Change to 3¼ mm (No 10/US 3) needles. Beg K row, cont in st st, inc one st at each end of every foll alt row until there are 62 (70) sts.

Cont without shaping until work measures 11 (13) cm/4¼ (5) in, ending with a P row. Now work 3 cm/1¼ in in rib as given for

Back welt, ending with a wrong side row. Cast off in rib.

BUTTONHOLE BAND

With 2¾ mm (No 12/US 1) needles, right side facing and M, pick up and K 14 (18) sts evenly along right front edge of opening for girl or left front edge of opening for boy. Beg with a 2nd row, work 3 rows in rib as given for Back welt.

1st buttonhole row (right side) Rib 3, cast off 2, rib to last 5 sts, cast off 2, rib to end.

2nd buttonhole row Rib to end, casting on 2 sts over those cast off in previous row. Rib a further 3 rows. Cast off in rib.

BUTTON BAND

With 2¾ mm (No 12/US 1) needles, right side facing and M, pick up and K 14 (18) sts evenly along left front edge of opening for girl or right front edge of opening for boy. Beg with a 2nd row, work 8 rows in rib as given for Back welt. Cast off in rib.

COLLAR

Join shoulder seams.

With 2¾ mm (No 12/US 1) needles, right side facing, M and beg at centre of buttonhole band for girl or button band for boy, pick up and K 23 (24) sts up right front neck, work across back neck sts as follows: [K1, K twice in next st] 13 (15) times, K1, pick up and K 23 (24) sts down left front neck to centre of button band for girl or buttonhole band for boy. 86 (94) sts. Beg with a 2nd row, work 7 cm/2¾ in in rib as given for Back welt. Cast off loosely in rib.

TO MAKE UP

Lap buttonhole band over button band, then catch down lower ends to cast off sts at base of opening. Sew on sleeves, placing centre of sleeves to shoulder seams. Beg at top of welt, join side then

sleeve seams. Sew on buttons. Embroider beak on each duck in B and bow around neck of each duck with C.

Pants

BACK AND FRONT ALIKE

With 3 mm (No 11/US 2) needles and M, cast on 62 (74) sts.

Beg with a K row, cont in st st until work measures 3 cm/1¼ in from beg, ending with a P row. Change to C and work 6 rows, inc 12 sts evenly across last row. 74 (86) sts.

Change to 3¼ mm (No 10/US 3) needles. Work in st st and stripe patt of 2 rows M and 6 rows C throughout, cont until work measures 24 (30) cm/9½ (11¾) in from beg, ending with a P row.

Divide for leg

Next row Patt 35 (41), K2 tog, turn. Work on first set of sts only. Work 1 row. Dec one st at end of next and every foll alt row until 33 (36) sts rem then at same edge on 2 (3) foll 3rd rows. 31 (33) sts. Cont without shaping for a few rows until work measures 29 (37) cm/11½ (14½) in from beg, ending with a P row. Cont in M only, K 1 row.

Change to 2¾ mm (No 12/US 1) needles.

1st row K1, [P1, K1] to end.

2nd row P1, [K1, P1] to end.

Rep last 2 rows 3 times more then work 1st row again. Cast off in rib.

With right side facing, join yarn to rem sts, K2 tog, patt to end. Complete to match first side, reversing shaping.

TO MAKE UP

Join side and inside leg seams. Join elastic to form ring. Fold first 3 cm/1¼ in from cast on edge to inside for waist band. Insert elastic, then slip stitch waist band in place.

Bee Cardigan, Bootees and Beanie Hat

See Page

12

MEASUREMENTS

To fit age	3	6:9	Mths
All round at chest	50	52:55	**cm**
	19½	20½:21½	**in**
Length to shoulder	24	26:29	**cm**
	9½	10¼:11½	**in**
Sleeve seam	12	13:15	**cm**
	4¾	5:6	**in**

MATERIALS

Cardigan: 2 (2:3) 50 g balls of Jaeger Matchmaker Merino 4 ply in main colour (M).
Bootees: 1 ball of Jaeger Matchmaker Merino 4 ply in main colour.
Hat: 1x50g ball of Jaeger Matchmaker Merino 4ply.
Oddments in Yellow and Black for embroidery for Cardigan and Bootees.
1 pair each of 2¾mm (No 12/US 1) and 3¼ mm (No 10/US 3) knitting needles. Medium size crochet hook. 5 buttons for cardigan and 2 buttons for bootees.

TENSION

28 sts and 36 rows to 10 cm/4 in over st st on 3¼mm (No 10/US 3) needles.

ABBREVIATIONS

See page 63.

Cardigan

BACK

With 2¾mm (No 12/US 1) needles and M, cast on 70 (74:78) sts. Work in K1, P1 rib for 5 cm/2 in.
Change to 3¼mm (No 10/US 3) needles. Beg with a K row, cont in st st until work measures 12 (13:15) cm/4¾ (5:6) in from beg, ending with a P row.
Shape Raglan Armholes
Next row K1, K2 tog tbl, K to last 3 sts, K2 tog, K1.
Next row P.
Rep last 2 rows until 34 (36:36) sts rem, ending with a P row. Cast off.

LEFT FRONT

With 2¾mm (No 12/US 1) needles and M, cast on 41 (43:45) sts.
1st row (right side) K1, [P1, K1] to last 6 sts, K6.
2nd row K6, P1, [K1, P1] to end.
Rep last 2 rows until work measures 5 cm/2 in from beg, ending with a wrong side row.
Change to 3¼mm (No 10/US 3) needles.
Next row K to end.
Next row K6, P to end.
Rep last 2 rows until work measures 12 (13:15) cm/4¾ (5:6) in from beg, ending with a wrong side row.
Shape Raglan Armhole
Next row K1, K2 tog tbl, K to end.
Next row K6, P to end.
Rep last 2 rows until 25 (26:26) sts rem, ending with a dec row.
Shape Neck
Cast off 20 (21:21) sts at beg of next row.
Next row K1, K2 tog tbl, K2 tog. P 1 row.
Next row K1, K2 tog. P 1 row.
K 2 tog and fasten off.

RIGHT FRONT

With 2¾mm (No 12/US 1) needles and M, cast on 41 (43:45) sts.
1st row (right side) K6, [K1, P1] to last st, K1.
2nd row P1, [K1, P1] to last 6 sts, P6.
Rep last 2 rows until work measures 5 cm/2 in from beg, ending with a wrong side row.
Change to 3¼mm (No 10/US 3) needles. Beg with a K row, cont in st st until work measures 12 (13:15) cm/4¾ (5:6) in from beg, ending with a P row.
Shape Raglan Armhole
Next row K to last 3 sts, K2 tog, K1.
Next row P.
Rep last 2 rows until 26 (27:27) sts rem, ending with a P row.

Shape Neck

Next row Cast off 20 (21:21), K to last 3 sts, K2 tog, K1. P 1 row.
Next row [K2 tog] twice, K1. P 1 row.
Next row K2 tog, K1. P 1 row.
K 2 tog and fasten off.

SLEEVES

With 3¼mm (No 10/US 3) needles and M, cast on 40 (44:48) sts.
Beg with a K row, work 12 rows in st st dec one st at each end of 3rd and foll 6th row.
Next row [K4, K2 tog, K3 (4:5) sts] to end. 32 (36:40) sts.
Change to 2¾mm (No 12/US 1) needles and work 3 rows in K1, P1 rib.
Next row [Rib 4, inc in next st, rib 3 (4:5) sts] to end, 36 (40:44) sts.
Change to 3¼mm (No 10/US 3) needles.
Beg with a K row, cont in st st inc one st at each end of 3rd and every foll 4th (5th:6th) row until there are 50 (54:58) sts.
Cont without shaping until work measures 12 (13:15) cm/4¾ (5:6) in from beg of rib, ending with a P row.
Shape Raglan Top
Next row K1, K2 tog tbl, K to last 3 sts, K2 tog, K1.
Next row P.
Rep last 2 rows until 14 (16:16) sts rem, ending with a P row. Cast off.

RIGHT FRONT BAND

With 3¼mm (No 10/US 3) needles and M, cast on 8 sts.
Work in st st until band when slightly stretched fits up Right Front to beg of neck shaping. Cast off.

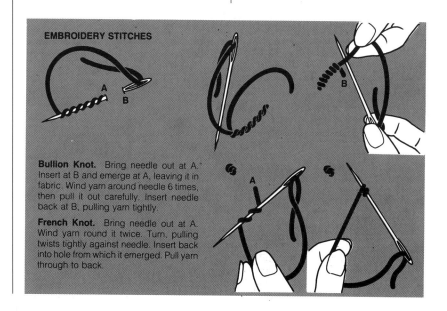

EMBROIDERY STITCHES

Bullion Knot. Bring needle out at A. Insert at B and emerge at A, leaving it in fabric. Wind yarn around needle 6 times, then pull it out carefully. Insert needle back at B, pulling yarn tightly.

French Knot. Bring needle out at A. Wind yarn round it twice. Turn, pulling twists tightly against needle. Insert back into hole from which it emerged. Pull yarn through to back.

With crochet hook, M and right side facing, work picot edging along long straight edge of band as follows:
[1 double crochet into next st, 3 chain, slip st in 3rd chain from hook] to end. Work other side in same way. Place band on top of last few sts at front edge of Right Front and sew in place.

COLLAR
Join All Raglan Seams.
With 3¼mm (No 10/US 3) needles, M and right side facing, pick up and K 54 (58:58) sts evenly around neck edge, omitting front bands.
Beg with a K row, work 2 rows in st st.
Next row K1, inc in next st, K to last 2 sts, inc in next st, K1.
Next row P.
Rep last 2 rows 4 times more. Work 2 rows straight. Cast off.
Work picot edging around collar as given for Right Front Band.

TO MAKE UP
Work picot edging along cast on edge of

Sleeves. Join side and sleeve seams, reversing seams on cuffs. Turn back cuffs. Make 5 buttonholes by pushing thick needle through 2 thicknesses of Right Front Band, first one 1 cm/¼ in up from cast on edge and last one 1 cm/¼ in down from cast off edge and rem 3 evenly spaced between. Neaten buttonholes. With Yellow and Black, embroider bees along Right Front Band, on each corner of Collar and on top of cuffs, with Bullion Knot, and wings with lazy daisy st (see diagram). Embroider heads.

Bootees

Using main colour throughout, work as Bootees of Striped Sweater with Zigzag Collar, omitting edging. Work picot edging around front edge of bootees as given for Right Front Band of Cardigan. Embroider bees on top of each bootee as given for Cardigan.

Beanie Hat

With 3¼mm (No 10/US 3) needles, cast on 115 sts.
1st row P1, [K1, P1] to end.
2nd row K1, [P1, K1] to end.
Rep these 2 rows until work measures 14 cm/5½ in from beg.
Shape Top
Dec row Rib 2, [work 3 tog, rib 3] 18 times, work 3 tog, rib 2. Work 3 rows straight.
Dec row Rib 1, [work 3 tog, rib 1] 19 times.
Dec row Rib 1, [work 2 tog] to end. 20 sts.
Break off yarn, thread end through rem sts, pull up and secure, then join seam, reversing seam at lower edge to allow for turning.

FEELERS (make 2)
With 3¼mm (No 10/US 3) needles, cast on 7 sts. Work 6 cm/2¼ in st st. Cast off. Roll lengthwise and slip stitch outside edge. Sew on top of hat.

Striped Sweater with Zig Zag Collar and Bootees

See Page
13

MEASUREMENTS			
To fit age	**3**	**6:9**	**Mths**
All round at chest	54	56:58	**cm**
	21¼	22:23	**in**
Length to shoulder	24	27:30	**cm**
	9½	10½:11¾	**in**
Sleeve seam	15	17:19	**cm**
	6¾	6¾:7½	**in**

MATERIALS
Sweater 2 (2-3) balls of Jaeger Matchmaker Merino 4 ply in each of 2 colours (A and B).
Bootees 1 ball of Jaeger Matchmaker Merino 4 ply in each of 2 colours (A and B).
1 pair each of 2¾mm (No 12/US 1) and 3¼mm (No 10/US 3) knitting needles.
2 buttons for Sweater and 2 buttons for Bootees.

TENSION
28 sts and 36 rows to 10 cm/4 in over st st on 3¼mm (No 10/US 3) needles.

ABBREVIATIONS
See page 63

Sweater

BACK
With 2¾mm (No 12/US 1) needles and A, cast on 75 (79:83) sts.
1st row (right side) K1, [P1, K1] to end.
2nd row P1, [K1, P1] to end.
Rep these 2 rows, until work measures 3 cm/1¼ in from beg, ending with a wrong side row.
Change to 3¼mm (No 10/US 3) needles.

Beg with a K row and working in st st and stripe patt of 2 rows B, 2 rows A throughout, cont until work measures 13 (15:17) cm/5 (6:6¾) in from beg, ending with a wrong side row.
Shape Armholes
Cast off 4 sts at beg of next 2 rows. 67 (71:75) sts.
Cont without shaping until work measures 24 (27:30) cm/9½ (10½:11¾) in from beg, ending with a wrong side row.

Shape Shoulders
Cast off 9 (9:10) sts at beg of next 2 rows and 9 (10:10) sts at beg of foll 2 rows.
Cast off rem 31 (33:35) sts.

FRONT
Work as given for Back until work measures 13 (15:17) cm/5 (6:6¾) in from beg, ending with a wrong side row.
Shape armholes and divide for front opening
Next row Cast off 4, K until there are 31 (33:35) sts on right hand needle, cast off next 5 sts, K to end.
Work on last set of 35 (37:39) sts only.
Cast off 4 sts at beg of next row. 31 (33:35) sts. Cont without shaping until work measures 19 (22:25) cm/7½ (8¾:10) in from beg, ending at inside edge.
Shape Neck
Cast off 4 (4:5) sts at beg of next row and 2 (3:3) sts at beg of foll alt row.
Dec one st at neck edge on next 5 rows, then on 2 foll alt rows. 18 (19:20) sts.
Cont without shaping until work measures same as Back to shoulder shaping, ending at armhole edge.
Shape Shoulder
Cast off 9 (9:10) sts at beg of next row. Work 1 row. Cast off rem 9 (10:10) sts.

With wrong side facing, rejoin yarn to rem sts and complete to match first side.

SLEEVES

With 2¾mm (No 12/US 1) needles and A, cast on 37 (39:41) sts.
Work in rib as given for Back for 3 cm/1¼ in, ending with a right side row.
Next row Rib 5 (5:4), [M1, rib 2, M1, rib 1] to last 5 (4:4) sts, M1, rib to end. 56 (60:64) sts.
Change to 3¼mm (No 10/US 3) needles.
Work in st st and stripe patt as given for Back, **at the same time**, inc one st at each end of every 9th row until there are 62 (68:74) sts.
Cont without shaping until work measures 16 (18:20) cm/6¼ (7:8) in from beg, ending with a wrong side row. Cast off.

COLLAR

Join Shoulder Seams.
With 2¾mm (No 12/US 1) needles, B and right side facing, pick up and K22 (22:24) sts up right front neck, 33 (33:36) sts across back neck and 22 (22:24) sts down left front neck. 77 (77:84) sts. K 3 rows.
Next row Rib 1 (1:2), M1, [rib 2, M1, rib 3, M1] to last 1 (1:2) sts, rib to end. 108 (108:117) sts.
K12 rows.
*1st row (right side) K9, turn. Work on these 9 sts only.
2nd row K2 tog tbl, K5, K2 tog.
3rd row K7.
4th row K2 tog tbl, K3, K2 tog.
5th row K5.
6th row K2 tog tbl, K1, K2 tog.
7th row K3.

8th row Slip 1, K2 tog, psso and fasten off. With right side facing, rejoin yarn to rem sts. Rep from * until all sts are worked off.

BUTTON BAND

With 2¾mm (No 12/US 1) needles, B and right side facing, pick up and K 18 (18:20) sts evenly along left side edge of front opening, omitting collar. K 12 rows. Cast off.

BUTTONHOLE BAND

With 2¾mm (No 12/US 1) needles, B and right side facing, pick up and K 18 (18:20) sts evenly along right side edge of front opening, omitting collar. K 5 rows, dec one st at each end of last row on 3rd size only.
**1st row K9, turn. Work on these 9 sts only.
2nd row (buttonhole) K2 tog tbl, K2, yf, K2 tog, K1, K2 tog.
Now work 3rd to 8th rows of collar.** With right side facing, rejoin yarn to rem sts. Rep from ** to ** once more.

TO MAKE UP

Sew on sleeves, placing centre of sleeves to shoulder seams. Join side and sleeve seams. Sew on buttons.

Bootees

With 3¼mm (No 10/US 3) needles and A, cast on 40 sts. K 1 row.
Cont in st st and stripe patt of 2 rows B, 2 rows A throughout, work as follows:
Next row Inc in first st, P18, inc in each of next 2 sts, P18, inc in last st. Work 1 row.

Next row Inc in first st, P20, inc in each of next 2 sts, P20, inc in last st. Work 1 row.
Next row Inc in first st, P22, inc in each of next 2 sts, P22, inc in last st. 52 sts. Work 6 rows.
Shape Instep
Next row K30, slip 1, K1, psso, turn.
Next row P9, P2 tog, turn.
Next row K9, slip 1, K1, psso, turn.
Rep last 2 rows 4 times more, then the 1st of the 2 rows again.
Next row K to end. 40 sts. Work 2 rows across all sts.
Shape Back Heel
Next row P8, turn. Work 7 rows on these 8 sts. Leave these sts on a spare needle. With wrong side facing, slip next 24 sts onto a holder, join yarn to rem 8 sts and work 8 rows.
Next row P to end then P across 8 sts of other side of back heel. 16 sts.
Cont in A only.
Next row Cast on 22 sts, P to end.
Buttonhole row K to last 3 sts, yf, K2 tog, K1. P1 row. Cast off.
With 2¾mm (No 12/US 1) needles, A and right side facing, pick up and K 8 sts down inside edge of back heel, K across 24 sts on a holder, pick up and K 8 sts up inside edge of back heel. 40 sts. Cast off knitwise.
With 2¾mm (No 12/US 1) needles and B, cast on 45 sts for edging. K 4 rows.
Now rep from * as given for Collar of Sweater until all sts are worked off.
Join back heel and sole seam. Sew on edging to strap. Sew on button.

Make another bootee, reversing strap.

Fair Isle Cardigan with Beret

See Page 14

MEASUREMENTS			
To fit age	**6–9**	**12:24:36**	**Mths**
All round at chest	56	61:67:72	**cm**
	22	12:26½:28½	**in**
Length to shoulder	27	31:35:39	**cm**
	10½	12¼:13¾:15¼	**in**
Sleeve seam	18	21:24:27	**cm**
	7	8¼:9½:10½	**in**

MATERIALS

Cardigan 1 (1:1:2) 50 g balls of Jaeger Baby Merino 4 ply in main colour (M).
1 x 50 g ball of same in 8 contrast colours (A, B, C, D, E, F, G and H).
1 pair each of 2¾mm (No 12/US 1) and 3¼mm (No 10/US 3) knitting needles.
4 buttons.

Beret Small amounts of Jaeger Baby Merino 4 ply in 9 colours (M, A, B, C, D, E, F, G and H).
Set of four 2¾mm (No 12/US 1) and 3¼ mm (No 10/US 3) double pointed knitting needles.

TENSION

32 sts and 32 rows to 10 cm/4 in over patt on 3¼mm (No 10/US 3) needles.

ABBREVIATIONS

See page 63.

NOTE

When working in patt, strand yarn not in use loosely across wrong side to keep fabric elastic.

Cardigan

BACK

With 2¾mm (No 12/US 1) needles and M, cast on 81 (87:93:99) sts.
1st row (right side) K1, [P1, K1] to end.
2nd row P1, [K1, P1] to end.
Rep these 2 rows until work measures 4 cm/1½ in from beg, ending with a right side row.
Next row Rib 4 (5:7:4), [inc in next st, rib 7 (6:5:5) sts] to last 5 (5:8:5) sts, inc in next st, rib to end. 91 (99:107:115) sts.
Change to 3¼mm (No 10/US 3) needles.
Beg with a K row and working in st st throughout, work in patt from chart 1 as indicated for Back, reading K rows from right to left and P rows from left to right until work measures 27 (31:35:39) cm/10½ (12¼:13¾:15¼) in from beg, ending with a wrong side row.

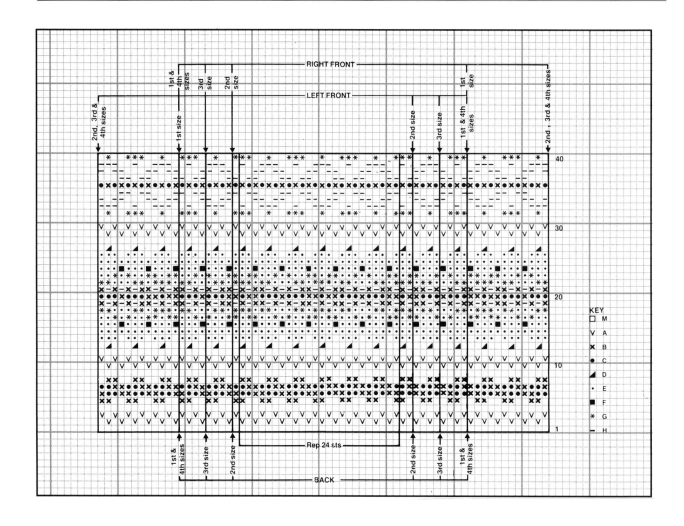

Shape Shoulders.
Cast off 15 (16:17:18) sts at beg of next 4 rows. Leave rem 31 (35:39:43) sts on a holder.

LEFT FRONT
With 2¾mm (No 12/US 1) needles and M, cast on 37 (41:43:47) sts.
Work in rib as given for Back for 4 cm/1½ in, ending with a right side row.
Next row Rib 3 (5:4:2), [inc in next st, rib 5 (5:4:5) sts] to last 4 (6:4:3) sts, inc in next st, rib to end. 43 (47:51:55) sts.
Change to 3¼mm (No 10/US 3) needles.
Beg with a K row and working in st st throughout, work in patt from chart 1 as indicated for Left Front until work measures 17 (19:21:23) cm/6¾ (7½:8¼:9) in from beg, ending with a wrong side row.
Shape Front
Dec one st at end (front edge) of next and every foll alt row until 30 (32:34:36) sts rem. Cont without shaping until work measures same as Back to shoulder shaping, ending with a wrong side row.
Shape shoulder
Cast off 15 (16:17:18) sts at beg of next row. Work 1 row.
Cast off rem 15 (16:17:18) sts.

RIGHT FRONT
Work as given for Left Front, following chart 1 as indicated for Right Front and reversing all shaping.

SLEEVES
With 2¾mm (No 12/US 1) needles and M, cast on 49 (51:53:55) sts.
Work in rib as given for Back for 4 cm/1½ in, ending with a wrong side row and inc 2 (8:6:12) sts evenly across last row. 51 (59:59:67) sts.
Change to 3¼mm (No 10/US 3) needles.
Beg with a K row and working in st st throughout, work in patt from chart 1 as indicated for 2nd (3rd:3rd:4th) sizes on Back, **at the same time**, inc one st at each end of every foll 2nd (3rd:3rd:5th) row until there are 79 (83:87:91) sts, working inc sts into patt.
Cont without shaping until work measures 18 (21:24:27) cm/7 (8¼: 9½: 10½) in from beg, ending with a wrong side row.
Cast off.

FRONT BAND
Join shoulder seams.
With 2¾mm (No 12/US 1) needles, M and right side facing, pick up and K 53 (59:65:71) sts evenly along straight edge of Right Front, 31 (37:43:49) sts along shaped edge to shoulder, K across 31 (35:39:43) sts on back neck, pick up and K 31 (37:43:49) sts along shaped edge of Left Front and 53 (59:65:71) sts down straight edge. 199 (227:255:283) sts.
Work 3 rows in rib as given for Back.
1st buttonhole row Rib 3, [cast off 2, rib 13 (15:17:19) sts more] 4 times, rib to end.
2nd buttonhole row Rib to end casting on 2 sts over those cast off in previous row.
Rib 3 rows. Cast off in rib.

TO MAKE UP
Sew on sleeves, placing centre of sleeves to shoulder seams.
Join side and sleeve seams. Sew on buttons.

Beret

With set of four 2¾mm (No 12/US 1) needles and M, cast on 92 (102:112:122) sts. Work 7 rounds in K1, P1 rib.
Next round *Rib 1 (2:3:4), [inc in each of next 3 sts, rib 1] 11 (12:13:14) times, inc in next st; rep from * once more. 160 (176:192:208) sts.
Change to set of four 3¼mm (No 10/US 3)

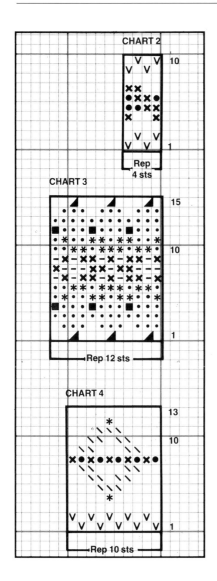

Fair Isle Sweater with Hat

See Page
15

MEASUREMENTS To fit age	1	2:3	Yrs
All round at chest	60	68:76	**cm**
	23½	26¾:30	**in**
Length to shoulder	30	33:37	**cm**
	11¾	13:14½	**in**
Sleeve seam	22	25:28	**cm**
	8¾	10:11	**in**

MATERIALS
Sweater 2 (2:3) 50 g balls of Rowan Designer DK Wool in main colour (A).
1 ball of same in each of 4 colours (B, C, D and E).
1 pair each of 3¼ mm (No 10/US 3) and 4 mm (No 8/US 5) knitting needles.

Set of four 3¼ mm (No 10/US 3) double pointed knitting needles.
Hat 1 x 50 g ball of Rowan Designer DK Wool in main colour (A).
Small amounts of same in each of 4 colours (B, C, D and E).
Set of four 4 mm (No 8/US 5) double pointed knitting needles.

TENSION
24 sts and 24 rows to 10 cm/4 in over patt on 4 mm (No 8/US 5) needles.

ABBREVIATIONS
See page 63.

NOTE
Strand yarn not in use loosely across wrong side to keep fabric elastic.

Sweater

BACK
With 3¼ mm (No 10/US 3) needles and A, cast on 65 (75:83) sts.
1st row (right side) K1, [P1, K1] to end.
2nd row P1, [K1, P1] to end.
Rep these 2 rows until work measures 5 cm/2 in from beg, ending with a wrong side row and inc 8 sts evenly across last row. 73 (83:91) sts.
Change to 4 mm (No 8/US 5) needles. Beg with a K row and working in st st throughout, cont in patt from chart 1 as indicated for Back, reading K rows from right to left and P rows from left to right until work measures 30 (33:37) cm/11¾ (13:14½) in from beg, ending with a wrong side row.
Shape Shoulders
Cast off 11 (13:14) sts at beg of next 4 rows. Leave rem 29 (31:35) sts on a holder.

FRONT
Work as given for Back until work measures 24 (27:31) cm/9½ (10½:12) in from beg, ending with a wrong side row.
Shape Neck
Next row Patt 29 (33:36), turn.
Work on this set of sts only. Keeping patt correct, dec one st at neck edge on every row until 22 (26:28) sts rem.
Cont without shaping until work measures same as Back to shoulder shaping, ending at side edge.
Shape Shoulder
Cast off 11 (13:14) sts at beg of next row. Work 1 row. Cast off rem 11 (13:14) sts.
With right side facing, slip centre 15

(17:19) sts onto a holder, rejoin yarn to rem sts and patt to end. Complete to match first side.

SLEEVES
With 3¼ mm (No 10/US 3) needles and A, cast on 33 (37:41) sts.
Work in rib as given for Back for 5 cm (2 in, ending with a wrong side row and inc 10 (12:12) sts evenly across last row. 43 (49:53) sts.
Change to 4 mm (No 8/US 5) needles. Beg with a K row and working in st st throughout, cont in patt from chart 1 as indicated for Sleeve, **at the same time**, inc one st at each end of every 2nd (3rd:3rd) row until there are 71 (75:79) sts, working inc sts into patt.
Cont without shaping until work measures 22 (25:28) cm/8¾ (10:11) in from beg, ending with a wrong side row. Cast off.

COLLAR
Join Shoulder Seams.
With set of four 3¼ mm (No 10/US 3) needles, A and a right side facing, slip first 8 (9:10) sts from holder at centre front onto a safety pin, join yarn to next st and K rem 7 (8:9) sts, pick up and K 16 sts up right front neck, K across 29 (31:35) sts on back neck, pick up and K 16 sts down left front neck then K sts from safety pin. 76 (80:86) sts. Work in rounds of K1, P1 rib for 2 cm/¾ in, dec one st at end of last round.
Turn and cont backwards and forwards as follows:
Next round Rib 3, work 3 times in next st, rib to last 4 sts, work 3 times in next st, rib 3. Rib 1 row.

needles.
Work in st st (every round K) throughout and patt from charts (read every row of chart from right to left) as follows:
Work 10 rounds from chart 2.
With M, work 2 (3:5:5) rounds, dec 4 sts evenly across last round on 1st and 4th sizes only and inc 4 sts evenly across last round on 2nd size only. 156 (180:192:204) sts.
Now work 15 rounds from chart 3.
With M, work 1 (2:3:4) rounds.
Dec round [K4, K2 tog] to end. 130 (150:160:170) sts.
Work 13 rounds from chart 4.
Dec round *[K1M, 1A] twice, with M, K3 tog, K1A, 1M, 1A; rep from * to end.
Dec round [K1A, 1M, 1A, with M, K3 tog, K1A, 1M] to end.
Cont in M only.
Dec round [K2, K3 tog, K1] to end.
Dec round [K1, K3 tog) to end.
Dec round [K2 tog] to end, 13 (15:16:17) sts.
Break off yarn, thread end through rem sts, pull up and secure.

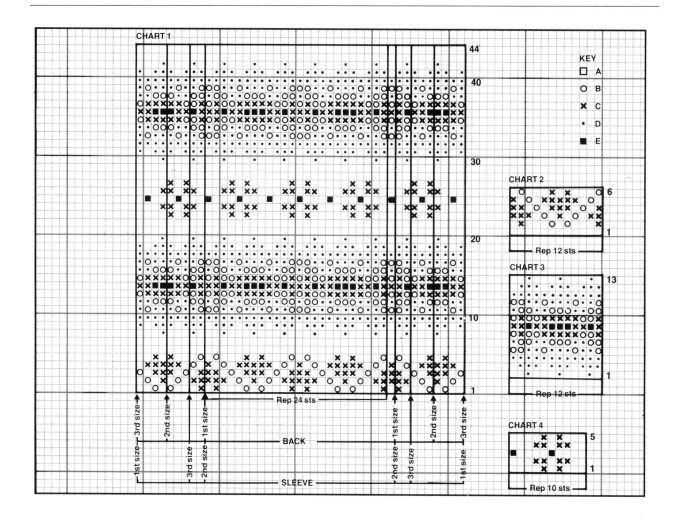

Rep last 2 rows until collar measures 8 (8:9) cm/3 (3:3½) in from beg. Cast off loosely.

TO MAKE UP
Sew on sleeves, placing centre of sleeves to shoulder seams. Join side and sleeve seams.

Hat

With set of four 4 mm (No 8/US 5) needles and A, cast on 80 (88:96) sts.
Work 8 rounds in K1, P1 rib.
Next round *[Inc in each of next 5 sts, rib 1] 3 (3:1) times, [inc in next st, rib 1] 1 (2:1) times; rep from * to end. 144 (156:168) sts. Cont in st st (every round K) throughout, reading every row of chart from right to left, work 6 rounds from chart 2, then work 2 (3:4) rounds in A. Now work 13 rounds from chart 3, then work 1 (2:3) rounds in A.
Next round With A, [K4, K3 tog, K5] to end. 120 (130:14)0) sts.

Work 5 rounds from chart 4.
Shape Crown
Next round With A, [K3, K3 tog, K4] to end. With A, K1 round.
Next round [With A, K2, K3 tog, K2, with D, K1] to end.
Next round [K1D, with A, K3 tog, with D, K2] to end.
Next round [With D, K3 tog, K1] to end.
Next round [With D, K2 tog] to end. 12 (13:14) sts.
Break off yarn, thread end through rem sts, pull up and secure.

Farm Animals Slippers

See Page
16

MEASUREMENTS

Duck and Rabbit

to fit age	**0–6 Mths**

Pig	
to fit age	**6–12 Mths**

MATERIALS

Duck 150 g ball of Rowan Designer DK Wool in each of Cream (A) and Orange (B).
Oddment of Black for embroidery.
Pair each of 3 mm (No 11/US 2) and 3¼mm (No 10/US 3) knitting needles.

Rabbit 150 g ball of Rowan Designer DK Wool in each of Brown (A) and Pink (B).
Oddments of Black and Cream.
Pair each of 2¾ mm (No 12/US 1), 3 mm (No 11/US 2) and 3¼mm (No 10/US 3) knitting needles.
Pig 250 g balls of Rowan DK Handknit Cotton in Pink.
Oddment of Black for embroidery.
Pair of 3 mm (No 11/US 2) knitting needles.

ABBREVIATIONS

See page 63.

Duck

MAIN PART

With 3 mm (No 11/US 2) needles and A, cast on 24 sts. K 40 rows. Cast off.
Make one more square in A and one in B.
Place B square on one A square and join them together. With A side on the outside, fold 3 corners of square into centre forming an open envelope.
Join the 2 seams. Fold rem A square diagonally to form triangle and join edges. Place joined edges of triangle to edges of open end of envelope, matching points. Sew in place.

BEAK

With 3¼mm (No 10/US 3) needles and B, cast on 14 sts. K 10 rows. Dec one st at each end of next row and 2 foll alt rows. K 1 row. Cast off. Make one more. Place pieces together and stitch all round, leaving cast on edges free. Turn to right side and join together cast on edges.
Sew to front of main part. With Black, embroider eyes.
Make one more.

Rabbit

MAIN PART

Work as given for Main Part of Duck.

OUTER EARS

With 3 mm (No 11/US 2) needles and A, cast on 7 sts. K 17 rows. Dec one st at each end of next row and foll 5th row. K 4 rows. K3 tog and fasten off. Make one more.

INNER EARS

With 2¾mm (No 12/US 1) needles and B, cast on 7 sts. K 17 rows. Dec one st at each end of next row and foll 5th row. K 2 rows. K3 tog and fasten off. Make one more.
Sew inner ears to outer ears. Fold cast on edges in half and stitch together along cast on edges and along first 1.5 cm/½ in. Sew in place.

NOSE

With 3¼mm (No 10/US 3) needles and Black, cast on one st.
Next row K into front, back, front, back

and front of st.
Next row (right side) K.
Next row P.
Next row K2 tog, K1, K2 tog.
Next row P3 tog and fasten off.
Run a gathering thread around edges, pull up and secure. Attach to front of main part.
With Black, embroider eyes. With Cream, make a small pompon and attach to back of main part.
Make one more.

Pig

MAIN PART

Work as given for Main Part of Duck, but using one colour throughout.

NOSE

With 3 mm (No 11/US 2) needles, cast on 4 sts. K 1 row. Inc one st at each end of next row and 2 foll alt rows, then at each end of foll row. 12 sts. K 6 rows. Dec one st at each end of next 2 rows then on 2 foll alt rows. K 1 row. Cast off. Make one more. Place pieces together and stitch all round, leaving cast on edges free. Turn to right side and join together cast on edges.
Sew to front of main part. With Black, embroider nostrils.

EARS

With 3 mm (No 11/US 2) needles, cast on 8 sts. K 2 rows. Dec one st at each end of next row and 2 foll alt rows. K2 tog and fasten off. Make one more. Sew in place.

TAIL

With 3 mm (No 11/US 2) needles, cast on 14 sts. Cast off. Sew to back of main part. Make one more.

Tyrolean Cardigan

See Page
19

MEASUREMENTS

To fit age	1	2:3	Yrs
All round at chest	66	72:76	cm
	26	28¼:30	in
Length to shoulder	31	34:37	cm
	12¼	13¼:14½	in
Sleeve seam	19	22:25	cm
	7½	8¾:10	in

MATERIALS
4 (5:5) 50 g balls of Jaeger Matchmaker Merino 4 ply in main colour (M). Oddments of DK yarn in 3 colours for embroidery.
Pair each of 2¾mm (No 12/US 1) and 3¼ mm (No 10/US 3) knitting needles.
5 buttons.

TENSION
28 sts and 36 rows to 10 cm/4 in over st st on 3¼mm (No 10/US 3) needles.

ABBREVIATIONS
T2F = K into front of second st, then K first st, slipping both sts off needle together.
T2B = K into back of second st, then K first st, slipping both sts off needle together.
MB = [K1, P1, K1, P1, K1] all in next st, turn, K5, turn, P5, turn, K2 tog, K1, K2 tog, turn, P3 tog.
Also see page 63.

PANEL A – worked over 4 sts.
1st row (right side) T2F, T2B.
2nd row P4.
3rd row T2B, T2F.
4th row As 2nd row.
These 4 rows form patt.

PANEL B – worked over 19 sts.
1st row (right side) P6, T2B, K1, MB, K1, T2F, P6.
2nd row K6, P7, K6.
3rd row P5, T2B, K5, T2F, P5.
4th row K5, P9, K5.
5th row P4, T2B, K1, MB, K3, MB, K1, T2F, P4.
6th row K4, P11, K4.
7th row P3, T2B, K9, T2F, P3.
8th row K3, P13, K3.
9th row P2, T2B, K1, MB, K7, MB, K1, T2F, P2.
10th row K2, P15, K2.
11th row P1, T2B, K13, T2F, P1.
12th row K1, P17, K1.
13th row P1, K2, MB, K11, MB, K2, P1.
14th row As 12th row.
15th row P1, K17, P1.
16th row as 12th row.
These 16 rows form patt.

BACK
With 2¾mm (No 12/US 1) needles and M, cast on 86 (94:102) sts.
1st row (right side) K2, [P2, K2] to end.
2nd row P2, [K2, P2] to end.
Rep these 2 rows until work measures 4 cm/1½ in from beg, ending with a right side row.
Next row Rib 8 (4:5) [inc in next st, rib 3 (4:5) sts] to last 6 (0:1) sts, rib 6 (0:1). 104 (112:118) sts.
Change to 3¼mm (No 10/US 3) needles.
Work in patt as follows:
1st row (right side P4 (8:11), work 1st row of Panel A, [work 1st row of Panel B, then Panel A] 4 times, P4 (8:11).
2nd row K4 (8:11), work 2nd row of Panel A, [work 2nd row of Panel B, then Panel A] 4 times, K4 (8:11).
These 2 rows set patt. Cont in patt as set, working appropriate rows of Panels until work measures 18 (20:22) cm/7 (8:8¾) in from beg, ending with a wrong side row.
Shape Armholes
Cast off 4 (5:5) sts at beg of next 2 rows. Keeping patt correct, dec one st at each end of every row until 88 (92:96) sts rem. Cont without shaping until work measures 31 (34:37) cm/12¼ (13¼:14½) in from beg, ending with a wrong side row.
Shape Shoulders
Cast off 9 (10:10) sts at beg of next 4 rows and 9 (9:10) sts at beg of foll 2 rows.
Leave rem 34 (34:36) sts on a holder.

LEFT FRONT
With 2¾mm (No 12/US 1) needles and M, cast on 42 (46:50) sts. Work in rib as given for Back for 4 cm/1½ in, ending with a right side row.
Next row Rib 3 (5:6), inc in next st, [rib 4 (4:5), inc in next st] to last 3 (5:7) sts, rib to end, 50 (54:57) sts.
Change to 3¼mm (No 10/US 3) needles.
Work in patt as follows:
1st row (right side) P4 (8:11), [work 1st row of Panel A, then Panel B] twice.
2nd row [Work 2nd row of Panel B, then Panel A] twice, K4 (8:11).
These 2 rows set patt. Cont in patt as set, working appropriate rows of Panels until work measures same as Back to armhole shaping, ending with a wrong side row.
Shape Armhole
Cast off 4 (5:5) sts at beg of next row. Dec one st at armhole edge on every row until 42 (44:46) sts rem.
Cont without shaping until work measures 27 (30:33) cm/10¾ (11¾:13) in from beg, ending with a right side row.

Shape Neck
Cast off 8 (8:9) sts at beg of next row. Dec one st at neck edge on next 7 rows. 27 (29:30) sts.
Cont without shaping until work measures same as Back to shoulder shaping, ending with a wrong side row.
Shape Shoulder
Cast off 9 (10:10) sts at beg of next row and foll alt row. Work 1 row. Cast off rem 9 (9:10) sts.

RIGHT FRONT
Work as given for Left Front, reversing all shaping and patt as follows:
1st row (right side) [Work 1st row of Panel B, then Panel A] twice, P4 (8:11).
2nd row K4 (8:11), [work 2nd row of Panel A, then Panel B] twice.

SLEEVES
With 2¾mm (No 12/US 1) needles and M, cast on 38 (42:42) sts. Work in rib as given for Back for 4 cm/1½ in, ending with a right side row.
Next row Rib 2 (4:4), [inc in next st, rib 1 (2:1), inc in next st, rib 2] to last 1 (2:3) sts, rib to end, 52 (54:56) sts.
Change to 3¼mm (No 10/US 3) needles.
Work in patt as follows:
1st row (right side) P1 (2:3), work 1st row of Panel A, [work 1st row of Panel B, then Panel A] twice, P1 (2:3).
2nd row K1 (2:3), work 2nd row of Panel A, [work 2nd row of Panel B, then Panel A] twice, K1 (2:3).
These 2 rows set patt. Cont in patt as set, working appropriate rows of Panels, at the same time, inc one st at each end of next and every foll 4th row until there are 72 (80 :86) sts, working inc sts into reverse st st. Cont without shaping until work measures 19 (22:25) cm/7½ (8¾:10) in from beg, ending with a wrong side row.
Shape Top
Cast off 4 (5:5) sts at beg of next 2 rows. Dec one st at each end of next 7 rows, then on every foll alt row until 28 (30:32) sts rem, ending with a wrong side row. Cast off.

BUTTONHOLE BAND
With 2¾mm (No 12/US 1) needles, right side facing and M, pick up and K 78 (86:94) sts evenly along front edge of Right Front. Work 3 rows in rib as given for Back.
1st buttonhole row Rib 3, [cast off 3, rib 15 (17:19) sts more] 3 times, cast off 3, rib to end.
2nd buttonhole row Rib to end, casting on 3 sts over those cast off in previous row. Rib 4 rows. Cast off in rib.

BUTTON BAND
Work to match Buttonhole Band, omitting buttonholes.

NECKBAND
Join shoulder seams.
With 2¾mm (No 12/US 1) needles, M and right side facing, pick up and K 32 (32:33) sts across Buttonhole Band and up right front neck, K across 34 (34:36) sts at back neck, pick up and K 32 (32:33) sts down left front neck and across Button Band. 98 (98:102) sts. Work 3 rows in rib as given for Back.
1st buttonhole row Rib 2, cast off 3, rib to end.
2nd buttonhole row Rib to last 2 sts, cast on 3, rib to end.
Rib 4 rows. Cast off in rib.

TO MAKE UP
With DK yarn, embroider flowers and leaves in lazy daisy stitch with french knot (see pages 77 and 99) in centre between bobbles of Panel B. Join side and sleeve seams. Set in sleeves. Sew on buttons.

Scandinavian Cardigan, Hat and Boots

See Page
20

MEASUREMENTS To fit age Mths	6–9	9–12	
All round at chest	65	71	**cm**
	25½	28	**in**
Length to shoulder	27	32	**cm**
	10½	12½	**in**
Sleeve seam	18	22	**cm**
	7	8¾	**in**
Hat To fit age Mths	**6–9**	**9–12**	
Boots To fit age Mths	**6–9**	**9–12**	

MATERIALS
Cardigan 3 (4) 50 g balls of Rowan Designer DK Wool in main colour (M).
1 (2) balls of same in contrast colour (A).
1 pair each of 3¼mm (No 10/US 3) and 4 mm (No 8/US 5) knitting needles.
5 (6) buttons.
Hat 1 x 50 g ball of Rowan Designer DK Wool in main colour (M).
1 ball of same in contrast colour (A).
Oddment of Red for pompons.
1 pair each of 3¼mm (No 10/US 3) and 4 mm (No 8/US 5) knitting needles.
Boots 1 x 50 g ball of Rowan True 4 ply Botany in main colour (M).
Oddment of Red for pompons.
1 pair of 2¾mm (No 12/US 1) knitting needles.

TENSION
24 sts and 25 rows to 10 cm/4 in over patt on 4 mm (No 8/US 5) needles using DK yarn.

ABBREVIATIONS
See page 63.

NOTE
When working motifs, use a separate length of yarn for each section and twist yarns together on wrong side when changing colour to avoid holes.
When working Fair Isle bands, strand yarn not in use loosely across wrong side to keep fabric elastic.

Cardigan

BACK
With 3¼mm (No 10/US 3) needles and M, cast on 69 (75) sts.
1st row (right side) K1, [P1, K1] to end.
2nd row P1, [K1, P1] to end.
Rep these 2 rows until work measures 3 cm/1¼in from beg, ending with a wrong side row and inc 6 sts evenly across last row. 75 (81) sts.
Change to 4 mm (No 8/US 5) needles.
Beg with a K row and working in st st throughout, cont in patt from chart as indicated for Back, reading K rows from right to left and P rows from left to right, until work measures 27 (32) cm/10½ (12½) in from beg, ending with a wrong side row.
Shape Shoulders
Cast off 21 (23) sts at beg of next 2 rows.
Leave rem 33 (35) sts on a holder.

LEFT FRONT
With 3¼mm (No 10/US 3) needles and M, cast on 37 (39) sts. Work in rib as given for Back for 3 cm./1¼in, ending with a wrong side row and inc 2 (3) sts evenly across last row. 39 (42) sts.
Change to 4 mm (No 8/US 5) needles.
Beg with a K row and working in st st throughout, cont in patt from chart as indicated for Left Front until work measures 21 (26) cm/8¼ (10¼) in from beg, ending with a right side row.

Shape Neck
Keeping patt correct, cast off 6 sts at beg of next row and 4 (5) sts at beg of foll alt row. Dec one st at neck edge on every row until 21 (23) sts rem.
Cont without shaping for a few rows until work measures same as Back to shoulder shaping, ending with a wrong side row.
Cast off.

RIGHT FRONT
Work as given for Left Front, reversing all shaping and working patt from chart as indicated for Right Front.

SLEEVES
With 3¼mm (No 10/US 3) needles and M, cast on 41 sts. Work in rib as given for Back for 3 cm/1¼in, ending with a wrong side row and inc 4 sts evenly across last row. 45 sts.
Change to 4 mm (No 8/US 5) needles.
Beg with a K row and working in st st throughout, cont in patt from chart as indicated for 2nd size on Back, **at the same time,** inc one st at each end of every foll alt row until there are 73 (77) sts, working inc sts into patt.
Cont without shaping until work measures 18 (22) cm/7 (8¾) in from beg, ending with a wrong side row. Cast off.

NECKBAND
Join shoulder seams.
With 3¼mm (No 10/US 3) needles, M and right side facing, pick up and K 26 sts up right front neck, K across 33 (35) sts on back neck, pick up and K 26 sts down left front neck. 85 (87) sts.
Beg with a 2nd row, work in rib as given for Back for 3 cm/1¼in. Cast off in rib.

BUTTONHOLE BAND
With 3¼mm (No 10/US 3) needles, M and right side facing, pick up and K 61 (73) sts along Right Front to top of neckband.
Beg with a 2nd row, work 3 rows in rib as given for Back.
1st buttonhole row Rib 3, [cast off 2, rib 10 sts more] 4 (5) times, cast off 2, rib to end.

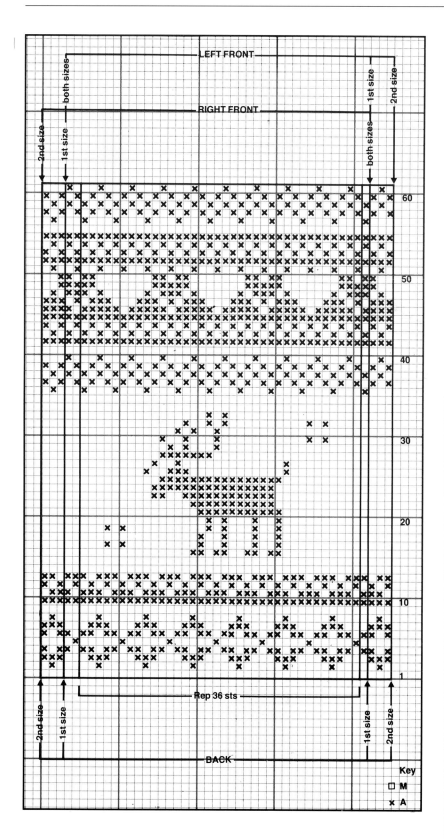

2nd buttonhole row Rib to end, casting on 2 sts over those cast off in previous row. Rib 4 rows. Cast off in rib.

BUTTON BAND
Work to match Buttonhole Band, omitting buttonholes.

TO MAKE UP
Sew on sleeves, placing centre of sleeves to shoulder seams. Join side and sleeve seams. Sew on buttons.

Hat   Pg 137

With 3¼-mm (No 10/US 3) needles and M, cast on 45 sts.
Work in rib as given for Back of Cardigan for 2 cm/¾-in, ending with a wrong side row.
Change to 4 mm (No 8/US 5) needles.
Beg with a K row and working in st st throughout, work 15th to 55th row of patt from chart as indicated for 2nd size on Back. Cast off.
Make another piece in same way. Join top and side seams. Make 2 pompons in Red and attach to each corner of hat.

Boots

With 2¾-mm (No 12/US 1) needles and M, cast on 53 sts. K 11 rows.
1st row (right side) K1, [P1, K1] to end.
2nd row P1, [K1, P1] to end.
Rep last 2 rows 3 times more.
Next row Rib 3, [P2 tog, yrn, rib 3, K2 tog, yf , rib 3] to end. Rib 5 rows.
Shape instep
Next row K20 M, 13A, turn.
Next row K13A, turn.
K 22 rows in A on these 13 sts. Break off yarn. Leave these sts on a holder.
With right side facing and M, pick up and K 12 sts evenly along side edge of instep, K 13 sts from holder, then pick up and K 12 sts evenly along other side edge of instep, K rem sts. 77 sts. Cont in M only, K 17 rows. Beg with K row, work 9 rows in st st.
Next row [P next st tog with corresponding st 9 rows below] to end. K 13 rows. Cast off.
Join back seam, reversing seam on cuff to allow for turning. Join under seam folding knitting carefully to lie flat to form mitred corners. With M, make cord approximately 40 cm/15¾-in long and thread through holes.

Long Line Fair Isle Sweater with Pockets and Socks

See Page 21

MEASUREMENTS

To fit age	**9**	**12:18**	**Mths**
All round at chest	60	64:70	**cm**
	$23\frac{1}{2}$	$25\frac{1}{4}$:$27\frac{1}{2}$	**in**
Length to shoulder	32	36:39	**cm**
	$12\frac{1}{2}$	14:$15\frac{1}{2}$	**in**
Sleeve seam	18	21:24	**cm**
	7	$8\frac{1}{4}$:$9\frac{1}{2}$	**in**
To fit foot		13	**cm**
		5	**in**
Length to base of heel		13	**cm**
		5	**in**

MATERIALS
Sweater 2 x 50 g balls of Jaeger Baby Merino 4 ply in main colour (M).
1 x 50 g ball of same in 7 contrast colours (A, B, C, D, E, F and G).
1 pair each of $2\frac{3}{4}$mm (No 12/US 1) and $3\frac{1}{4}$ mm (No 10/US 3) knitting needles.
Set of four $2\frac{3}{4}$mm (No 12/US 1) double pointed knitting needles.
Socks 1 x 50 g ball of Jaeger Baby Merino 4 ply in main colour (M).
Small amounts of same in 6 contrast colours (B, C, D, E, F and G).
1 pair each of $2\frac{3}{4}$mm (No 12/US 1) and $3\frac{1}{4}$mm (No 10/US 3) knitting needles.
Set of four $3\frac{1}{4}$mm (No 10/US 3) double pointed knitting needles.

TENSION
32 sts and 32 rows to 10 cm/4 in over patt on $3\frac{1}{4}$mm (No 10/US 3) needles.

ABBREVIATIONS
See page 63.

NOTE
When working in patt, strand yarn not in use loosely across wrong side to keep fabric elastic.

Sweater

BACK
With $2\frac{3}{4}$mm (No 12/US 1) needles and M, cast on 81 (85:93) sts.
1st row (right side) K1, [P1, K1] to end.
2nd row P1, [K1, P1] to end.
Rep these 2 rows until work measures 4 cm/$1\frac{1}{2}$ in from beg, ending with a right side row.
Next row Rib 1 (4:3), [inc in next st, rib 4 (3:3), inc in next st, rib 4] to end. 97 (103:113) sts.
Change to $3\frac{1}{4}$mm (No 10/US 3) needles.
Beg with a K row and working in st st throughout, work patt from chart as indicated for Back, reading K rows from right to left and P rows from left to right until work measures 32 (36:39) cm/$12\frac{1}{2}$ (14:$15\frac{1}{2}$) in from beg, ending with a wrong side row.
Shape Shoulders
Cast off 15 (16:18) sts at beg of next 4 rows. Leave rem 37 (39:41) sts on a holder.

POCKET LININGS (make 2)
With $3\frac{1}{4}$mm (No 10/US 3) needles and M, cast on 26 sts. Work in st st until work measures 6 cm/$2\frac{1}{4}$in from beg, ending with a P row. Leave these sts on a holder.

FRONT
Work as given for Back until work measures 11 cm/$4\frac{1}{4}$in from beg, ending with a wrong side row.
Place Pockets
Next row Patt 9 (10:11), *slip next 26 sts onto a holder, patt across sts on one pocket lining*, patt 27 (31:39), rep from * to * once, patt to end.
Cont in patt until work measures 27 (31:34) cm/$10\frac{1}{2}$ (12:$13\frac{1}{2}$) in from beg, ending with a wrong side row.
Shape Neck
Next row Patt 39 (41:45), turn. Work on this set of sts only.
Keeping patt correct, dec one st at neck edge on every row until 30 (32:36) sts rem. Cont without shaping until work measures same as Back to shoulder shaping, ending with a wrong side row.
Shape Shoulder
Cast off 15 (16:18) sts at beg of next row. Patt 1 row. Cast off rem 15 (16:18) sts.
With right side facing, slip centre 19 (21:23) sts onto a holder, rejoin yarn to rem sts and patt to end. Complete to match first side, reversing shaping.

SLEEVES
With $2\frac{3}{4}$mm (No 12/US 1) needles and M, cast on 49 (51:53) sts.
Work in rib as given for Back for 4 cm/$1\frac{1}{2}$ in, ending with a wrong side row and inc 10 sts evenly across last row. 59 (61:63) sts.
Change to $3\frac{1}{4}$mm (No 10/US 3) needles.
Beg with a K row and working in st st throughout, work in patt from chart as indicated for Sleeve, **at the same time**, inc one st at each end of every foll 3rd row until there are 83 (89:95) sts, working inc sts into patt.
Cont without shaping until work measures 18 (21:24) cm/7 ($8\frac{1}{4}$:$9\frac{1}{2}$) in from beg, ending with a wrong side row. Cast off.

COLLAR
Join shoulder seams.
With right side facing, slip first 9 (10:11) sts from centre front holder onto a safety pin, join M yarn to next st, and with set of four $2\frac{3}{4}$mm (No 12/US 1) needles, K rem 10 (11:12) sts, pick up and K 18 sts up right front neck, K across 37 (39:41) sts on back neck inc 4 sts evenly, pick up and K 18 sts down left front neck, then K9 (10:11) sts from safety pin. 96 (100:104) sts.
Work in rounds of K1, P1 rib for 2 cm/$\frac{3}{4}$in, inc one st at end of last round, turn. 97 (101:105) sts.
Work backwards and forwards in rib until collar measures 6 (7:8) cm/$2\frac{1}{4}$($2\frac{3}{4}$:3) in.
Cast off loosely in rib.

POCKET TOPS
With $2\frac{3}{4}$mm (No 12/US 1) needles, M and right side facing, K across sts on pocket top, inc one st at centre, 27 sts.
Beg with a 2nd row, work 7 rows in rib as given for Back. Cast off in rib.

TO MAKE UP
Sew on sleeves, placing centre of sleeves to shoulder seams. Join side and sleeve seams. Catch down pocket linings and sides of pocket tops.

Socks

With $2\frac{3}{4}$mm (No 12/US 1) needles and M, cast on 49 sts for cuff.
Work in rib as given for Back of Sweater for 4 rows.
Change to $3\frac{1}{4}$mm (No 10/US 3) needles.
Beg with a K row and working in st st throughout, work 13th to 29th rows of chart as indicated for 1st size on Back, dec 6 sts evenly across last row. 43 sts.
Cont in M only. Change to $2\frac{3}{4}$mm (No 12/US 1) needles.
Beg with a 1st row (thus reversing the fabric), work in rib as given for Back of Sweater until work measures 12 cm/$4\frac{3}{4}$in from beg, ending with a wrong side row.
Change to $3\frac{1}{4}$mm (No 10/US 3) needles.
Beg with a K row, work 4 rows in st st.
Break off yarn.

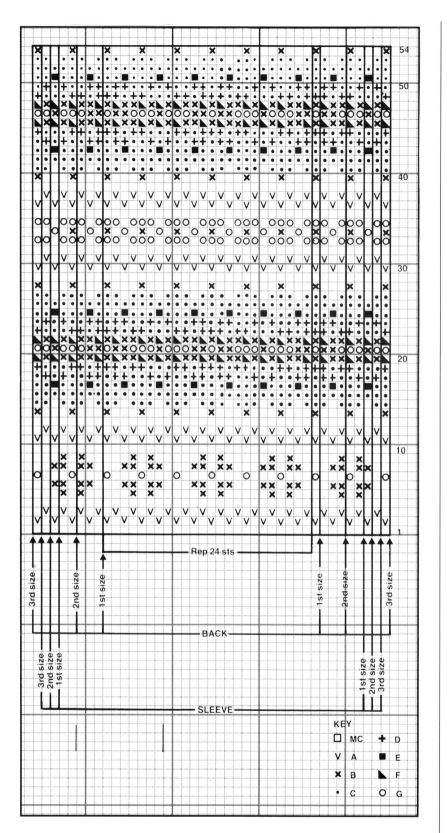

With set of four 3¼mm (No 10/US 3) needles, divide sts onto 3 needles as follows:

Slip first 9 sts onto first needle, next 12 sts onto second needle and next 12 sts onto third needle, slip last 10 sts onto other end of first needle.

Shape Heel
With right side facing, join M yarn to 19 sts on first needle, K9, K2 tog, K8, turn. Work on these 18 sts only.

Beg with a P row, work 9 rows in st st.

Next row K13, K2 tog tbl, turn.

Next row Sl 1, P8, P2 tog, turn.

Next row Sl 1, K8, K2 tog tbl, turn.

***Next row** Sl 1, P8, P2 tog turn.*

Rep from * to * twice 10 sts. Break off yarn.

Next round Reset sts on 3 needles as follows: Slip first 5 sts of heel sts onto a safety pin. Place marker here to indicate beg of round, join M yarn to rem sts, with first needle K5, then pick up and K 8 sts along side of heel, K5, with second needle, K14, with 3rd needle K5, then pick up and K 8 sts along other side of heel, K5 from safety pin. 50 sts. K 1 round.

Next round K12, K2 tog, K to last 14 sts, K2 tog tbl, K12, K 1 round.

Next round K11, K2 tog, K to last 13 sts, K2 tog tbl, K11.

Cont in this way dec one st at each side of heel on every alt round until 40 sts rem. Cont without shaping until work measures 11 cm/4¼in from back of heel.

Shape Toe
Next round [K7, K2 tog, K2, K2 tog tbl, K7] twice, K 1 round.

Next round [K6, K2 tog, K2, K2 tog tbl, K6] twice.

Cont in this way dec 4 sts on every alt round until 20 sts rem. Divide sts onto 2 needles (sole and instep) and graft sts.

Join back seam, reversing seam on cuff to allow for turning.

Mexican Jacket

See Page
22

MEASUREMENTS

To fit age	6–12	12–24:24–36	Mths
All round at chest	62 / 24½	66:70 / 26:27½	cm / in
Length to shoulder	25 / 10	28:32 / 11:12½	cm / in
Sleeve seam	16 / 6¼	22:25 / 8½:10	cm / in

MATERIALS
3 (3:4) 50 g balls of Rowan Designer DK Wool in main colour (M)

Small amount of same in 5 colours (A, B, C, D and E).
1 pair each of 3¼ mm (No 10/US 3) and 4 mm (No 8/US 5) knitting needles.

TENSION
22 sts and 28 rows to 10 cm/4 in over st st on 4 mm (No 8/US 5) needles.

NOTE
Use a separate length of yarn for each motif and twist yarns together on wrong side when changing colour to avoid holes. If preferred, motifs may be Swiss Darned when knitting is complete.

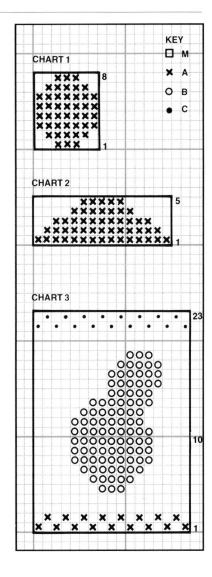

KEY
□ M
✗ A
○ B
● C

CHART 1

CHART 2

CHART 3

BACK
With 4 mm (No 8/US 5) needles and M, cast on 69 (73:77) sts.
1st row K1, [P1, K1] to end.
This row forms moss st. Moss st 3 more rows.
Next row K1M, [1A, 1M] to end.
Next row P1A, [1M, 1A] to end.
Cont in st st and M only until work measures 25 (28:32) cm/10 (11:12½) in from beg, ending with a wrong side row.
Shape Shoulders
Cast off 10 (11:11) sts at beg of next 2 rows and 11 (11:12) sts at beg of foll 2 rows. Leave rem 27 (29:31) sts on a holder.

LEFT FRONT
With 4 mm (No 8/US 5) needles and M, cast on 35 (37:39) sts.
Work 4 rows in moss st as given for Back.
Next row (right side) K1 M, [1A, 1M] to last 4 sts, with M, moss st 4.
Next row With M, moss st 4, P1A, [1M, 1A] to end.
Cont in M only.
Next row K to last 4 sts, moss st 4.
Next row Moss st 4, P to end.
Rep last 2 rows until work measures 15 (17:20) cm/6 (6¾:8) in from beg, ending with a wrong side row.
Work patt from chart 1, reading K rows from right to left and P rows from left to right, as follows:
1st row With M, K13 (14:15), K across 1st row of chart 1, with M, K to last 4 sts, moss st 4.
2nd row With M, moss st 4, P11 (12:13), P across 2nd row of chart 1, with M, P to end.
3rd to 8th row Rep 1st and 2nd rows 3 times more, but working 3rd to 8th rows of chart 1.
Keeping the 4 sts at front edge in moss st and remainder in st st, cont in M only until work measures 20 (23:27) cm/8 (9:10½) in from beg, ending with a right side row.
Shape Neck
Cast off 4 (5:6) sts at beg of next row and

3 sts at beg of foll alt row. Dec one st at neck edge on every row until 21 (22:23) sts rem. Cont without shaping until work measures same as Back to shoulder shaping, ending with a wrong side row.
Shape Shoulder
Cast off 10 (11:11) sts at beg of next row. Work 1 row. Cast off rem 11 (11:12) sts.

RIGHT FRONT
With 4 mm (No 8/US 5) needles and M, cast on 35 (37:39) sts.
Work 4 rows in moss st as given for Back.
Next row (right side) With M, moss st 4, K1M, [1A, 1M] to end.
Next row P1A, [1M, 1A] to last 4 sts, with M, moss st 4.
Cont in M only.
Next row Moss st 4, K to end.
Next row P to last 4 sts, moss st 4.
Complete as Left Front, reversing all shaping and working patt from chart 1 as follows:
1st row With M, moss st 4, K11 (12:13), K across 1st row of chart 1, with M, K to end.
2nd row With M, P13 (14:15), P across 2nd row of chart 1, with M, P to last 4 sts, moss st 4.

SLEEVES
With 4 mm (No 8/US 5) needles and M, cast on 33 (35:37) sts. Work 4 rows in moss st as given for Back.
Next row K1C, [1M, 1C] to end.
Next row With M, P twice in first st, [P1C, 1M] to last 2 sts, P1C, with M, P twice in last st.
With M, work 2 rows in st st.
Work patt from chart 2 as follows:
1st row With M, K twice in first st, K9 (10:11), K across 1st row of chart 2, with M, K to last st, K twice in last st.
2nd row With M, P11 (12:13), P across 2nd row of chart 2, with M, P to end.
These 2 rows set patt from chart 2. Work a further 3 rows as set, inc one st at each

end of 2nd row. 39 (41:43) sts.
Cont in st st and M only, inc one st at each end of 2nd and every foll 3rd (4th:5th) row until there are 57 (61:65) sts.
Cont without shaping for a few rows until work measures 16 (22:25) cm/6¼ (8½:10) in from beg, ending with a P row. Cast off.

POCKETS
With 4 mm (No 8/US 5) needles and M, cast on 23 sts.
1st row With M, K1, P1, K1, K across 1st row of chart 3, with M, K1, P1, K1.
2nd row With M, K1, P1, K1, P across 2nd row of chart 3, with M, K1, P1, K1.
3rd to 23rd rows Rep last 2 rows 10 times more then work 1st row again, but working 3rd to 23rd row of chart 3. Cont in M only, P 1 row, then work 4 rows in moss st. Cast off.
Make another pocket, reversing patt from chart 3 by reading K rows from left to right and P rows from right to left.

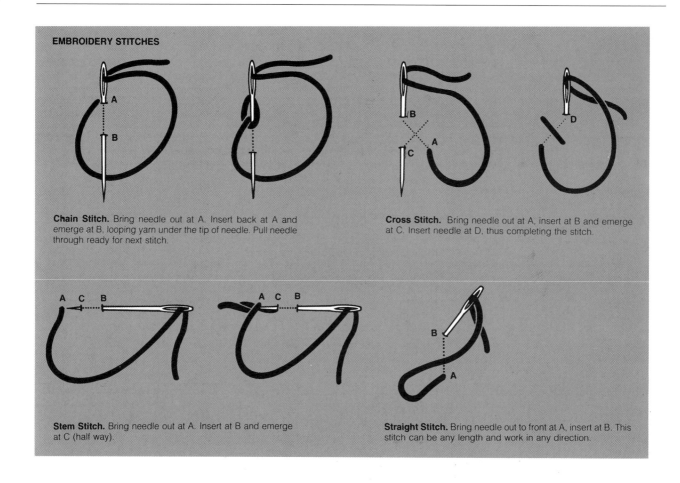

EMBROIDERY STITCHES

Chain Stitch. Bring needle out at A. Insert back at A and emerge at B, looping yarn under the tip of needle. Pull needle through ready for next stitch.

Cross Stitch. Bring needle out at A, insert at B and emerge at C. Insert needle at D, thus completing the stitch.

Stem Stitch. Bring needle out at A. Insert at B and emerge at C (half way).

Straight Stitch. Bring needle out to front at A, insert at B. This stitch can be any length and work in any direction.

NECKBAND

Join shoulder seams.
With 3¼-mm (No 10/US 3) needles, M and right side facing, pick up and K 23 sts up right front neck, K across 27 (29:31) sts on back neck, pick up and K 23 sts down left front neck. 73 (75:77) sts.
Work 4 rows in moss st. Cast off, working 2 sts tog at beg and end.

TO MAKE UP

Sew on sleeves, placing centre of sleeves to shoulder seams. Join side and sleeve seams. If necessary, work Swiss Darning (see diagram page 111). Embroider cactus flowers in E and lazy daisy stitch (see diagram page 99) and spikes in D and straight stitches (see diagram above). Embroider sunrays in A and straight stitches. With D, work cross stitches around outside edges of each pocket, omitting cast on edge. Sew on pockets. Now work cross stitch with D along cast on edge of Right Front, up straight edge, around neck edge, down Left Front, along cast on edge of Left Front and Back. Work cross stitch with D along cast on edge of each sleeve.

Hooded Fair Isle Jacket

See Page
23

MEASUREMENTS

To fit age	1	2:3	Yrs
All round at chest	70	75:80	cm
	$27\frac{1}{2}$	$29\frac{1}{2}$:$31\frac{1}{2}$	in
Length to shoulder	34	37:40	cm
	$13\frac{1}{2}$	$14\frac{1}{2}$:$15\frac{3}{4}$	in
Sleeve seam	21	23:25	cm
	$8\frac{1}{4}$	9:10	in

MATERIALS

3 (4:4) 50 g balls of Rowan Designer DK Wool in main colour (M).
3 balls of same in colour A.
2 (2:3) balls of same in colour B.
2 balls of same in colour C.
1 ball of same in 2 colours D and E.
1 pair each of $3\frac{1}{4}$ mm (No 10/US 3) and 4 mm (No 8/US 5) knitting needles.
6 buttons.

TENSION

23 sts and 24 rows to 10 cm/4 in over patt using 4 mm (No 8/US 5) needles.

ABBREVIATIONS

See page 63.

NOTE

When working in pattern, strand yarn not in use loosely across wrong side to keep fabric elastic.

BACK

With $3\frac{1}{4}$ mm (No 10/US 3) needles and M, cast on 81 (87:93) sts.
Beg with a K row, work 7 rows in st st.
Next row K to end for hem line.
Change to 4 mm (No 8/US 5) needles.
Beg with a K row and working in st st throughout, cont in patt from chart as indicated for Back, reading K rows from right to left and P rows from left to right, until work measures 34 (37:40) cm/$13\frac{1}{2}$ ($14\frac{1}{2}$:$15\frac{3}{4}$) in from hem line, ending with a wrong side row. Cast off.

RIGHT FRONT

With $3\frac{1}{4}$ mm (No 10/US 3) needles and M, cast on 55 (58:61) sts.
Beg with a K row, work 7 rows in st st.
Next row K to end for hem line.
Change to 4 mm (No 8/US 5) needles.
Beg with a K row and working in st st throughout, cont in patt from chart as indicated for Right Front until work measures 11.5 cm/$4\frac{1}{2}$ in from hem line, ending with a wrong side row.
1st buttonhole row Patt 3, cast off 3, patt to end.
2nd buttonhole row Patt to last 3 sts, cast on 3, patt 3.

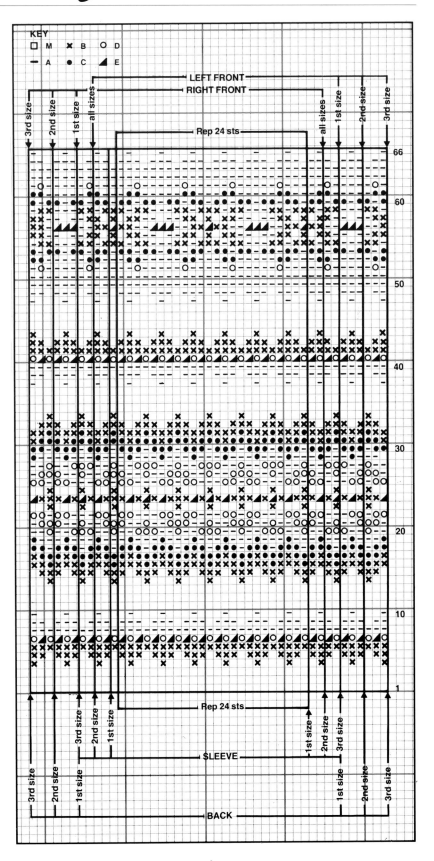

Patt 10 (12:14) rows. Rep the 2
buttonhole rows again. Patt 2 rows.
Shape Collar
Cast on 7 sts at beg of next row. Keeping
patt correct, inc one st at front edge on
next 10 rows then on every foll alt row
until there are 84 (89:94) sts.
Cont without shaping until work measures
same as Back to cast off edge, ending
with a right side row.
Shape Shoulder
Cast off 26 (28:30) sts at beg of next row.
58 (61:64) sts.
Shape Right Side Hood
Cast on 15 (16:17) sts at beg of next 2
rows. 88 (93:98) sts.
Cont without shaping until hood
measures 18 (20:23) cm/7 (8:9) in, ending
with a wrong side row.
Shape Top
Cast off 8 (9:9) sts at beg of next 8 rows.
Cast off rem 24 (21:26) sts.

LEFT FRONT
Following chart as indicated for Left Front,
work as given for Right Front, reversing
buttonhole rows and all shaping.

SLEEVES
With 3¼mm (No 10/US 3) needles and M,
cast on 41 (45:49) sts.
1st row (right side) K1, [P1, K1] to end.
2nd row P1, [K1, P1] to end.
Rep these 2 rows until work measures 4
cm/1½ in from beg, ending with a wrong
side row and inc 8 sts evenly across last
row. 49 (53:57) sts.
Change to 4 mm (No 8/US 5) needles.
Beg with a K row and working in st st
throughout, cont in patt from chart as
indicated for Sleeves, **at the same time**,
inc one st at each end of 3rd (4th:4th) and
3 foll alt rows then on every 3rd row until
there are 69 (73:79) sts, working inc sts
into patt. Cont without shaping until work
measures 21 (23:25) cm/8¼ (9:10) in from
beg, ending with a wrong side row. Cast
off.

FRONT FACINGS (make 2)
With 3¼mm (No 10/US 3) needles and M,
cast on 9 sts.
Work 8.5 cm/3½ in in st st, ending with a P
row.
1st buttonhole row K 3, cast off 3, K to end.

2nd buttonhole row P3, cast on 3, P to
end.
Work 10 (12:14) rows, then rep the 2
buttonhole rows again. Work 2 rows. Cast
off.

TO MAKE UP
Join shoulder seams. Join back, top and
inside back seam of hood. Fold hood in
half to inside, folding shaped part of collar
to wrong side of fronts. Join cast on
edges of hood to back neck then slip
stitch collar in position. Sew on sleeves,
placing centre of sleeves to shoulder
seams. Join side and sleeve seams.
Fold hem to wrong side and slip stitch in
place, closing opening at front edges.
Sew on facings, sewing cast on edges to
top of hem and cast off edges to cast on
sts for collar. Neaten buttonholes. Sew on
2 buttons to right side of Left Front and 2
to wrong side of Right Front to correspond
with buttonholes, then sew 2 buttons to
right side of Right Front in same place as
buttons on wrong side.

Aran Sweater with Farmyard Panel

See Page 24

MEASUREMENTS
To fit age	2	Yrs
Actual chest measurement	76	cm
	30	in
Length	41	cm
	16	in
Sleeve seam	25	cm
	10	in

MATERIALS
950 g balls of Rowan DK Handknit
Cotton in Brown (MC).
150 g ball of same in each of Red,
Cream, Black, Yellow and Blue.
Pair each of 3¼mm (No 10/US 3) and 4
mm (No 8/US 5) knitting needles.
Cable needle.

TENSION
20 sts and 28 rows to 10 cm/4 in square
over st st on 4 mm (No 8/US 5) needles.

ABBREVIATIONS
C2B = slip next st onto cable needle
and leave at back of work, K1, then K1
from cable needle;
C2F = slip next st onto cable needle
and leave at front of work, K1, then K1
from cable needle;
Cr2L = slip next st onto cable needle
and leave at front of work, P1, then K1
from cable needle;
Cr2R = slip next st onto cable needle
and leave at back of work, K1, then P1
from cable needle;
MB = make bobble, [K1, P1, K1, P1] all
in next st, turn, P4, turn, K4, turn, [P2 tog]
twice, turn, K2 tog.
Also see page 63.

NOTE
Read Chart from right to left on right side
rows and from left to right on wrong side
rows. When working motifs, use separate
lengths of contrast yarn for each
coloured area and twist yarns together
on wrong side when changing colour to
avoid holes.

PANEL – worked over 18 sts.
1st row (wrong side) K8, P2, K8.
2nd row P7, C2B, C2F, P7.
3rd row K6, Cr2L, P2, Cr2R, K6.
4th row P5, Cr2R, C2B, C2F, Cr2L, P5.
5th row K4, Cr2L, K1, P4, K1, Cr2R, K4.
6th row P3, Cr2R, P1, Cr2R, K2, Cr2L, P1, Cr2L, P3.
7th row K3, P1, K2, P1, K1, P2, K1, P1, K2, P1, K3.
8th row P3, MB, P1, Cr2R, P1, K2, P1, Cr2L, P1, MB, P3.
9th row K5, P1, K2, P2, K2, P1, K5.
10th row P5, MB, P2, K2, P2, MB, P5.
These 10 rows form patt.

BACK
With 3¼mm (No 10/US 3) needles and
MC, cast on 74 sts.
1st row (wrong side) K2, [P2, K2] to end.
2nd row P2, [K2, P2] to end.
Rep last 2 rows until work measures
4 cm/1½ in from beg, ending with a wrong
side row.
Inc row Rib 3, [m1, rib 5] 3 times, rib 5,
m1, rib 9, [m1, rib 3] 4 times, rib 7, m1, rib
5, [rib 5, m1] 3 times, rib 3. 86 sts.
Change to 4 mm (No 8/US 5) needles.
Work in patt as follows:
1st row (wrong side) With MC, K1, work

1st row of Panel, [P across 1st row of Chart, with MC, work 1st row of Panel] twice, K1MC.

2nd row With MC, P1, work 2nd row of Panel, [K across 2nd row of Chart, with MC, work 2nd row of Panel] twice, P1MC.

These 2 rows set position of Panels and Charts. Cont in patt as set until work measures 41 cm/16 in from beg, ending with a wrong side row.

Shape Shoulders

Cast off 13 sts at beg of next 2 rows and 14 sts at beg of foll 2 rows.

Leave rem 32 sts on a holder.

FRONT

Work as given for Back until Front measures 35 cm/13¾ in from beg, ending with a wrong side row.

Shape Neck

Next row Patt 35, turn.

Work on this set of sts only. Keeping patt correct, dec one st at neck edge on every row until 27 sts rem. Cont straight until Front matches Back to shoulder shaping, ending at side edge.

Shape Shoulder

Cast off 13 sts at beg of next row. Patt 1 row. Cast off rem 14 sts.

With right side facing, slip centre 16 sts onto a holder, rejoin yarn to rem sts and patt to end. Complete to match first side.

SLEEVES

With 3¼ mm (No 10/US 3) needles and MC, cast on 42 sts. Work 3 cm/1¼ in in rib as given for Back welt, ending with a wrong side row.

Inc row Rib 1, [m1, rib 5] to last st, m1, rib

1. 51 sts.

Change to 4 mm (No 8/US 5) needles. Work in patt as follows:

1st row (wrong side) With MC, work 1st row of Panel, P across 1st row of Chart, with MC, work 1st row of Panel.

2nd row With MC, work 2nd row of Panel, K across 2nd row of Chart, with MC, work 2nd row of Panel.

These 2 rows set position of Panels and Chart. Cont in patt as set, inc one st at each end of next row and 8 foll 3rd rows, then on every foll 4th row until there are 79 sts, working inc sts into patt from Chart. Cont straight until Sleeve measures 25 cm/10 in from beg, ending with a wrong side row. Cast off.

NECKBAND

Join right shoulder seam.

With 3¼ mm (No 10/US 3) needles, MC and right side facing, pick up and K 17 sts down left front neck, K centre front sts, pick up and K 17 sts up right front neck, K back neck sts. 82 sts.

Beg with a 1st row, work 11 rows in rib as given for Back welt. Beg with a K row, work 5 rows in st st. Cast off purlwise.

TO MAKE UP

Join left shoulder and neckband seam, reversing seam on st st section of neckband. Allow top of neckband to roll back. Sew on sleeves, placing centre of sleeves to shoulder seams. Join side and sleeve seams. With Black, embroider eyes and legs on chicks and eyes on ducklings.

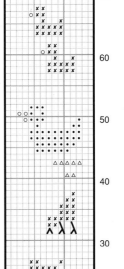

KEY

□ = Brown
○ = Red
• = Cream
▲ = Black
✗ = Yellow
△ = Blue

∧ = λ
embroidery stitches

Cotton Smock

See Page
25

MEASUREMENTS To fit age	2–3	3–4	Years
Actual chest measurement	69	77	cm
	27	30¼	in
Length	50	56	cm
	19¾	22	in
Sleeve seam	22	25	cm
	8¾	10	in

MATERIALS

11(13) 50 g balls of Rowan Cotton Glace.
Pair each of 2¼ mm (No 13/US 0) and 3 mm (No 11/US 2) knitting needles.
Cable needle.
6 buttons.

TENSION

28 sts and 34 rows to 10 cm/4 in square over st st on 3 mm (No 11/US 2) needles.

ABBREVIATIONS

Cr2L = sl next st onto cable needle and leave at front of work, P1, then K1 from cable needle;
Cr2R = sl next st onto cable needle and leave at back of work, K1, then P1 from cable needle;
C2B = sl next st onto cable needle and leave at back of work, K1, then K1 from cable needle;
C2F = sl next stitch onto cable needle and leave at front of work, K1, then K1 from cable needle.
Also see page 63.

PATTERN A

Rep of 8 sts.
1st row (right side) [P3, C2F, P3] to end.
2nd row [K2, Cr2L, Cr2R, K2] to end.
3rd row [P1, Cr2R, P2, Cr2L, P1] to end.
4th row [Cr2L, K4, Cr2R].
5th row K1, P6, [C2B, P6] to last st, K1.
6th row [Cr2R, K4, Cr2L] to end.
7th row [P1, Cr2L, P2, Cr2R, P1] to end.
8th row [K2, Cr2R, Cr2L, K2] to end.
These 8 rows form patt.

HEART MOTIF

Worked over 13 sts.
1st row (right side) K3, P1, K5, P1, K3.
2nd row P2, K3, P3, K3, P2.
3rd row K1, [P2, K1] 4 times.
4th row K2, P3, K3, P3, K2.
5th row P2, K4, P1, K4, P2.
6th row P1, K2, P7, K2, P1.
7th row K2, P2, K5, P2, K2.
8th row P3, [K2, P3] twice.
9th row K4, P2, K1, P2, K4.
10th row P5, K3, P5.
11th row K6, P1, K6.
12th row P13.
13th row K13.
14th row P13.
15th and 16th rows As 13th and 14th rows.
17th row As 11th row.
18th row As 10th row.
19th row As 9th row.
20th row As 8th row.
21st row As 7th row.
22nd row As 6th row.
23rd row As 5th row.
24th row As 4th row.
25th row As 3rd row.
26th row As 2nd row.
27th row As 1st row.

BACK

With 3 mm (No 11/US 2) needles, cast on 146(162) sts.
**Beg with a K row, work 7 rows in st st.
Next row (fold line) K.
Beg with a K row, work in st st until Back measures 32(37) cm/12½(14½) in from fold line, ending with a K row. **
Dec row P19(21), [P2 tog, P1] 36(40) times, P19(21). 110(122) sts.
Work in patt as follows:
1st row (right side) K18(20), P1, work 1st row of patt A across next 72(80) sts, P1, K18(20).
2nd row P18(20), K1, work 2nd row of patt A across next 72(80) sts, K1, P18(20).
Work a further 8 rows as set.
11th row K3(4), work 1st row of Heart Motif, K2(3), P1, work 72(80) sts in patt A, P1, K2(3), work 1st row of Heart Motif, K3(4).
12th row P3(4), work 2nd row of Heart Motif, P2(3), K1, work 72(80) sts in patt A, K1, P2(3), work 2nd row of Heart Motif, P3(4).
Work a further 25 rows as set.
38th row P18(20), K1, work 72(80) sts in patt A, K1, P18(20).

39th row K18(20), P1, work 72(80) sts in patt A, P1, K18(20).
Cont as now set until work measures 49(55) cm/19¼(21½) in from fold line, ending with a right side row.
Shape Neck and Shoulders
Next row Patt 44(49), cast off next 22(24) sts, patt to end.
Work on last set of sts only. Patt 1 row.
Cast off 5 sts at beg of next row, 16(18) sts at beg of foll row and 5 sts at beg of foll row. Cast off rem 18(21) sts.
With right side facing, rejoin yarn to rem sts and patt 2 rows. Cast off 5 sts at beg of next row, 16(18) sts at beg of foll row and 5 sts at beg of foll row. Cast off rem 18(21) sts.

LEFT FRONT

With 3 mm (No 11/US 2) needles, cast on 69(77) sts.
Work as given for Back from ** to **.
Dec row [P2 tog] 1(2) times, [P1, P2 tog] 15 times, P1, [P2 tog] 1(3) times, P19(21). 52(57) sts.
Work in patt as follows:
1st row (right side) K18(20), P1, work 1st row of patt A across next 32 sts, P1(4).
2nd row K1(4), work 2nd row of patt A across next 32 sts, K1, P18(20).
Work a further 8 rows as set.
11th row K3(4), work 1st row of Heart Motif, K2(3), P1, work 32 sts in patt A, P1(4).
12th row K1(4), work 32 sts in patt A, K1, P2(3), work 2nd row of Heart Motif, P3(4).
Work a further 25 rows as set.
38th row K1(4), work 32 sts in patt A, K1, P18(20).
39th row K18(20), P1, work 32 sts in patt A, P1(4).
Cont as now set until work measures 45(51) cm/17¾(20) in from fold line, ending with a right side row.
Shape Neck
Keeping patt correct, cast off 9 sts at beg of next row. Dec one st at neck edge on every row until 34(39) sts rem. Cont straight until Front matches Back to shoulder shaping, ending with a wrong side row.
Shape Shoulder
Cast off 16(18) sts at beg of next row. Work 1 row. Cast off rem 18(21) sts.

RIGHT FRONT

With 3 mm (No 11/US 2) needles, cast on 69(77) sts.
Work as given for Back from ** to **.
Dec row P19(21), [P2 tog] 1(3) times, P1, [P2 tog, P1] 15 times, [P2 tog] 1(2) times. 52(57) sts.
Work in patt as follows:
1st row (right side) P1(4), work 1st row of patt A across next 32 sts, P1, K18(20).
2nd row P18(20), K1, work 2nd row of patt A across next 32 sts, K1(4).
Work a further 8 rows as set.
11th row P1(4), work 32 sts in patt A, P1, K2(3), work 1st row of Heart Motif, K3(4).
12th row P3(4), work 2nd row of Heart

Motif, P2(3), K1, work 32 sts in patt A, K1(4).
Work a further 25 rows as set.
38th row P18(20), K1, work 32 sts in patt A, K1(4).
39th row P1(4), work 32 sts in patt A, P1, K18(20).
Cont as now set and complete as given for Left Front, reversing shapings.

SLEEVES

With 3 mm (No 11/US 2) needles, cast on 42(49) sts.
Beg with a K row, work 7 rows in st st.
Next row (fold line) K.
Inc row P4, *[K twice in next st, P6] 1(2) times, K twice in next st, P2, P twice in next st, P2; rep from * once, [K twice in next st, P6] 1(0) time, K twice in next st, P4. 50(58) sts.
Next row K1, work 2nd row of patt A across next 48(56) sts, K1.
Next row P1, work 3rd row of patt A across next 48(56) sts, P1.
Work a further 14 rows as set.
Inc row P1(2), [P twice in each of next 2 sts, P1] to last 1(2) sts, P1(2). 82(94) sts.
Beg with a K row, work in st st, inc one st at each end of 5th row and every foll 6th(8th) row until there are 92(104) sts.
Cont straight for a few rows until Sleeve measures 15(18) cm/6(7) in from fold line, ending with a P row.
Next row K21(23), P1, work 1st row of patt A across next 48(56) sts, P1, K21(23).
Next row P21(23), K1, work 2nd row of patt A across next 48(56) sts, K1, P21(23).
Work a further 23 rows as set. Cast off.

COLLAR

With 3 mm (No 11/US 2) needles, cast on 64(72) sts.
Beg with a K row, work 7 rows in st st inc one st at each end of 2nd row and every foll row. 76(84) sts.
Next row (fold line) K.
Next row P4, K twice in next st, P4, K58(66), P4, K twice in next st, P4. 78(86) sts.
Work in patt as follows:
1st row (wrong side) K3, Cr2L, Cr2R, K3, P58(66), K3, Cr2L, P2, Cr2R, K3.
2nd row P2, Cr2R, P2, Cr2L, P2, K58(66), P2, Cr2R, P2, Cr2L, P2.
3rd row K1, Cr2L, K4, Cr2R, K1, P58(66), K1, Cr2L, K4, Cr2R, K1.
4th row P1, K1, P6, K1, P1, K58(66), P1, K1, P6, K1, P1.
5th row K1, Cr2R, K4, Cr2L, K1, P58(66), K1, Cr2R, K4, Cr2L, K1.
6th row P2, Cr2L, P2, Cr2R, P2, K58(66), P2, Cr2L, P2, Cr2R, P2.
7th row K3, Cr2R, Cr2L, K3, P58(66), K3, Cr2R, Cr2L, K3.
8th row P4, C2F, P4, K58(66), P4, C2F, P4.
These 8 rows form patt. Work a further 34(42) rows.
Shape Neck
Next row Patt 30(33), cast off next 18(20) sts, patt to end.
Cont on last set of sts only for right side of

collar. Patt 1 row. Cast off 3 sts at beg of next row and foll alt row. 24(27) sts. Patt 11 rows straight. Inc one st at beg of next row and at same edge on every row until there are 31(34) sts. Patt 1 row. Cast on 8(9) sts at beg of next row. 39(43) sts. Patt 28(36) rows straight.

Next row P4, K2 tog, P4, K29(33).

Next row (fold line) K.

Beg with a K row, work 7 rows in st st, dec one st at end of 2nd row and at same edge of every foll row. 32(36) sts. Cast off. With right side facing, rejoin yarn to rem sts and patt to end. Complete to match first side, reversing shapings.

COLLAR FACINGS

With 3 mm (No 11/US 2) needles and right side facing, pick up and K 67 (79) sts evenly along one outside edge between fold lines.

Next row (fold line) K.

Beg with a K row, work 7 rows in st st, dec one st at each end of 2nd row and every foll row. 55(67) sts. Cast off.

Work other outside edge in same way.

With 3 mm (No 11/US 2) needles and right side facing, pick up and K 21(27) sts evenly along inside edge between fold line and cast on sts at neck.

Next row (fold line) K.

Beg with a K row, work 7 rows in st st, dec one st at end of 2nd row and at same edge of every foll row. 15(21) sts. Cast off.

POCKETS (make 2)

With 3 mm (No 11/US 2) needles, cast on 30(32) sts. Beg with a K row, work 7 rows in st st.

Next row (fold line) K.

Beg with a K row, work 36(40) rows in st st. Cast off.

BUTTONHOLE BAND

With 2¼ mm (No 13/US 0) needles and right side facing, pick up and K 120 (140) sts along front edge of Right Front from fold line to beg of neck shaping. Beg with a P row, work 2 rows in st st.

1st buttonhole row P2, [cast off 2, P9(11) sts more] 6 times, P to end.

2nd buttonhole row K to end, casting on 2

sts over those cast off in previous row. Work 3 rows in st st.

Next row (fold line) P.

Beg with a P row, work 3 rows in st st.

1st buttonhole row K56(66), [cast off 2, K9(11) sts more] 5 times, cast off 2, K1 st more.

2nd buttonhole row P to end, casting on 2 sts over those cast off in previous row. Work 2 rows in st st. Cast off.

BUTTON BAND

Work to match Buttonhole Band, omitting buttonholes.

TO MAKE UP

Join shoulder seams. Sew on sleeves, placing centre of sleeves to shoulder seams. Join side and sleeve seams. Fold all hems and facings at fold line to wrong side and slip stitch in positions, joining open ends of front bands together and mitring corners of collar facings. Neaten buttonholes. Sew on pockets, collar and buttons.

Cable Sweater with Chicken Panel

See Page
26

MEASUREMENTS			
To fit age	18–24	24–36	Months
Actual chest measurement	69	73	**cm**
	27¼	28¾	**in**
Length	36	40	**cm**
	14¼	15¾	**in**
Sleeve seam	20	23	**cm**
	8	9	**in**

MATERIALS

7(8) 50 g balls of Rowan DK Handknit Cotton in Orange (MC).
1(1) 50 g ball of same in each of Cream (A), Yellow (B) and Black (C). Pair each of 3¼ mm (No 10/US 3) and 4 mm (No 8/US 5) knitting needles. Cable needle.

TENSION

20 sts and 28 rows to 10 cm/4 in square over st st on 4 mm (No 8/US 5) needles.

ABBREVIATIONS

Cr4L = slip next 3 sts onto cable needle and leave at front of work, K1, then K1 tbl, P1, K1 tbl sts from cable

needle;
Cr4R = slip next st onto cable needle and leave at back of work, K1 tbl, P1, K1 tbl, then K1 from cable needle;
C7F = slip next 3 sts onto cable needle and leave at front of work, [K1 tbl, P1] twice, then K1 tbl, P1, K1 tbl sts from cable needle;
MB = make bobble, [K1, yf, K1, yf, K1] all in next st, turn, P5, turn, K3, K2 tog, then pass 2nd, 3rd and 4th st over first st. Also see page 63.

NOTE

Read Charts from right to left on right side rows and from left to right on wrong side rows. When working motifs, use separate lengths of A, B and C yarn for each coloured area and twist yarns together on wrong side when changing colour to avoid holes.

PANEL A – worked over 21 sts.
1st row (wrong side) K7, P1, K1, P3, K1, P1, K7.
2nd row P6, Cr4R, K1 tbl, Cr4L, P6.
3rd row K6, [P1, K1] 4 times, P1, K6.
4th row P5, Cr4R, K1, K1 tbl, K1, Cr4L,

P5.
5th row K5, P1, K1, [P1, K2] twice, P1, K1, P1, K5.
6th row P4, Cr4R, K2, K1 tbl, K2, Cr4L, P4.
7th row K4, P1, K1, P2, K2, P1, K2, P2,

K1, P1, K4.
8th row P3, Cr4R, [K1 tbl, K2] twice, K1 tbl, Cr4L, P3.
9th row K3, [P1, K1] twice, [P1, K2] twice, [P1, K1] twice, P1, K3.
10th row P2, Cr4R, K1, [K1 tbl, K2] twice,

K1 tbl, K1, Cr4L, P2.
11th row K2, P1, K1, [P1, K2] 4 times, P1, K1, P1, K2.
12th row P1, Cr4R, [K2, K1 tbl] 3 times, K2, Cr4L, P1.
13th row [K1, P1] twice, K3, [P1, K2] 3 times, K1, [P1, K1] twice.
14th row [P1, K1 tbl] twice, K3, [MB, K2] 3 times, K1, [K1 tbl, P1] twice.
15th row [K1, P1] twice, K3, [P1 tbl, K2] 3 times, K1, [P1, K1] twice.
16th row [P1, K1 tbl] twice, P3, K1 tbl, P1, K3 tbl, P1, K1 tbl, P3,[K1 tbl, P1] twice.
These 16 rows form patt.

PANEL B – worked over 13 sts.
1st row (wrong side) P1 tbl, K2, [P1 tbl, K1] 4 times, K1, P1 tbl.
2nd row K1 tbl, P2, C7F, P2, K1 tbl.
3rd row As 1st row.
4th row K1 tbl, P2, [K1 tbl, P1] 4 times, P1, K1 tbl.
5th to 10th rows Rep 3rd and 4th rows 3 times.
These 10 rows form patt.

BACK

With 3¼mm (No 10/US 3) needles and MC, cast on 65(69) sts.
1st row (wrong side) K1, [P1 tbl, K1] to end.
2nd row P1, [K1 tbl, P1] to end.
Rep last 2 rows until work measures 4 cm/1½in from beg, ending with a wrong side row and inc 4 sts evenly across last row. 69(73) sts.
Change to 4 mm (No 8/US 5) needles.
Work border patt as follows:
1st row K in MC.
2nd row P in MC. **
3rd row K7(9)MC, [K across 1st row of Chart 1, K8MC] twice, K across 1st row of Chart 1, K7(9)MC.
4th row P7(9)MC, [P across 2nd row of Chart 1, P8MC] twice, P across 2nd row of Chart 1, P7(9)MC.
5th to 17th rows Rep 3rd and 4th rows 6 times, then work 3rd row again but working 3rd to 15th rows of Chart 1.
*** 18th row P in MC.
19th and 20th rows As 1st and 2nd rows.
Cont in MC only.
Inc row K0(2), [K twice in next st, K1, K twice in next st, K2] 13 times, [K twice in next st, K1(2)] twice. 97(101) sts.
Work in main patt as follows:
1st row (wrong side) K1, [P1, K1] 1(2) times, P1 tbl, [work 1st row of Panel A, then Panel B] twice, work 1st row of Panel A, P1 tbl, [K1, P1] 1(2) times, K1.
2nd row P1, [K1, P1] 1(2) times, K1 tbl, [work 2nd row of Panel A, then Panel B] twice, work 2nd row of Panel A, K1 tbl, [P1, K1] 1(2) times, P1.
3rd row P1, [K1, P1] 1(2) times, P1 tbl, [work 3rd row of Panel A, then Panel B] twice, work 3rd row of Panel A, P1 tbl, [P1, K1] 1(2) times, P1.
4th row K1, [P1, K1] 1(2) times, K1 tbl, [work 4th row of Panel A, then Panel B]

twice, work 4th row of Panel A, K1 tbl, [K1, P1] 1(2) times, K1.
These 4 rows set position of Panels and form double moss st at each side. *******
Cont in patt as set until work measures 36(40) cm/14¼(15¾) in from beg, ending with a wrong side row.
Shape Shoulders
Cast off 14(15) sts at beg of next 2 rows and 14 sts at beg of foll 2 rows.
Leave rem 41(43) sts on a holder.

FRONT

Work as given for Back to **.
3rd row K6(8)MC, K across 1st row of Chart 2, K7MC, K across 1st row of Chart 1, K8MC, K across 1st row of Chart 1, K7(9)MC.
4th row P7(9)MC, P across 2nd row of Chart 1, P8MC, P across 2nd row of Chart 1, P7MC, P across 2nd row of Chart 2, P6(8)MC.
5th to 10th rows Rep 3rd and 4th rows 3 times, but working 3rd to 8th rows of Charts.
11th row K28(30)MC, K across 9th row of Chart 1, K8MC, K across 9th row of Chart 1, K7(9)MC.
12th row P7(9)MC, P across 10th row of Chart 1, P8MC, P across 10th row of Chart 1, P28(30)MC.
13th to 17th rows Rep 11th and 12th rows twice, then work 11th row again, but working 11th to 15th rows of Chart 1.
Work as given for Back from *** to ***.
Cont in patt as set until work measures 30(34) cm/11¾(13½) in from beg, ending with a wrong side row.
Shape Neck
Next row Patt 39(40), turn.
Work on this set of sts only. Keeping patt correct, dec one st at neck edge on every row until 28(29) sts rem. Cont straight until Front matches Back to shoulders, ending at side edge.
Shape Shoulder
Cast off 14(15) sts at beg of next row. Patt 1 row. Cast off rem 15 sts.
With right side facing, slip centre 19(21) sts onto a holder, rejoin yarn to rem sts and patt to end. Complete to match first side.

SLEEVES

With 3¼mm (No 10/US 3) needles and MC, cast on 43(47) sts. Work 5 cm/2 in in rib as given for Back welt, ending with a wrong side row.
Inc row Rib 4(6), inc in next st, rib 7, inc in next st, [rib 2, inc in next st] twice, rib 2, work 3 times in next st, rib 2, [inc in next st, rib 2] twice, inc in next st, rib 7, inc in next st, rib 4(6). 53(57) sts.
Change to 4 mm (No 8/US 5) needles.
Work in patt as follows:
1st row P1, [K1, P1] 1(2) times, work 1st row of Panel B, Panel A, then Panel B, [P1, K1] 1(2) times, P1.
2nd row K1, [P1, K1] 1(2) times, work 2nd row of Panel B, Panel A, then Panel B, [K1, P1] 1(2) times, K1.
3rd row K1, [P1, K1] 1(2) times, work 3rd row of Panel B, Panel A, then Panel B, [K1, P1] 1(2) times, K1.
4th row P1, [K1, P1] 1(2) times, work 4th row of Panel B, Panel A, then Panel B, [P1, K1] 1(2) times, P1.
These 4 rows set position of Panels and form double moss st at each side.
Cont in patt as set, inc one st at each end of next row and every foll alt row until there are 81(85) sts, working inc sts into double moss st.
Cont straight until Sleeve measures 20(23) cm/8(9) in from beg, ending with a wrong side row. Cast off.

NECKBAND

Join right shoulder seam.
With 3¼mm (No 10/US 3) needles, MC and right side facing, pick up and K 16 sts down left front neck, K across centre front sts, pick up and K 15 sts up right front neck, K back neck sts. 91(95) sts.
Beg with a 1st row, work 11 rows in rib as given for Back welt. Cast off in rib.

TO MAKE UP

Join left shoulder and neckband seam. Sew on sleeves, placing centre of sleeves to shoulder seams. Join side and sleeve seams. With B, embroider beaks on hens and chicks. With C, embroider chicks' eyes.

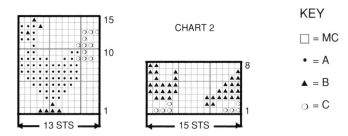

CHART 1

CHART 2

15

10

1

8

1

13 STS

15 STS

KEY

□ = MC

• = A

▲ = B

○ = C

Cow Sweater

See Page
27

MEASUREMENTS

To fit age	6–12	12–18	Months
Actual chest measurement	69	75	cm
	27	29½	in
Length	29	32	cm
	11½	12½	in
Sleeve seam	19	22	cm
	7½	8½	in

MATERIALS

4(5) 50 g balls of Rowan Cotton Glace in Black (MC).
2(3) 50 g balls of same in Cream (A).
1(1) 50 g ball of same in Green.
Small amount of 4 ply cotton in Pink.
Pair each of 2¾ mm (No 12/US 1) and 3¼ mm (No 10/US 3) knitting needles.
6 buttons.

TENSION

26 sts and 30 rows to 10 cm/4 in square over check pattern on 3¼ mm (No 10/US 3) needles.

ABBREVIATIONS

See page 63.

NOTE

Read Chart from right to left on right side rows and from left to right on wrong side rows. When working check pattern, strand yarn not in use loosely across wrong side to keep fabric elastic. When working motif, use separate small balls of yarn for each coloured area and twist yarns together on wrong side when changing colour to avoid holes.

FRONT

With 2¾ mm (No 12/US 1) needles and MC, cast on 83(91) sts.
1st row (right side) K1, [P1, K1] to end.
2nd row P1, [K1, P1] to end.
Rep last 2 rows until welt measures 3 cm/1¼ in from beg, ending with a right side row.
Inc row Rib 8(6), inc in next st, [rib 10(12), inc in next st] 6 times, rib 8(6). 90(98) sts.
Change to 3¼ mm (No 10/US 3) needles.
Work in check patt as follows:
1st row (right side) K3A, [4MC, 4A] to last 7 sts, 4MC, 3A.
2nd row P3A, [4MC, 4A] to last 7 sts, 4MC, 3A.
3rd and 4th rows As 1st and 2nd rows.
5th row K3MC, [4A, 4MC] to last 7 sts, 4A, 3MC.
6th row P3MC, [4A, 4MC] to last 7 sts, 4A, 3MC.
7th and 8th rows As 5th and 6th rows.
These 8 rows form check patt.** Cont in check patt, work a further 16(20) rows. Place motif as follows:
Next row Patt 27(31), K across 1st row of Chart, patt 27(31).
Next row Patt 27(31), P across 2nd row of Chart, patt 27(31).
Cont working from Chart as set until 32nd row of Chart has been worked.
Work in check patt across all sts until Front measures 24(27) cm/9½(10½) in from beg, ending with a wrong side row.

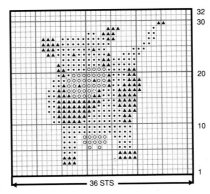

KEY

▲ = Black □ = Green
• = Cream ○ = Pink

← 36 STS →

Shape Neck

Next row Patt 36(39), turn.
Work on this set of sts only. Keeping patt correct, dec one st at neck edge on every row until 31(34) sts rem. Cont straight until Front measures 28(31) cm/11(12) in from beg, ending with a wrong side row. Leave these sts on a spare needle.
With right side facing, slip centre 18(20) sts onto a holder, rejoin yarn to rem sts, patt to end. Complete to match first side.

BACK

Work as given for Front to **.
Cont in check patt until Back measures 26(29) cm/10¼(11¼) in from beg, ending with a wrong side row.
Shape Neck
Next row Patt 36(39), turn.
Work on this set of sts only. Dec one st at neck edge on next 5 rows. 31(34) sts. Leave these sts on a spare needle.
With right side facing, slip centre 18(20) sts onto a holder, rejoin yarn to rem sts, patt to end. Complete to match first side.

SLEEVES

With 2¾ mm (No 12/US 1) needles and MC, cast on 37(41) sts. Work 3 cm/1¼ in in rib as given for Front welt, ending with a right side row.
Inc row Rib 7(5), [inc in next st, rib 5(3)] to end. 42(50) sts.
Change to 3¼ mm (No 10/US 3) needles. Work in check patt as given for Front, inc one st at each end of 5(10) foll 2nd(3rd) rows, then on every foll 3rd(4th) row until there are 70(78) sts, working inc sts into patt. Cont straight until Sleeve measures 19(22) cm/7½(8½) in from beg, ending with a wrong side row. Cast off.

BACK NECKBAND

With 2¾ mm (No 12/US 1) needles, MC and right side facing, pick up and K 6 sts down right back neck, K across back neck sts dec one st, pick up and K 6 sts up left back neck. 29(31) sts. Beg with a 2nd row, work 7 rows in rib as given for Front welt. Cast off in rib.

FRONT NECKBAND

With 2¾ mm (No 12/US 1) needles, MC and right side facing, pick up and K 14 sts down left front neck, K across front neck sts dec one st, pick up and K 14 sts up right front neck. 45(47) sts. Complete as given for Back Neckband.

BUTTONHOLE BANDS

With 2¾ mm (No 12/US 1) needles, MC and right side facing, K across left front shoulder sts, dec 2(3) sts evenly then pick up and K 6 sts along row ends of neckband. 35(37) sts. Beg with a 2nd row, work 3 rows in rib as given for Front welt.
1st buttonhole row Rib 5, [cast off 2, rib until there are 10(11) sts] twice, cast off 2, rib until there are 4 sts.
2nd buttonhole row Rib to end, casting on 2 sts over those cast off in previous row. Rib 3 rows. Cast off in rib.
Work right front shoulder to match.

BUTTON BANDS

With 2¾ mm (No 12/US 1) needles, MC and right side facing, K across right back

shoulder sts, dec 2(3) sts evenly then pick up and K 6 sts along row ends of neckband. 35(37) sts. Beg with a 2nd row, work 8 rows in rib as given for Front welt. Cast off in rib.
Work left back shoulder to match.

TO MAKE UP

Lap buttonhole bands over button bands and catch down at side edges. Sew on sleeves, placing centre of sleeves in line with buttonholes. Join side and sleeve seams. Sew on buttons.

Classic J

sport yarn
23 sts - 4 in.
on 3¾ mm needles

See Page
28

MEASUREMENTS

To fit age	6–12	12–24:24–
All round at chest	59 23¼	64:69 25¼:27¼
Length to shoulder	26 10¼	30:34 11¾:13½
Sleeve seam	16 6¼	20:24 8:9½

BACK

With 4 mm (No 8/US 5) needles, cast on 67 (73:79) sts.
1st row K1, [P1, K1] to end.
This row forms moss st patt. Cont in moss st until work measures 26 (30:34) cm/10¼ (11¾:13½) in from beg.

Shape Shoulders

Cast off 10 (11:12) sts at beg of next 4 rows. Cast off rem 27 (29:31) sts.

POCKET FLAPS (make 4)

With 4 mm (No 8/US 5) needles, cast on 17 sts.
Work 10 rows in moss st patt as given for Back. Leave these sts on a holder.

LEFT FRONT

With 4 mm (No 8/US 5) needles, cast on 37 (41:43) sts.
Cont in moss st patt as given for Back until work measures 8 (9:10) cm/3 (3½:4) in from beg, ending at side edge.
** Place Pocket Flap
Next row (right side) Moss st 8 (10:10) sts, now place one pocket flap sts in front of work, then taking on st from each needle and working them together, moss st across these 17 sts, moss st to end.**

Cont in moss st until work measures 20 (23:26) cm/8 (9:10¼) in from beg, ending with a wrong side row.
Rep from ** to ** once more.
Cont in moss st until work measures 22 (26:30) cm/8¾ (10¼:11¾) in from beg, ending at front edge.

Shape Neck

Cast off 7 (9:9) sts at beg of next row. Keeping moss st correct, dec one st at neck edge on every row until 20 (22:24) sts rem. Cont without shaping until work measures same as Back to shoulder shaping, ending at side edge.

Shape Shoulder

Cast off 10 (11:12) sts at beg of next row. Moss st 1 row. Cast off rem 10 (11:12) sts.
Mark front edge with pins indicating buttons, first one to come 7 (8:9) cm/2¾ (3:3½) in up from cast on edge and last one 1 cm/¼ in down from neck edge and rem 2 spaced evenly between.

RIGHT FRONT

With 4 mm (No 8/US 5) needles, cast on 37 (41:43) sts.
Cont in moss st patt as given for Back until work measures 7 (8:9) cm/2¾ (3:3½) in from beg, ending at front edge.

1st buttonhole row (right side) Moss st 2, cast off 3, moss st to end.
2nd buttonhole row Moss st to end, casting on 3 sts over those cast off in previous row. Moss st 2 rows.
***Place Pocket Flap
Next row Moss st 12 (14:16), now place one pocket flap sts in front of work, then taking one st from each needle and working them together, moss st across these 17 sts, moss st to end.***
Complete to match Left Front, making 3 more buttonholes at pin positions as before and placing 2nd flap as given from *** to ***.

SLEEVES

With 4 mm (No 8/US 5) needles, cast on 37 (39:41) sts.
Work in moss st patt as given for Back, **at the same time,** inc one st at each end of every foll 5th (6th:7th) row until there are 53 (57:61) sts.
Cont without shaping until work measures 16 (20:24) cm/6¼ (8:9½) in from beg. Cast off.

TO MAKE UP

Join shoulder seams. Sew on sleeves, placing centre of sleeves to shoulder seams. Join side and sleeve seams.

Crochet Edging

With crochet hook and right side facing, work 1 row of double crochet along cast on edge of Back, Right Front, up Right Front, around neck, down Left Front, then along cast on edge of Left Front. DO NOT TURN. Now work 1 row of backward double crochet (double crochet worked from left to right-corded st). Fasten off. Work crochet edging along cast on edge of Sleeves and round 3 free edges of each Pocket Flap.
Sew on 4 buttons to front edge of Left Front and one to centre of each Flap.

Hen and Chick Cardigan

See Page 29

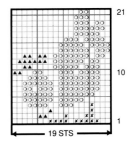

CHART 1

19 STS

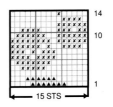

CHART 2

15 STS

MEASUREMENTS To fit age	1	2	Years
Actual chest measurement	72	78	cm
	28¼	30½	in
Length to shoulder	31	34	cm
	12¼	13½	in
Sleeve seam	21	25	cm
	8¼	10	in

MATERIALS

6(6) 50 g balls of Rowan DK Handknit Cotton in Blue (MC).
1(1) 50 g ball of same in each of Yellow (A), Red (B) and Cream (C).
Pair of 4 mm (No 8/US 5) knitting needles.
Medium size crochet hook.
3 buttons.

TENSION

20 sts and 28 rows to 10 cm/4 in square over st st on 4 mm (No 8/US 5) needles.

ABBREVIATIONS

Ch = chain; dc = double crochet; tr = treble; ss = slip stitch.
Also see page 63.

NOTE

Read Charts from right to left on K rows and from left to right on P rows. Use separate lengths of A, B and C yarn for each motif and twist yarns together on wrong side when changing colour to avoid holes. If preferred the motifs may be Swiss Darned when knitting is complete.

KEY

□ = MC   x = A   ▲ = B   ○ = C

BACK

With 4 mm (No 8/US 5) needles and MC, cast on 72(78) sts.
Beg with a K row, work in st st until Back measures 17(19) cm/6¾(7½) in from beg, ending with a P row.
Shape Armholes
Cast off 4(5) sts at beg of next 2 rows. 64(68) sts. Cont straight until Back measures 30(33) cm/12(13¼) in from beg, ending with a P row.
Shape Shoulders
Cast off 10(11) sts at beg of next 2 rows and 10 sts at beg of foll 2 rows. Cast off rem 24(26) sts.

LEFT FRONT

With 4 mm (No 8/US 5) needles and MC, cast on 34(37) sts.
Beg with a K row, work 14 rows in st st.**
Place Hen motif as follows:
1st row (right side) K11(14)MC, K across 1st row of Chart 1, K4MC.
2nd row P4MC, P across 2nd row of Chart 1, P11(14)MC.
Work a further 19 rows from Chart 1 as set.
Now cont in st st and MC only until Front measures 15(17) cm/6(6¾) in from beg, ending with a P row.
Shape Front
Dec one st at end (front edge) of next row and foll 3rd row. Work 2 rows.

Shape Armhole
Next row Cast off 4(5) sts, K to last 2 sts, K2 tog. 27(29) sts.
Keeping armhole edge straight, cont to dec at front edge on every foll 3rd row until 20(21) sts rem.
Cont straight until Front matches Back to shoulder shaping, ending with a P row.
Shape Shoulder
Cast off 10(11) sts at beg of next row. Work 1 row. Cast off rem 10 sts.

RIGHT FRONT

Work as for Left Front to **.
Place Chick motif as follows:
1st row (right side) K6MC, K across 1st row of Chart 2, K13(16)MC.

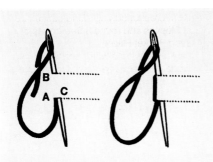

Satin Stitch. Bring needle out of A. Insert at B and emerge at C ready for next stitch.

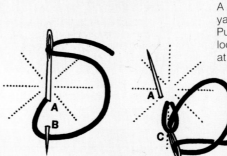

Lazy Daisy Stitch. Bring needle out at A. Insert back at A and emerge at B, looping yarn under the tip of needle. Pull needle through and over loop and insert at C. Emerge at A for next chain stitch.

2nd row P13(16)MC, P across 2nd row of Chart 2, P6MC.
Work a further 12 rows from Chart 2 as set. Complete to match Left Front, reversing shapings.

SLEEVES
With 4 mm (No 8/US 5) needles and MC, cast on 40(44) sts.
Beg with a K row, work in st st, inc one st at each end of 3rd row and every foll 6th(7th) row until there are 54(58) sts.
Cont straight until Sleeve measures 22(27) cm/8¾(10¾) in from beg, ending with a P row. Cast off.

TO MAKE UP
Work Swiss Darning (see diagram page 111) if necessary. Join shoulder seams. Sew on sleeves, placing centre of sleeves to shoulder seams and sewing ends of last 6(8) rows to cast off sts at armholes. Join side and sleeve seams.
Crochet Edging
With right side facing and crochet hook, join MC yarn to Right Front side seam. Work 1 round of dc (the number of dc should be divisible by 3) along cast on edge of Right Front, front edge to shoulder, across back neck, down front edge of Left Front, then along cast on edge of Left Front and Back, working 3 dc in each corner, ss in first dc.
Next round [2 tr in same dc as ss, miss 2 dc, ss in next dc] to end, making 3 buttonhole loops along straight edge of Right Front by working 3 ch, miss 2 dc, ss in next dc. Fasten off.
Work crochet edging along lower edge of sleeves. With A, B or C, embroider flowers in lazy daisy stitch (see page 99) along lower edge of Back, Fronts and Sleeves. Fill centre of flowers with B or A and satin st (see page 99). With B, embroider beaks. Sew on buttons.

Farmyard Picture Book Sweater
See Page 30

MEASUREMENTS

To fit age	18–24	24–36	Months
Actual chest measurement	70	78	cm
	27½	30¾	in
Length	38	40	cm
	15	15¾	in
Sleeve seam	20	24	cm
	8	9½	in

MATERIALS
5(6) 50 g balls of Rowan DK Handknit Cotton in Red (MC).
1(1) 50 g ball of same in each of Cream, Yellow, Black, Dark Pink, Blue, Green and Light Pink.
Pair each of 3¼ mm (No 10/US 3) and 4 mm (No 8/US 5) knitting needles.

TENSION
20 sts and 28 rows to 10 cm/4 in square over st st on 4 mm (No 8/US 5) needles.

ABBREVIATIONS
See page 63.

NOTE
Read Chart from right to left on right side rows and from left to right on wrong side rows. When working in pattern, use separate small balls of yarn for each coloured area and twist yarns together on wrong side when changing colour to avoid holes.

BACK
With 3¼ mm (No 10/US 3) needles and MC, cast on 66(74) sts.
1st row (right side) K2, [P2, K2] to end.
2nd row P2, [K2, P2] to end.
Rep last 2 rows until work measures 4 cm/1½ in from beg, ending with a wrong side row and inc 4 sts evenly across last row. 70(78) sts.
Change to 4 mm (No 8/US 5) needles.
Beg with a K row, work 2(4) rows in st st.
Cont in st st and patt from Chart until 92nd row of Chart has been worked.
Cont in MC only, work 2(6) rows.
Shape Shoulders
Cast off 10(11) sts at beg of next 2 rows and 10(12) sts at beg of foll 2 rows. Leave rem 30(32) sts on a holder.

FRONT
Work as given for Back until 84th row of Chart has been worked.
Shape Neck
Next row Patt 26(29), K2 tog, turn.
Work on this set of sts only. Keeping patt correct, dec one st at neck edge on every row until 20(23) sts rem, ending with 92nd row of Chart.
Cont in MC only, work 2(6) rows straight.
Shape Shoulder
Cast off 10(11) sts at beg of next row.
Work 1 row. Cast off rem 10(12) sts.
With right side facing, slip centre 14(16) sts onto a holder, rejoin MC yarn to rem sts, K2 tog, K to end. Complete to match first side, reversing shoulder shaping.

LEFT SLEEVE
With 3¼ mm (No 10/US 3) needles and MC, cast on 34(38) sts. Work 5 cm/2 in in rib as given for Back welt, ending with a right side row.
Inc row Rib 2(5), inc in next st, [rib 3, inc in next st] to last 3(4) sts, rib 3(4). 42(46) sts.
Change to 4 mm (No 8/US 5) needles.
Beg with a K row, work 10(14) rows in st st inc one st at each end of 3rd row and 3(5) foll alt rows. 50(58) sts. **
Place sheep motif as follows:
Next row With MC, K twice in first st, K10(14), K 6th(10th) to 32nd(36th) sts of 12th row of Chart for Back, with MC, K to last st, K twice in last st.
Next row P13(17) MC, P 39th(43rd) to 65th(69th) sts of 13th row of Chart for Back, with MC, P to end.
These 2 rows set the patt. Cont as set until 33rd row of Chart has been worked, **at the same time**, inc one st at each end of next row and every foll 2nd(3rd) row until there are 70(74) sts, working inc sts in MC. With MC only, work 10(18) rows. Cast off.

RIGHT SLEEVE
Work as given for Left Sleeve to **.
Place cow motif as follows:
Next row With MC, K twice in first st, K9(13), K 34th(38th) to 63rd(67th) sts of 58th row of Chart for Back, with MC, K to last st, K twice in last st.
Next row P11(15)MC, P 8th(12th) to 37th(41st) sts of 59th row of Chart for Back, with MC, P to end.
These 2 rows set the patt. Cont as set until 81st row of Chart has been worked, **at the same time**, inc one st at each end of next row and every foll 2nd(3rd) row until there are 70(74) sts, working inc sts in MC. With MC, work 8(16) rows.
Cast off.

NECKBAND
Join right shoulder seam.
With 3¼ mm (No 10/US 3) needles, MC

KEY

- ☐ = Red
- ○ = Cream
- ━ = Yellow
- ▲ = Black
- ▪ = Dark Pink
- • = Blue
- v = Green
- ✳ = Light Pink
- ∧, ⋋ or ⟋ = embroidery sts

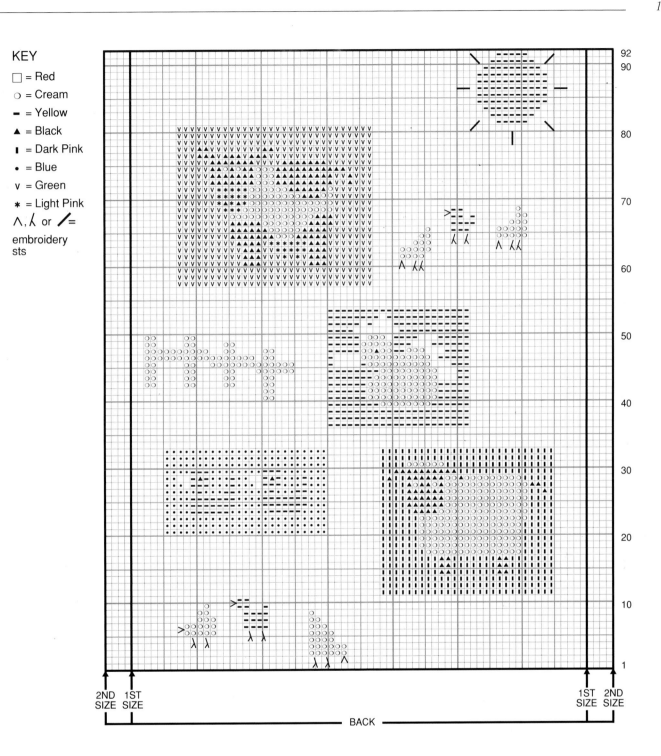

2ND SIZE 1ST SIZE   1ST SIZE 2ND SIZE

BACK

and right side facing, pick up and K16(18) sts down left front neck, K centre front neck sts, pick up and K16(18) sts up right front neck, K back neck sts. 76(84) sts. Work 12 rows in K2, P2 rib. Cast off in rib.

TO MAKE UP

Join left shoulder and neckband seam. Sew on sleeves, placing centre of sleeves to shoulder seams. Join side and sleeve seams.

With Black, embroider feet and eyes on chicks. Embroider chicks' beaks in Black or Yellow. With Yellow, work a few straight stitches (see page 90) around the sun for rays.

Patchwork Sweater

See Page
31

MEASUREMENTS

To fit age	2–3	3–4	4–5	Years
Actual chest measurement	72	78	84	cm
	28¼	30¾	33	in
Length	44	47	50	cm
	17¼	18½	19¾	in
Sleeve seam	27	29	31	cm
	10¾	11½	12¼	in

MATERIALS

6(6:7) 50 g balls of Rowan DK Handknit Cotton in Cream (MC).
2(2:2) 50 g balls of same in Blue.
1(1:1) 50 g ball of same in each of Rust, Red, Brown and Pink.
Pair each of 3¼mm (No 10/US 3) and 4 mm (No 8/US 5) knitting needles.

TENSION

20 sts and 28 rows to 10 cm/4 in square over st st on 4 mm (No 8/US 5) needles.

ABBREVIATIONS

See page 63.

NOTE

Read Charts from right to left on right side rows and from left to right on wrong side rows. When working in pattern, use separate small balls of yarn for each coloured area and twist yarns together on wrong side when changing colour to avoid holes.

BACK

With 3¼mm (No 10/US 3) needles and MC, cast on 70(78:82) sts.
1st row (right side) K2, [P2, K2] to end.
2nd row P2, [K2, P2] to end.
Rep last 2 rows until work measures 4 cm/1½ in from beg, ending with a 2nd row and inc 2 sts evenly across last row on **1st** and **3rd** sizes only. 72(78:84) sts.
Change to 4 mm (No 8/US 5) needles.
Beg with a K row, work 4(6:10) rows in st st.
Place Chart 1 as follows:
Next row K32(35:38)MC, K across 1st row of Chart 1, K2(5:8)MC.
Next row P2(5:8)MC, P across 2nd row of Chart 1, P32(35:38)MC.
Cont working from Chart as set, work a further 6 rows.
Place Chart 2 as follows:
Next row K2(2:5)MC, K across 1st row of Chart 2, K4(7:7)MC, K across 9th row of Chart 1, K2(5:8) MC.
Next row P2(5:8)MC, P across 10th row of Chart 1, P4(7:7)MC, P across 2nd row of Chart 2, P2(2:5)MC.
Cont working from Charts as set, work a further 30 rows, working sts in MC when Chart 2 has been completed.
With MC only, work 10(12:14) rows in st st.
Place Chart 3 as follows:
Next row K3MC, K across 1st row of Chart 3, K39(45:51)MC.
Next row P39(45:51)MC, P across 2nd row of Chart 3, P3MC.
Cont working from Chart as set, work a further 6 rows.

Place Chart 4 as follows:
Next row K3MC, K across 9th row of Chart 3, K8(11:14)MC, K across 1st row of Chart 4, K4(7:10)MC.
Next row P4(7:10)MC, P across 2nd row

of Chart 4, P8(11:14)MC, P across 10th row of Chart 3, P3MC.
Cont working from Charts as set, work a further 28 rows, working sts in MC when Chart 4 has been completed.
Cont in st st and MC only until work measures 44(47:50) cm/17¼(18½:19¾) in from beg, ending with a P row.
Shape Shoulders
Cast off 23(26:28) sts at beg of next 2 rows. Leave rem 26(26:28) sts on a holder.

FRONT

Work as given for Back until Front measures 39(41:44) cm/15¼(16:17¼) in from beg, ending with a P row.
Shape Neck
Next row K30(33:35), turn.
Work on this set of sts only. Dec one st at neck edge on every row until 23(26:28) sts rem. Cont straight until Front matches Back to shoulders, ending at side edge. Cast off.
With right side facing, slip centre 12(12:14) sts onto a holder, rejoin yarn to rem sts and K to end. Complete to match first side.

SLEEVES

With 3¼mm (No 10/US 3) needles and MC, cast on 38(38:42) sts.
Work 4 cm/1½ in in rib as given for Back welt, ending with a 1st row.

CHART 1

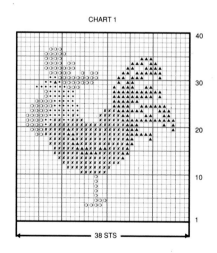

38 STS

CHART 2

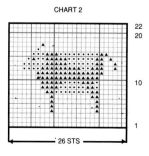

26 STS

CHART 3

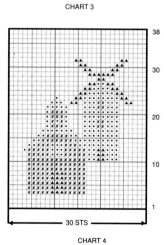

30 STS

CHART 4

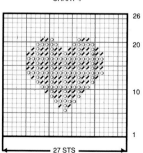

27 STS

KEY

☐	= Blue
•	= Cream
▲	= Rust
○	= Red
✗	= Brown
✔	= Pink

Inc row Rib 5(4:3), inc in next st, [rib 8(5:6), inc in next st] to last 5(3:3) sts, rib 5(3:3). 42(44:48) sts.
Change to 4 mm (No 8/US 5) needles.
Beg with a K row, work 4(4:6) rows in st st.
Place Chart 2 as follows:
Next row With MC, K twice in first st, K5(6:8), K across 1st row of Chart 2, with MC, K to last st, K twice in last st.
Next row P11(12:14)MC, P across 2nd row of Chart 2, with MC, P to end.
Cont working from Chart as set until 22nd row of Chart 2 has been worked, **at the same time**, inc one st at each end of 3rd row and every foll 4th row, working inc sts in MC. 54(56:60) sts.
With MC only, work 10(12:14) rows in st

st, inc one st at each end of 3rd row and 1(2:2) foll 4th rows. 58(62:66) sts.
Place Chart 4 as follows:
Next row K18(20:22)MC, K across 1st row of Chart 4, K13(15:17)MC.
Next row P13(15:17)MC, P across 2nd row of Chart 4, P18(20:22)MC.
Cont working from Chart as set until 26th row of Chart 4 has been worked, **at the same time**, inc one st at each end of next row and 1(1:2) foll 6th rows, working inc sts in MC. 62(66:72) sts.
Cont in MC only, work 4(6:8) rows in st st. Cast off.

NECKBAND

Join right shoulder seam.

With 3¼mm (No 10/US 3) needles, MC and right side facing, pick up and K 16(18:18) sts down left front neck, K centre front sts, pick up and K16 (18:18) sts up right front neck, K back neck sts. 70(74:78) sts.
Beg with a 2nd row, work 7 cm/2¾ in in rib as given for Back welt. Cast off loosely in rib.

TO MAKE UP

Join left shoulder and neckband seam.
Sew on sleeves, placing centre of sleeves to shoulder seams.
Join side and sleeve seams. With Rust, embroider stitching around each motif rectangle.

Knitted Toys

See Page
32

MATERIALS
Cat 1x50 g ball of Rowan Designer DK Wool.
Oddment of White for embroidery.
Lamb 1x50 g ball of Rowan Designer DK Wool in Cream (A).
Small amount of same in Black.
Pig 1x50 g ball of Rowan Designer DK Wool.
Oddment of Black for embroidery.

Medium size crochet hook.
Pair of 3¾mm (No 9/US 4) knitting needles.
Kapok for stuffing.
4 pipe cleaners.
Length of ribbon.

ABBREVIATIONS
See page 63.

attach to body. With White, embroider eyes. Place ribbon around cat's neck and tie into a bow.

Little Lamb

BODY AND LEGS
Cast on 40 sts. Cont in garter st (every row K) until work measures a square. Cast off.

HEAD, EARS AND TAIL
With Black, work as given for Head, Ears and Tail of Cat.

TO MAKE UP
Work as given for To Make Up of Cat.

Little Pig

BODY AND LEGS
Work as given for Body and Legs of Lamb.

HEAD
Cast on 7 sts. Work in garter st, inc one st at each end of next 5 rows. 17 sts. K 14 rows straight. Dec one st at each end of next 3 rows. K 2 rows.
Inc one st at each end of next 3 rows. 17 sts. K 14 rows straight.
Dec one st at each end of next 5 rows. 7 sts. Cast off.

SNOUT
Cast on 4 sts for outside. K 18 rows. Cast off.
Cast on 3 sts for centre. K 1 row. Cont in garter st, inc one st at each end of next row. K 2 rows. Dec one st at each end of next row. K 1 row. Cast off.

Cat

BODY AND LEGS
Cast on 40 sts. Cont in st st until work is a square. Cast off.

HEAD
Cast on 5 sts. P 1 row.
1st row (right side) K twice in first st, [K1, m1] twice, K1, K twice in last st.
2nd row P twice in first st, P to last st, P twice in last st.
3rd row K twice in first st, K4, m1, K1, m1, K4, K twice in last st.
4th row As 2nd row.
5th row K twice in first st, K7, m1, K1, m1, K7, K twice in last st. 21 sts.
Work 3 rows in st st.
9th row K8, K2 tog, K1, sl 1, K1, psso, K8.
10th row P.
11th row K7, K2 tog, K1, sl 1, K1, psso, K7. 17 sts.
Work 7 rows in st st.
Dec one st at each end of next 4 rows. 9 sts. K 1 row.
Inc one st at each end of next 4 rows. 17 sts. Work 13 rows in st st.
Dec one st at each end of next 6 rows. 5 sts. Cast off.

EARS (make 2)
Cast on 4 sts. K 1 row.
Next row K1, [m1, K1] 3 times. 7 sts.
K 3 rows.
Next row Sl 1, K1, psso, K3, K2 tog.
K 1 row.
Next row Sl 1, K1, psso, K1, K2 tog.
K 1 row. K3 tog and fasten off.

TAIL
Cast on 12 sts. Work 5 rows in st st. Cast off.

TO MAKE UP
Join each of the 4 corners of body and leg pieces together for approximately 6 cm/2¼ in to form legs. Twist together 2 pairs of pipe cleaners and bend them in half.
Insert ends of one pair of pipe cleaners in back legs and other in front legs. Stuff and join opening. Wrap tightly a length of yarn twice around each leg approximately 3 cm/1¼ in from lower edge and secure. Fold head piece in half widthwise and join side seams. Stuff firmly and sew to body.
** Fold cast on edge of ears in half and stitch together, then sew them in place. With P side on the outside, join cast on and cast off edges of tail together and

EARS (make 2)

Cast on 3 sts. K 1 row. Cont in garter st, inc one st at each end of next row and foll alt row. K 6 rows. Dec one st at each end of next row and foll alt row. Break off yarn, thread end through rem sts, pull up and secure.

TO MAKE UP

Work as given for To Make Up of Cat to **. Join cast on and cast off edges of outside of snout together. Sew in centre at one end. Stuff and sew other end to head. Sew on ears. With Black, embroider eyes and nostrils. Place ribbon around pig's

neck and tie into à bow. Using a crochet hook and 2 strands of yarn together, work a chain approximately 6 cm/2¼ in long for tail. Fasten off and attach to body.

Sheep

See Page
32

MATERIALS

350 g balls of Rowan Designer DK Wool in Cream (MC).
150 g ball of same in Black (A).
Small amount of same in Brown.
Pair of 3¼ mm (No 10/US 3) knitting needles.
Stuffing.

TENSION

26 sts and 50 rows to 10 cm/4 in square over garter st (every row K).

ABBREVIATIONS

See page 63.

UPPER BODY

With MC, cast on 58 sts. K1 row. Mark centre of last row. Cont in garter st.

Shape Back Legs

Cast on 6 sts at beg of next 4 rows and 3 sts at beg of foll 2 rows. 88 sts.
Work 20 rows straight. Cast off 3 sts at beg of next 2 rows. Dec one st at each end of next row, 2 foll alt rows, then on foll 3 rows. 70 sts.
Inc one st at each end of 7th row and 2 foll 6th rows. 76 sts.
Work 29 rows straight. Dec one st at each end of next row and 2 foll 6th rows. 70 sts.
Work 7 rows straight.

Shape Front Legs

Cast on 3 sts at beg of next 6 rows. 88 sts.
Work 20 rows straight. Cast off 3 sts at beg of next 4 rows. Dec one st at each end of next row and 5 foll alt rows, then on every row until 38 sts rem. Work 3 rows. Cast off.

UNDERSIDE

With MC, cast on 5 sts. Mark centre st of cast on row. Work in garter st, inc one st at each end of 3rd row, foll alt row and 3 foll 8th rows. 15 sts.
Work 9 rows straight.

Shape Back Legs

Cast on 6 sts at beg of next 4 rows and 3 sts at beg of foll 2 rows. 45 sts.
Work 1 row.
Next row K15, K2 tog tbl, K11, K2 tog, K15.
Work 3 rows.
Next row K14, K2 tog tbl, K11, K2 tog, K14.
Cont in this way, dec 2 sts as set on every foll 4th row until 35 sts rem.
Work 2 rows. Cast off 3 sts at beg of next row.

Next row Cast off 3 sts, K6 sts more, K2 tog tbl, K11, K2 tog, K to end.
Dec one st at each end of next row and 2 foll alt rows, then on foll 3 rows. 15 sts.
Inc one st at each end of 7th row and 2 foll 6th rows. 21 sts. Work 29 rows straight. Dec one st at each end of next row and 2 foll 6th rows. 15 sts.
Work 7 rows straight.

Shape Front Legs

Cast on 3 sts at beg of next 6 rows. 33 sts.
Work 20 rows straight. Cast off 3 sts at beg of next 4 rows. Dec one st at each end of next row and every foll 6th row until 9 sts rem. Work 3 rows straight. Cast off.

HEAD

With A, cast on 47 sts.
Next row K37, turn.
Next row P27, turn.
Next row K23, turn.
Next row P19, turn.
Next row K15, turn.
Next row P11, turn.
Next row K to end.
Beg with a P row, work 5 rows in st st.
Next row K7, K2 tog, K6, K2 tog tbl, K13, K2 tog, K6, K2 tog tbl, K7.
Next row P14, P2 tog, P11, P2 tog tbl, P14.
Next row K6, K2 tog, K6, K2 tog tbl, K9, K2 tog, K6, K2 tog tbl, K6.
Next row P13, P2 tog, P7, P2 tog tbl, P13.
Next row K5, [K2 tog, K6, K2 tog tbl, K5] twice.
P 1 row.
Next row K4, K2 tog, K6, K2 tog tbl, K3, K2 tog, K6, K2 tog tbl, K4.
Work 3 rows in st st.
Next row K10, K2 tog, K3, K2 tog tbl, K10.
Work 9 rows in st st, dec one st at centre

of 7th row. 24 sts.

Shape Muzzle

Next row K3, cast off 6, K5 sts more, cast off 6, K to end.
Work 3 rows on last set of 3 sts. Leave these sts on a holder. With wrong side facing, rejoin yarn to centre 6 sts and work 3 rows. Leave these sts on a holder. With wrong side facing, rejoin yarn to rem 3 sts and work 3 rows.
Slip these 3 sts and last 3 sts onto one needle. Place these sts to centre 6 sts with right sides together, then cast them off together.

FEET (make 8)

With A, cast on 14 sts. Work 14 rows in st st. Cast off.

HORNS (make 2)

With Brown, cast on 12 sts. P1 row. K1 row. P2 rows. These 4 rows form patt. Cont in patt, work 6 rows. Dec one st at each end of next row and every foll 4th row until 2 sts rem, ending with a wrong side row. P2 tog and fasten off.

EARS (make 2)

With MC, cast on 6 sts. Work in garter st, dec one st at each end of 5th row and foll alt row. Work 1 row. K2 tog and fasten off.

TO MAKE UP

Join upper body to underside, matching marker and legs and leaving row ends of legs free. Fold first 2 sts of row ends of legs to inside and slip stitch in place. Join paired pieces of feet together, leaving one row end edge open. Place feet inside legs and sew in position. Fold last 2 rows of cast off edge of body and underside to inside and slip stitch in place. Join head seam. Place cast off seam of muzzle at centre, then join row ends to cast off sts. Stuff body and head. Sew head to body. Roll horns widthwise and slip stitch top edge, then pull thread, thus curling the horns. Sew horns and ears in place. With MC, embroider eyes.

Cow

See Page

32

MEASUREMENTS
Approximate height 23 cm/9 in.

MATERIALS
3x50 g balls of Rowan Designer DK
Wool in Cream (MC).
1x50 g ball of same in Black (A).
Small amount of same in each of Pink,
Brown and Rust.
Pair of 3¼mm (No 10/US 3) knitting
needles.
Stuffing.

TENSION
26 sts and 50 rows to 10 cm/4 in square
over garter st (every row K).

ABBREVIATIONS
See page 63.

NOTE
When working in pattern, use separate
small balls of yarn for each coloured
area and twist yarns together on wrong
side when changing colour to avoid
any holes.

UPPER BODY
Left Back Leg
With MC, cast on 20 sts. K 1 row. Cont in
garter st, inc one st at beg of next row and
at same edge on every row until there are
31 sts. K1 row. Leave these sts on a
holder.
Right Back Leg
With MC, cast on 20 sts. K1 row. Cont in
garter st, inc one st at end of next row and
at same edge on every row until there are
31 sts. K1 row.
Shape Body
Next row (right side) K across sts of Right
Back Leg, cast on 58 sts, K across sts of
Left Back Leg. 120 sts. Mark centre of last
row.
K 3 rows. Cast off 13 sts at beg of next 2
rows. Dec one st at each end of next row
and 3 foll alt rows. 86 sts. K 1 row.
Place Chart 1 as follows:
Next row With MC, K2 tog, K14, reading
Chart 1 from right to left, K across 1st row,
K8MC, reading Chart 1 from left to right, K
across 1st row, with MC, K14, K2 tog.
Next row K15MC, reading Chart 1 from
right to left, K across 2nd row, K8MC,
reading Chart 1 from left to right, K across
2nd row, K15MC.

Cont working from Chart 1 as set, dec one
st at each end of next row and 3 foll alt
rows, then at each end of foll 2 rows. 72
sts. Patt 11 rows straight.
Now inc one st at each end of next row
and 2 foll alt rows then on foll 4th row. 80
sts. Patt 1 row.
Place Chart 2 as follows:
Next row Reading Chart 2 from right to
left, K across 1st row, patt to last 10 sts,
reading Chart 2 from left to right, K across
1st row.
Cont working from Charts as set, inc one
st at each end of 2nd row and foll 4th row,
working inc sts in A. 84 sts.
Patt 21 rows straight, working sts in MC
when Chart 1 has been completed.
Dec one st at each end of next row and 3
foll 4th rows. 76 sts. Patt 1 row.
Place Chart 3 as follows:
Next row Patt 11, reading Chart 3 from
right to left, K across 1st row, reading
Chart 3 from left to right, K across 1st row,
patt 11.
Cont working from Charts as set, patt 3
rows, thus completing Chart 2.
Shape Front Legs
Cast on 4 sts at beg of next 6 rows and 10
sts at beg of foll 2 rows. 120 sts.

Patt 14 rows straight. Cast off 22 sts at
beg of next 2 rows. 76 sts.
Dec one st at each end of 5th row and
every foll alt row until 52 sts rem.
Patt 1 row. Cast off 2 sts at beg of next 2
rows. 48 sts. Patt 1 row.
Mark each end of last row.
Shape Head
Next row Patt 16, cast off 16, patt 16.
Work on last set of 16 sts only for right
side of head. Inc one st at beg of next row
and 3 foll alt rows, **at the same time**, cast
off 2 sts at beg of 4 foll alt rows. 12 sts.
Cont in MC only. Dec one st at end of 3rd
row, then at each end of 3 foll 4th rows. K
2 rows. Mark each end of last row.
Inc one st at beg of next row. K 1 row.
Cast off.
With right side of work facing, rejoin yarn
to rem sts for left side of head and
complete to match right side, reversing
shaping.

UNDERSIDE
With MC, cast on 3 sts. Mark centre st.
Work in garter st, inc one st at each end of
3rd row, foll 6th row, foll 8th row, then foll
10th row and foll 14th row. 13 sts. K 5
rows. Leave these sts on a holder.
Left Back Leg
Work as for Left Back Leg of Upper Body.
Right Back Leg
Work as for Right Back Leg of Upper
Body.
Next row K across sts of Right Back Leg,
K13 sts from holder, K across sts of Left
Back Leg. 75 sts.
K 3 rows. Cast off 13 sts at beg of next 2
rows. 49 sts.
Next row K2 tog, K16, K2 tog tbl, K9, K2
tog, K16, K2 tog.
K 1 row.
Next row K2 tog, K14, K2 tog tbl, K9, K2
tog, K14, K2 tog.
K 1 row.
Next row K2 tog, K12, K2 tog tbl, K9,

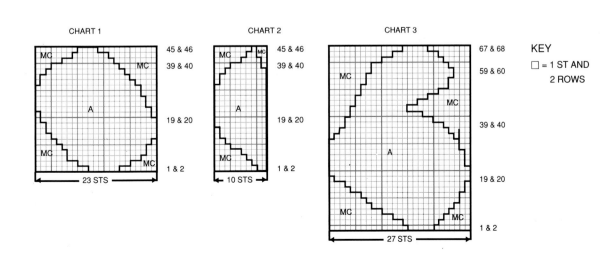

CHART 1   45 & 46   39 & 40   19 & 20   1 & 2   23 STS

CHART 2   45 & 46   39 & 40   19 & 20   1 & 2   10 STS

CHART 3   67 & 68   59 & 60   39 & 40   19 & 20   1 & 2   27 STS

KEY
☐ = 1 ST AND
2 ROWS

K2 tog, K12, K2 tog. Cont in this way, dec 4 sts as set on every alt row until 21 sts rem.
Dec one st at each end of 2 foll alt rows, then at each end of next 2 rows. 13 sts.
Inc one st at each end of 4 foll 6th rows. 21 sts. K 27 rows straight.
Dec one st at each end of next row and 3 foll 4th rows. 13 sts. K 3 rows.

Shape Front Legs
Cast on 4 sts at beg of next 6 rows and 10 sts at beg of foll 2 rows. 57 sts.
K 14 rows. Cast off 22 sts at beg of next 2 rows. 13 sts.
Dec one st at each end of 7th row and 3 foll 6th rows. 5 sts. K 9 rows straight.
Mark each end of last row.
Inc one st at each end of next row and foll alt row, then on 2 foll 4th rows. 13 sts.
Dec one st at each end of 2 foll 4th rows. K 3 rows.
Cast off 2 sts at beg of next 2 rows. 5 sts. K 2 rows. Mark each end of last row. Inc one st at each end of next row. 7 sts. K 13 rows.
Dec one st at each end of next row. 5 sts. Mark each end of last row.
Inc one st at each end of 6 foll 4th rows. 17 sts. K 5 rows. Cast off.

UDDER
With MC, cast on 46 sts.
Next 2 rows K3, turn, P to end.
Next 2 rows K6, turn, P to end.
Next 2 rows K10, turn, P to end.
Next 2 rows K16, turn, P to end.
Next row K to end.
Next 2 rows P3, turn, K to end.
Next 2 rows P6, turn, K to end.
Next 2 rows P10, turn, K to end.
Next 2 rows P16, turn, K to end.
Beg with a P row, work 7 rows in st st.
Next row K1, [K2 tog, K3] to end.
Work 3 rows straight.
Next row K1, [K2 tog, K2] to end.
Work 1 row.
Next row K1, [K2 tog, K1] to end.
Work 1 row.
Next row K1, [K2 tog] to end. 10 sts.
Break off yarn, thread end through rem sts, pull up and secure.

TEATS (make 4)
With Pink, cast on 5 sts. Beg with a K row, work 6 rows in st st.
Next row K1, [K2 tog] twice.
Break off yarn, thread end through rem sts, pull up and secure.

EARS (make 2)
With MC, cast on 5 sts. K 10 rows. Dec one st at each end of next row.
K3 tog and fasten off.

HORNS (make 2)
With Brown, cast on 4 sts. Beg with a K row, work 4 rows in st st.
Next row [K2 tog] twice.
Break off yarn, thread end through rem sts, pull up and secure.

TAIL
With MC, cast on 30 sts. Cast off.

TO MAKE UP
Join upper body to underside, matching legs and markers and leaving an opening. Stuff firmly and close opening. Join back seam of udder, stuff lightly and sew in place. Join seam of teats and sew in place. Join seam of horns and sew in position. Sew on ears. With MC, work fringe along top of head. With Rust, embroider eyes. Make small tassel with MC and attach to one end of tail. Attach other end to body.

Pig

See Page
32

MEASUREMENTS
Approximate height 23 cm/9 in.

MATERIALS
3x50 g balls of Rowan Designer DK Wool.
Oddment of Black for embroidery.
Pair of 3¼ mm (No 10/US 3) knitting needles.
Stuffing.

TENSION
26 sts and 50 rows to 10 cm/4 in square over garter st (every row K).

ABBREVIATIONS
See page 63.

UPPER BODY
Cast on 76 sts. Mark centre and 6th sts from each end. K 1 row.

Shape Back Legs
Cont in garter st, cast on 6 sts at beg of next 4 rows and 12 sts at beg of foll 2 rows. 124 sts. K 22 rows. Cast off 12 sts at beg of next 2 rows and 6 sts at beg of foll 4 rows. 76 sts. K 66 rows.

Shape Front Legs
Cast on 24 sts at beg of next 2 rows. 124 sts. K 18 rows. Cast off 24 sts at beg of next 2 rows. 76 sts. K 19 rows.

Shape Head
Next row (wrong side) K16, [K2 tog tbl, K9] twice, [K9, K2 tog] twice, K16.
K5 rows straight.
Next row K16, [K2 tog tbl, K8] twice, [K8, K2 tog] twice, K16.
K 5 rows straight. Mark each end of last row.
Next row K16, [K2 tog tbl, K7] twice, [K7, K2 tog] twice, K16.
Cont in this way, dec 4 sts as set on 2 foll alt rows and 3 foll 4th rows. 44 sts. K 14 rows.
Next row K6, [K twice in next st, K5] 6 times, K2. 50 sts.
K3 rows. Cast off.

UNDERSIDE
Cast on 3 sts. Mark centre st. K 1 row.
Cont in garter st, inc one st at each end of next 3 rows and 4 foll alt rows. 17 sts. K 13 rows straight. Dec one st at each end of next row and 2 foll 4th rows. 11 sts. K 7 rows straight. Mark each end of last row.

Shape Back Legs
Cast on 6 sts at beg of next 6 rows and 12 sts at beg of foll 2 rows. 71 sts.
Next row K30, K2 tog tbl, K7, K2 tog, K30.
K 5 rows straight.
Next row K29, K2 tog tbl, K7, K2 tog, K29.
K 5 rows straight.
Next row K28, K2 tog tbl, K7, K2 tog, K28.
K 5 rows straight.
Next row K27, K2 tog tbl, K7, K2 tog, K27.
K 3 rows straight. Cast off 12 sts at beg of next 2 rows.
Next row Cast off 6 sts, K until there are 8 sts on right-hand needles, K2 tog tbl, K7, K2 tog, K14.
Cast off 6 sts at beg of next 3 rows. 13 sts. K 66 rows.

Shape Front Legs
Cast on 24 sts at beg of next 2 rows. 61 sts. K 18 rows. Cast off 24 sts at beg of next 2 rows. 13 sts. K 8 rows.
Dec one st at each end of next row and 4 foll 4th rows. 3 sts. K 1 row.
K3 tog and fasten off.

SNOUT
Cast on 3 sts. K 1 row. Cont in garter st, inc one st at each end of next 3 rows and 3 foll alt rows. 15 sts. K 7 rows. Dec one st

at each end of next row and 2 foll alt rows,
then on 3 foll rows. 3 sts. K 1 row. Cast off.

EARS (make 2)
Cast on 17 sts. K 6 rows. Dec one st at
each end of next row, 2 foll 4th rows, then
4 foll alt rows. 3 sts. K 1 row. K3 tog and
fasten off.

TAIL
Cast on loosely 20 sts. Cast off tightly.

TO MAKE UP
Join seam from cast off edge to first
marker. Sew in snout. Join upper body to
underside, matching legs and markers
and leaving an opening. Stuff firmly and

close opening. Fold sides of each ear to
centre at cast on edge and secure. Sew
on ears and tail. With Black, embroider
eyes, nostrils and mouth.

Farmyard Jacket

See Page *34*

MEASUREMENTS

To fit age	2	3	Years
Actual chest measurement	74	79	cm
	29	31	in
Length	31	34	cm
	12¼	13½	in
Sleeve seam	23	26	cm
	9	10¼	in

MATERIALS
5(6) 50 g balls of Rowan Designer DK
Wool in Green (MC).
1(1) 50 g ball of same in each of Brown,
Yellow, Cream, Black, Blue, Red and
Pink.
Pair each of 3¼mm (No 10/US 3) and 4
mm (No 8/US 5) knitting needles.
5 buttons.

TENSION
24 sts and 32 rows to 10 cm/4 in square
over st st on 4 mm (No 8/US 5) needles.

ABBREVIATIONS
See page 63.

NOTE
Read Chart from right to left on right
side rows and from left to right on
wrong side rows. When working in
pattern, use separate lengths of yarn
for each coloured area and twist yarns
together on wrong side when changing
colour to avoid holes.

BACK
With 3¼mm (No 10/US 3) needles and
MC, cast on 87(93) sts.
1st row (right side) K1, [P1, K1] to end.
2nd row P1, [K1, P1] to end.
Rep last 2 rows until work measures 4(5)
cm/1½ (2) in from beg, ending with a 2nd
row.
Change to 4 mm (No 8/US 5) needles.
Beg with a K row, cont in st st throughout,
work 4(8) rows.
Now work patt from Chart until 70th row
of Chart has been worked.
Cont in MC only, work 14 rows.
Shape Shoulders
Cast off 14(16) sts at beg of next 2 rows
and 15 sts at beg of foll 2 rows.
Leave rem 29(31) sts on a holder.

LEFT FRONT
With 3¼mm (No 10/US 3) needles and
MC, cast on 43(45) sts.
Work 4(5) cm/1½(2) in in rib as given for
Back welt, ending with a 2nd row and inc
one st at centre of last row on **2nd** size

only. 43(46) sts.
Change to 4 mm (No 8/US 5) needles.
Beg with a K row, cont in st st throughout,
work 4(8) rows.
Now work patt from Chart until 58th row
of Chart has been worked.
Shape Neck
Keeping patt correct, dec one st at front
edge on every row until 70th row of Chart
has been worked.
Cont in MC only, work 2(3) rows, dec one
st at front edge of every row. 29(31) sts.
Work 12(11) rows straight.
Shape Shoulder
Cast off 14(16) sts at beg of next row.
Work 1 row. Cast off rem 15 sts.

RIGHT FRONT
Work to match Left Front, reversing
shoulder shaping.

SLEEVES
With 3¼mm (No 10/US 3) needles and
MC, cast on 43(45) sts.
Work 4(5) cm/1½(2) in in rib as given for

Back welt, ending with a 2nd row and inc
2 sts evenly across last row. 45(47) sts.
Change to 4 mm (No 8/US 5) needles.
Beg with a K row, cont in st st throughout,
work 4(8) rows, inc one st at each end of
0(5th) row. 45(49) sts.
Now work patt from Chart until 52nd row
of Chart has been worked, **at the same
time**, inc one st at each end of 3rd row
and every foll 4th row until there are
69(73) sts, working inc sts into patt. Cont
in MC only, work 4(8) rows. Cast off.

FRONT BANDS AND COLLAR
Join shoulder seams.
With 3¼mm (No 10/US 3) needles, MC
and right side facing, pick up and K 55
(61) sts along straight edge of Right
Front, 38 sts along shaped edge to
shoulder, K back neck sts inc 8 sts
evenly, pick up and K 38 sts down
shaped edge of Left Front and 55(61) sts
along straight edge. 223(237) sts.
Beg with a 2nd row, work 3 rows in rib as
given for Back welt.
1st buttonhole row Rib 3, [cast off 2, rib
9(11) sts more] 5 times, rib to end.
2nd buttonhole row Rib to end, casting
on 2 sts over those cast off in previous
row.
Next 2 rows Rib to last 55(61) sts, turn, sl
1, rib to last 55(61) sts, turn.
Next 2 rows Sl 1, rib to last 57(63) sts,
turn.
Next 2 rows Sl 1, rib to last 59(65) sts, ,
turn.
Cont in this way, working 2 sts less at
end of every row on next 12(14) rows.
Next row Rib to end.
Rib 2 rows. Cast off in rib.

TO MAKE UP
Sew on sleeves, placing centre of
sleeves to shoulder seams. Join side and
sleeve seams. Sew on buttons.
Embroider eyes with Black and
moustache with Brown on each farmer's
face. With Black, embroider scarecrow's
eyes and nose and with Yellow
embroider straw hands. Sew small dot in
Black on each cockerel's eye and with
Yellow embroider beak and back claw.

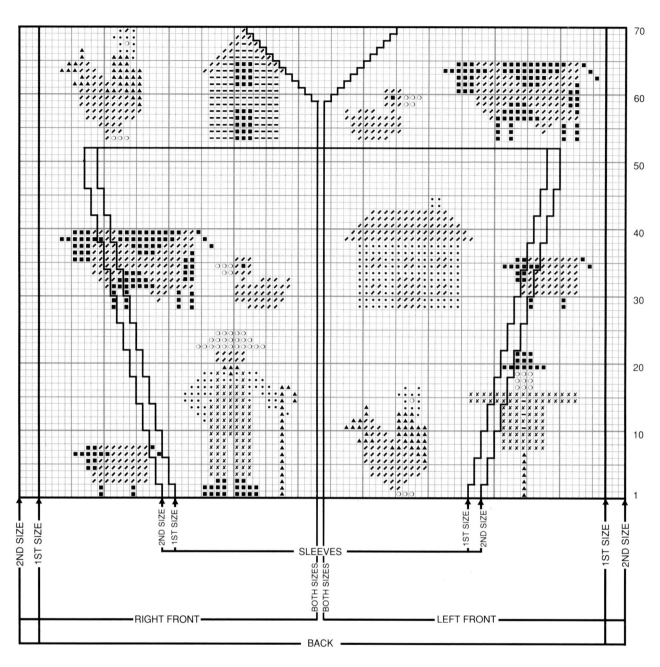

70

60

50

40

30

20

10

1

2ND SIZE

1ST SIZE

2ND SIZE

1ST SIZE

SLEEVES

1ST SIZE

2ND SIZE

1ST SIZE

2ND SIZE

BOTH SIZES
BOTH SIZES

RIGHT FRONT

LEFT FRONT

BACK

KEY

☐ = Green   ■ = Black

▲ = Brown   ✗ = Blue

○ = Yellow   • = Red

✦ = Cream   ▬ = Pink

108

Duck and Sheep Fair Isle Cardigan

See Page
35

MEASUREMENTS To fit age	3–4	5–6	Years
Actual chest measurement	78	89	cm
	30¾	35	in
Length to shoulder	46	49	cm
	18	19¼	in
Sleeve seam	25	28	cm
	10	11	in

MATERIALS
4(5) 50 g balls of Rowan DK Handknit Cotton in Navy (MC).
3(4) 50 g balls of same in Green (A).
2(2) 50 g balls of same in Cream (B).
1(2) 50 g balls of same in each of Rust (C) and Brown (D).
1(1) 50 g ball of same in Blue (E).
Pair each of 3¼ mm (No 10/US 3) and 4 mm (No 8/US 5) knitting needles.
One 3¼ mm (No 10/US 3) circular needle.
5 buttons.

TENSION
22 sts and 24 rows to 10 cm/4 in square over patt on 4 mm (No 8/US 5) needles.

ABBREVIATIONS
See page 63.

NOTE
Read Chart from right to left on K rows and from left to right on P rows. Strand yarn not in use loosely across wrong side when working in pattern to keep fabric elastic.

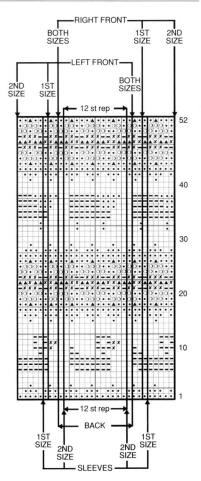

BACK
With 3¼ mm (No 10/US 3) needles and MC, cast on 78(90) sts.
1st row (right side) K2, [P2, K2] to end.
2nd row P2, [K2, P2] to end.
Rep these 2 rows until work measures 4 cm/1½ in from beg, ending with a right side row.
Inc row Rib 7(9), inc in next st, [rib 8(9), inc in next st] 7 times, rib 7(10). 86(98) sts.
Change to 4 mm (No 8/US 5) needles.
Beg with a K row, work in st st and patt from Chart as indicated for Back until Back measures 46(49) cm/18(19¼) in from beg, ending with a wrong side row.
Shape Shoulders
Cast off 14(16) sts at beg of next 4 rows.
Leave rem 30(34) sts on a holder.

LEFT FRONT
With 3¼ mm (No 10/US 3) needles and MC, cast on 38(42) sts.
Work 4 cm/1½ in in rib as on Back welt, ending with a right side row.
Inc row Rib 9(5), inc in next st, [rib 18(9), inc in next st] 1(3) times, rib 9(6). 40(46) sts.
Change to 4 mm (No 8/US 5) needles.
Beg with a K row, work in st st and patt from Chart as indicated for Left Front until Front measures 25(26) cm/10(10¼) in from beg, ending with a wrong side row.
Shape Front
Dec one st at end (front edge) of next row and 1(3) foll alt rows then on every foll 4th

row until 28(32) sts rem.
Cont straight until Front matches Back to shoulder shaping, ending with a wrong side row.
Shape Shoulder
Cast off 14(16) sts at beg of next row.
Work 1 row. Cast off rem 14(16) sts.

RIGHT FRONT
Work as for Left Front, working patt from Chart as indicated for Right Front and reversing shapings.

SLEEVES
With 3¼ mm (No 10/US 3) needles and MC, cast on 38(42) sts.
Work 5 cm/2 in in rib as on Back welt, ending with a right side row.
Inc row Rib 3, inc in next st, [rib 5(6), inc in next st] 5 times, rib 4(3). 44(48) sts.
Change to 4 mm (No 8/US 5) needles.
Beg with a K row, work in st st and patt from Chart as indicated for Sleeves, **at the same time**, inc one st at each end of every foll 3rd row until there are 72(76) sts, working inc sts into patt.
Cont straight until Sleeve measures 25(28) cm/10 (11) in from beg, ending with a wrong side row. Cast off.

FRONT BAND
Join shoulder seams.
With right side of work facing, 3¼ mm (No 10/US 3) circular needle and MC, pick up and K 52(54) sts up straight front edge of

Right Front, 52(56) sts up shaped edge to shoulder, K across back neck sts dec 4 sts evenly, pick up and K 52(56) sts down shaped edge of Left Front and 52(54) sts down straight front edge. 234(250) sts.
Beg with a 2nd row, work 3 rows in rib as on Back welt.
1st buttonhole row Rib 3(4), [cast off 2, rib 8 sts more] 5 times, rib to end.
2nd buttonhole row Rib to end casting on 2 sts over those cast off in previous row.
Rib 3 rows. Cast off in rib.

TO MAKE UP
Sew on sleeves, placing centre of sleeves to shoulder seams. Join side and sleeve seams. Sew on buttons.

KEY
• = MC
□ = A
– = B
✗ = C
○ = D
▲ = E

Double Moss Stitch and Cable Jacket

See Page
36

MEASUREMENTS

To fit age	2	3	4	Years
Actual chest measurement	76	80	83	cm
	30	31½	32¾	in
Length to shoulder	36	39	43	cm
	14¼	15½	17	in
Sleeve seam	24	27	30	cm
(with cuff turned back)	9½	10½	11¾	in

MATERIALS

6(7:7) 50 g balls of Rowan Designer DK Wool in Red (MC).
1(1:1) 50 g ball of same in Black (A).
Small amount of same in each of Cream (B), Green (C), Pale Blue (D) and Gold (E).
Pair of 4 mm (No 8/US 5) knitting needles.
Medium size crochet hook.
Cable needle.
5 buttons.

TENSION

26 sts and 34 rows to 10 cm/4 in square over double moss st patt on 4 mm (No 8/US 5) needles.

ABBREVIATIONS

C4B = slip next 2 sts onto cable needle and leave at back of work, K2, then K2 from cable needle;
C4F = slip next 2 sts onto cable needle and leave at front of work, K2, then K2 from cable needle;
Cr3L = slip next 2 sts onto cable needle and leave at front of work, P1, then K2 from cable needle;
Cr3R = slip next st onto cable needle and leave at back of work, K2, then P1 from cable needle;
MB = make bobble, [K1, P1, K1, P1, K1, P1, K1] all in next st, then pass 2nd, 3rd, 4th, 5th, 6th and 7th st over first st;
ch = chain; **dc** = double crochet; **ss** = slip stitch.
Also see page 63.

NOTE

Read Chart from right to left on right side rows and from left to right on wrong side rows. Use separate lengths of A, B, C, D and E yarn for each motif and twist yarns together on wrong side when changing colour to avoid holes. If preferred the motifs may be Swiss Darned when knitting is complete.

KEY
□ = MC
✎ = A
× = B
● = C
• = D
▲ = E

12 STS

CABLE PANEL – worked over 23 sts.

1st row (wrong side) P4, K5, P5, K5, P4.
2nd row K4, P5, K2, MB, K2, P5, K4.
3rd row As 1st row.
4th row C4B, P5, MB, K3, MB, P5, C4F.
5th row As 1st row.
6th row As 2nd row.
7th row As 1st row.
8th row C4B, P4, Cr3R, P1, Cr3L, P4, C4F.
9th row P4, K4, P2, K1, P1, K1, P2, K4, P4.
10th row K4, P3, Cr3R, K1, P1, K1, Cr3L, P3, K4.
11th row P4, K3, P3, K1, P1, K1, P3, K3, P4.
12th row C4B, P2, Cr3R, P1, [K1, P1] twice, Cr3L, P2, C4F.
13th row P4, K2, P2, K1, [P1, K1] 3 times, P2, K2, P4.
14th row K4, P2, K3, [P1, K1] 3 times, K2, P2, K4.
15th row As 13th row.

16th row C4B, P2, Cr3L, P1, [K1, P1] twice, Cr3R, P2, C4F.
17th row As 11th row.
18th row K4, P3, Cr3L, K1, P1, K1, Cr3R, P3, K4.
19th row As 9th row.
20th row C4B, P4, Cr3L, P1, Cr3R, P4, C4F.
These 20 rows form Cable Panel patt.

RIGHT FRONT

With 4 mm (No 8/US 5) needles and MC, cast on 57(59:61) sts.
Work in patt as follows:
1st row (wrong side) With MC, [K1, P1] 6(7:8) times, K1, work 1st row of Cable Panel, K1, P2, P across 1st row of Chart, P6MC.
2nd row K6MC, K across 2nd row of Chart, with MC, K2, P1, work 2nd row of Cable Panel, P1, [K1, P1] 6(7:8) times.
3rd row With MC, [P1, K1] 6(7:8) times, K1, work 3rd row of Cable Panel, K1, P2, P across 3rd row of Chart, P6MC.
4th row K6MC, K across 4th row of Chart, with MC, K2, P1, work 4th row of Cable Panel, P1, [P1, K1] 6(7:8) times.
These 4 rows set position of Cable Panel and Chart and form double moss st at side edge. Cont in patt as set, working appropriate rows of Cable Panel and Chart until 17th(19th:23rd) row has been worked.
1st buttonhole row With MC, K2, cast off 2, patt to end.
2nd buttonhole row Patt to last 2 sts, with MC, cast on 2 sts, P2.
Patt 18(20:22) rows.
Rep last 20(22:24) rows 3 times more, then the 2 buttonhole rows again.

Patt 2 rows.
Shape Neck
Cast off 9(10:11) sts at beg of next row and 3 sts at beg of 4 foll alt rows. Dec one st at neck edge on next 6 rows. Patt 2(4:6) rows. Cast off rem 30(31:32) sts.

LEFT FRONT
With 4 mm (No 8/US 5) needles and MC, cast on 57(59:61) sts.
Work in patt as follows:
1st row (wrong side) P6MC, P across 1st row of Chart, with MC, P2, K1, work 1st row of Cable Panel, K1, [P1, K1] 6(7:8) times.
2nd row With MC, [P1, K1] 6(7:8) times, P1, work 2nd row of Cable Panel, P1, K2, K across 2nd row of Chart, K6MC.
3rd row P6MC, P across 3rd row of Chart, with MC, P2, K1, work 3rd row of Cable Panel, K1, [K1, P1] 6(7:8) times.
4th row With MC, [K1, P1] 6(7:8) times, P1, work 4th row of Cable Panel, P1, K2, K across 4th row of Chart, K6MC.
Complete to match Right Front, reversing shapings and omitting buttonholes.

BACK
With 4 mm (No 8/US 5) needles and MC, cast on 97(101:107) sts.
Work in patt as follows:
1st row (wrong side) K1, [P1, K1] to end.
2nd row P1, [K1, P1] to end.
3rd row As 2nd row.
4th row As 1st row.

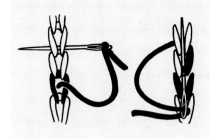

Swiss Darning. Bring needle out to front at base of stitch to be covered. Insert needle under the base of stitch above, then back at base. Emerge at base of next stitch to be covered.

These 4 rows form double moss st patt. Cont in patt until Back measures same as Front to cast off edge, ending with a wrong side row.
Shape Shoulders
Cast off 30(31:32) sts at beg of next 2 rows. Cast off rem 37(39:43) sts.

SLEEVES
With 4 mm (No 8/US 5) needles and MC, cast on 47(49:51) sts.
Work 6 cm/2¼ in in double moss st patt as on Back for cuff. Cont in patt, inc one st at each end of 13th row and every foll 4th row until there are 77(81:87) sts, working inc sts into patt.
Cont straight until Sleeve measures 30(33:36)cm 11¾(13:14¼) in from beg, ending with a wrong side row. Cast off.

TO MAKE UP
Work Swiss Darning (see diagram) if necessary. Join shoulder seams. Sew on sleeves, placing centre of sleeves to shoulder seams. Join side and sleeve seams, reversing seams on cuffs.
Crochet Edging
With right side facing and crochet hook, join MC yarn to Right Front side seam. Work 1 round of dc (the number of dc should be divisible by 3) along cast on edge of Right Front, along straight front edge, around neck edge and down straight front edge of Left Front, then along cast on edge of Left Front and Back, working 3 dc in every corner, ss in first dc. Fasten off.
Next round Join A in same place as ss, *3 ch, 1 dc in first of 3 ch (picot made), miss 2 dc, 1 dc in next dc; rep from * to end. Fasten off. With wrong side of sleeve facing, work crochet edging along lower edge of sleeves. Turn back cuffs. Sew on buttons.

Mexican Sweater

See Page
37

MEASUREMENTS To fit age	2–3	Years
Actual chest measurement	78 30¾	cm in
Length	37 14½	cm in
Sleeve seam	22 8¾	cm in

MATERIALS
650 g balls of Rowan DK Handknit Cotton in Blue (MC).
150 g ball of same in each of Red (A), Brown, Green, Pink, Yellow, White and Black.
Pair each of 3¾ mm (No 9/US 4) and 4 mm (No 8/US 5) knitting needles.
4 Mexican dolls.

TENSION
20 sts and 28 rows to 10 cm/4 in square over st st on 4 mm (No 8/US 5) needles.

ABBREVIATIONS
See page 63.

NOTE
Read Charts from right to left on right side rows and from left to right on wrong side rows. When working in pattern, use separate lengths of contrast yarns for each coloured area and twist yarns together on wrong side when changing colour to avoid holes.

BACK
With 3¾ mm (No 9/US 4) needles and MC, cast on 78 sts.
Stranding yarn not in use loosely across wrong side of work, work in rib patt as follows:
1st row (right side) P2MC, [K2A, P2MC] to end.
2nd row K2MC, [P2A, K2MC] to end.
Rep last 2 rows until welt measures 4 cm/1½ in from beg, ending with a wrong side row.
Change to 4 mm (No 8/US 5) needles. Beg with a K row, work in st st and patt from Chart 1 until 92nd row of Chart 1 has been worked.
Shape Shoulders
With MC, cast off 24 sts at beg of next 2 rows. Leave rem 30 sts on a holder.

FRONT
Work as given for Back until 76th row of Chart 1 has been worked.
Shape Neck
Next row Patt 31, turn.
Work on this set of sts only. Cont working from Chart 1, cast off 2 sts at beg of next row and foll alt row. Dec

one st at neck edge on 3 foll alt rows. 24
sts. Patt 6 rows straight. With MC, cast
off.

With right side facing, slip centre 16 sts
onto a holder, rejoin yarn to rem sts and
patt to end. Patt 1 row. Complete to
match first side.

SLEEVES

With 3¾ mm (No 9/US 4) needles and MC,
cast on 46 sts. Work 4 cm/1½ in in rib as
given for Back welt, ending with a right
side row.

Inc row Rib 4, [work twice in next st, rib
7] 5 times, work twice in next st, rib 1.
52 sts.
Change to 4 mm (No 8/US 5) needles.
Beg with a K row, work in st st and patt
from Chart 2, inc one st at each end of 5th
row and every foll 4th row until there are
72 sts. Cont straight until 50th row of
Chart 2 has been worked. Cast off.

NECKBAND

Join right shoulder seam.
With 3¾ mm (No 9/US 4) needles, MC and
right side facing, pick up and K 16 sts
down left front neck, K centre front sts,
pick up and K 16 sts up right front neck,
K back neck sts. 78 sts. P 1 row.
Beg with a 1st row, work 6 rows in rib as
given for Back welt.
With MC, cast off in rib.

TO MAKE UP

Join left shoulder and neckband seam.
Sew on sleeves, placing centre of sleeves
to shoulder seams. Join side and sleeve
seams. With Black, outline baskets,
melons, butterfly wings and heads, trees,
houses and house features. With Yellow,
work chain st (see diagram page 114)
between butterfly wings for body and 2
straight sts (see diagram page 90) with
French Knot (see diagram page 77) at
end of each for antennae. Work few
French Knots in Red, Yellow or Green in
baskets for fruit and in Red on trees.
With Yellow, work straight sts around sun
for rays. Sew Mexican dolls in the area as
indicated by dotted lines on Chart 1.

CHART 1

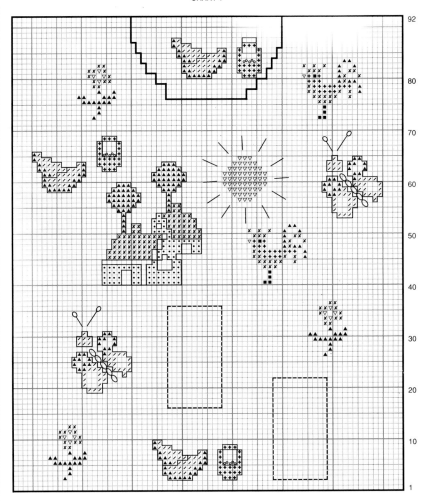

KEY

□ = Blue   x = Red   + = Brown
▲ = Green   ╱ = Pink   ▽ = Yellow
• = White   ■ = Black

Embroidery sts

— = Outlines   ○ = French Knot

∞ = Chain St   〉= Straight Sts

CHART 2

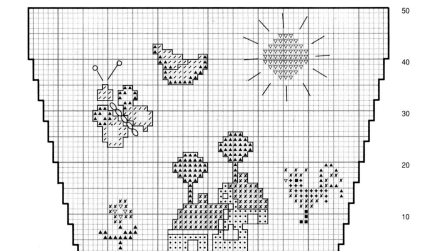

Wheatsheaf Sweater

MEASUREMENTS

To fit age	3–4	5–6	Years
Actual chest measurement	90	94	cm
	35¼	37	in
Length	43	48	cm
	17	19	in
Sleeve seam	26	30	cm
	10¼	11¾	in

MATERIALS
13(14) 50 g balls of Rowan DK Handknit Cotton.
Pair each of 3¼ mm (No 10/US 3) and 4 mm (No 8/US 5) knitting needles.
Cable needle.

TENSION
20 sts and 28 rows to 10 cm/4 in square over st st on 4 mm (No 8/US 5) needles.

ABBREVIATIONS
C4B = sl next 2 sts onto cable needle and leave at back of work, K2, then K2 from cable needle;
C4F = sl next 2 sts onto cable needle and leave at front of work, K2, then K2 from cable needle;
Cr3L = sl next 2 sts onto cable needle and leave at front of work, P1, then K2 from cable needle;
Cr3R = sl next st onto cable needle and leave at back of work, K2, then P1 from cable needle;
Cr4L = sl next 2 sts onto cable needle and leave at front of work, P2, then K2 from cable needle;
Cr4R = sl next 2 sts onto cable needle and leave at back of work, K2, then P2 from cable needle;
MB = make bobble as follows: [K1, P1, K1, P1, K1, P1, K1] all in next st, pass 2nd, 3rd, 4th, 5th, 6th and 7th sts over first st.
Also see page 63.

PANEL A – worked over 16 sts.
1st row (wrong side) K5, P6, K5.
2nd row P5, K2, C4B, P5.
3rd row As 1st row.
4th row P5, C4B, K2, P5.
5th to 12th rows Rep 1st to 4th rows twice.
13th row As 1st row.
14th row P4, Cr3R, K2, Cr3L, P4.
15th row K4, P2, [K1, P2] twice, K4.
16th row P3, Cr3R, P1, K2, P1, Cr3L, P3.
17th row K3, P2, [K2, P2] twice, K3.
18th row P2, Cr3R, P2, K2, P2, Cr3L, P2.
19th row K2, P2, [K3, P2] twice, K2.
20th row P2, Cr3L, P2, K2, P2, Cr3R, P2.
21st row As 17th row.
22nd row P3, Cr3L, P1, K2, P1, Cr3R, P3.
23rd row As 15th row.
24th row P4, Cr3L, K2, Cr3R, P4.
These 24 rows form patt.

PANEL B – worked over 12 sts.
1st row (wrong side) K2, P2, K4, P2, K2.
2nd row P2, K2, P4, K2, P2.
3rd row As 1st row.
4th row P2, Cr4L, Cr4R, P2.
5th row K4, P4, K4.
6th row P4, Cr4L, P4.
7th row K4, P2, K6.
8th row P6, Cr3L, P3.
9th row K3, P2, K7.
10th row P7, Cr3L, P2.
11th row K2, P2, K8.
12th row P3, MB, P4, K2, P2.
13th row As 11th row.
14th row P7, Cr3R, K2.
15th row As 9th row.
16th row P6, Cr3R, P3.
17th row As 7th row.
18th row P4, C4B, P4.
19th row As 5th row.
20th row P2, Cr4R, Cr4L, P2.
21st to 25th rows Work 1st to 5th rows.
26th row P4, Cr4R, P4.
27th row K6, P2, K4.
28th row P3, Cr3R, P6.
29th row K7, P2, K3.
30th row P2, Cr3R, P7.
31st row K8, P2, K2.
32nd row P2, K2, P4, MB, P3.
33rd row As 31st row.
34th row P2, Cr3L, P7.
35th row As 29th row.
36th row P3, Cr3L, P6.
37th row As 27th row.
38th row P4, C4F, P4.
39th row As 5th row.
40th row As 20th row.
These 40 rows form patt.

BACK
With 3¼ mm (No 10/US 3) needles, cast on 101(107) sts.
1st row (wrong side) K2, [P1 tbl, K2] 6(7) times, * P4, K2, [P1 tbl, K2] 3 times, P4, * K2, [P1 tbl, K2] 7 times, rep from * to *, K2, [P1 tbl, K2] 6(7) times.
2nd row P2, [K1 tbl, P2] 6(7) times, * C4F, P2, [K1 tbl, P2] 3 times, C4B *; P2, [K1 tbl, P2] 7 times, rep from * to *, P2, [K1 tbl, P2] 6(7) times.
3rd row As 1st row.
4th row P2, [K1 tbl, P2] 6(7) times, * K4, P2, [K1 tbl, P2] 3 times, K4 *; P2, [K1 tbl, P2] 7 times, rep from * to *, P2, [K1 tbl, P2] 6(7) times.
These 4 rows form rib patt. Rep them twice more, then work 1st row again.
Inc row [Patt 15(33), m1] 2(1) times, patt 12, [m1, patt 4] 5 times, patt 9, [m1, patt 15(33)] 2(1) times. 110(114) sts.
Change to 4 mm (No 8/US 5) needles.
Work in main patt as follows:
1st row (wrong side) K1, [P1, K1] 2(3) times, work 1st row of Panel A, * P4, work 1st row of Panel B, P4 *; K28, rep from * to *, work 1st row of Panel A, K1, [P1, K1] 2(3) times.
2nd row P1, [K1, P1] 2(3) times, work 2nd row of Panel A, * K4, work 2nd row of Panel B, K4 *; P 28, rep from * to *, work 2nd row of Panel A, P1, [K1, P1] 2(3) times.
3rd row P1, [K1, P1] 2(3) times, work 3rd row of Panel A, * P4, work 3rd row of Panel B, P4 *; K28, rep from * to *, work 3rd row of Panel A, P1, [K1, P1] 2(3) times.
4th row K1, [P1, K1] 2(3) times, work 4th row of Panel A, * C4F, work 4th row of Panel B, C4B *; P28, rep from * to *, work 4th row of Panel A, K1, [P1, K1] 2(3) times.
These 4 rows set position of Panels and form double moss st at sides.
Cont in patt as set until Back measures 43(48) cm/17(19) in from beg, ending with a wrong side row.

Shape Shoulders
Cast off 20(21) sts at beg of next 2 rows and 21 sts at beg of foll 2 rows. Leave rem 28(30) sts on a holder.

FRONT
Work as given for Back until Front measures 36(41) cm/14¼(16¼) in from beg, ending with a wrong side row.

Shape Neck
Next row Patt 49(50), turn.
Work on this set of sts only. Keeping patt correct, dec one st at neck edge on every row until 41(42) sts rem. Cont straight until Front matches Back to shoulder shaping, ending at side edge.

Shape Shoulder
Cast off 20(21) sts at beg of next row. Work 1 row. Cast off rem 21 sts.
With right side facing, slip centre 12(14) sts onto a holder, rejoin yarn to rem sts and patt to end. Complete to match first side.

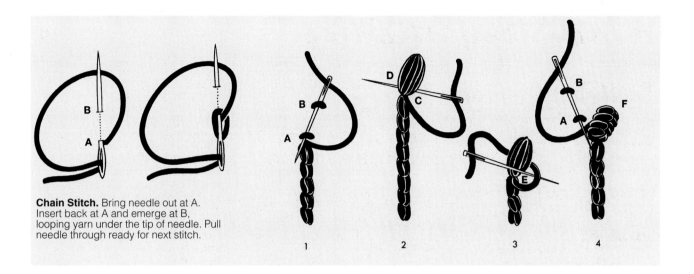

Chain Stitch. Bring needle out at A. Insert back at A and emerge at B, looping yarn under the tip of needle. Pull needle through ready for next stitch.

1   2   3   4

SLEEVES

With 3¼ mm (No 10/US 3) needles, cast on 47 sts.

1st row (wrong side) K2, [P1 tbl, K2] 4 times, P4, K2, [P1 tbl, K2] 3 times, P4, K2, [P1 tbl, K2] 4 times.

2nd row P2, [K1 tbl, P2] 4 times, C4F, P2, [K1 tbl, P2] 3 times, C4B, P2, [K1 tbl, P2] 4 times.

3rd row As 1st row.

4th row P2, [K1 tbl, P2] 4 times, K4, P2, [K1 tbl, P2] 3 times, K4, P2, [K1 tbl, P2] 4 times.

These 4 rows form rib patt. Rep them twice more, then work 1st row again.

Inc row Patt 1, m1, [patt 3, m1] 4 times, patt 10, m1, patt 11, [m1, patt 3] 4 times, m1, patt 1. 58 sts.

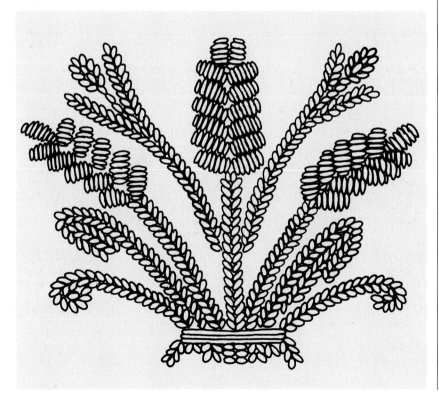

Change to 4 mm (No 8/US 5) needles. Work in main patt as follows:

1st row (wrong side) K1, P1, K1, work 1st row of Panel A, P4, work 1st row of Panel B, P4, work 1st row of Panel A, K1, P1, K1.

2nd row P1, K1, P1, work 2nd row of Panel A, K4, work 2nd row of Panel B, K4, work 2nd row of Panel A, P1, K1, P1.

3rd row P1, K1, P1, work 3rd row of Panel A, P4, work 3rd row of Panel B, P4, work 3rd row of Panel A, P1, K1, P1.

4th row K1, P1, K1, work 4th row of Panel A, C4F, work 4th row of Panel B, C4B, work 4th row of Panel A, K1, P1, K1.

These 4 rows set position of Panels and form double moss st at sides.

Cont in patt as set, inc one st at each end of next row and every foll 3rd row until

there are 88(92) sts, working inc sts into double moss st.

Cont straight until Sleeve measures 26(30) cm/10¼(11¾) in from beg, ending with a wrong side row. Cast off.

NECKBAND

Join right shoulder seam.

With 3¼ mm (No 10/US 3) needles and right side facing, pick up and K 21 sts down left front neck, P4(14), [m1, P4] 2(0) times across centre front sts, pick up and K 21 sts up right front neck, [K2(3), m1, K2(3)] 7(5) times across back neck sts. 91 sts.

1st row K1, * P4, K2, [P1 tbl, K2] 3 times; rep from * to end.

2nd row * P2, [K1 tbl, P2] 3 times, K4; rep from * to last st, P1.

3rd row As 1st row.

4th row * P2, [K1 tbl, P2] 3 times, C4F, P2, [K1 tbl, P2] 3 times, C4B; rep from * to last st, P1.

These 4 rows form rib patt. Rep them twice more, then work 1st row again. Cast off in patt.

TO MAKE UP

Join left shoulder and neckband seam. Sew on sleeves, placing centre of sleeves to shoulder seams. Join side and sleeve seams. Embroider wheatsheaf as shown on diagram.

Wheatsheaf Work laid threads (diagram 1, above) as follows: bring needle out at A, * catch loop of knitted st at B, then catch loop of knitted st at A *; rep from * to * 2 or 3 times more.

Couch laid threads (diagrams 2 and 3) as follows: * insert needle under laid threads at C and bring out at D, pull through leaving small loop. Insert needle into loop at E and pull up tightly *; rep from * to * until laid threads are covered, taking care to keep sts close together.

Insert needle at F (diagram 4) and bring needle out at A, laid threads and couch them as before working in reverse direction.

Aran Sweater Dress

See Page
39

MEASUREMENTS

To fit age	1	2:3	Yrs
All round at chest	64	78–80	**cm**
	25¼	28¼:31½	**in**
Length to shoulder	38	44:50	**cm**
	15	17¼:19¾	**in**
Sleeve seam	22	24:26	**cm**
	8½	9½:10¼	**in**

MATERIALS
6 (6:7) 100 g balls of Rowan Magpie.
1 pair each of 3¾ mm (No 9/US 4) and 4½ mm (No 7/US 6) knitting needles.
One 3¾ mm (No 9/US 4) circular needle 40 cm long.
Cable needle.

TENSION
19 sts and 25 rows to 10 cm/4 in over st

st using 4½ mm (No 7/US 6) needles.

ABBREVIATIONS
C4F = slip next 2 sts onto cable needle and leave at front, K2, then K2 from cable needle.
C4B = slip next 2 sts onto cable needle and leave at back, K2, then K2 from cable needle.
FC = slip next 2 sts onto cable needle and leave at front, P1, then K2 from cable needle.
BC = slip next st onto cable needle and leave at back, K2, then P1 from cable needle.
TW2L = slip next st onto cable needle and leave at front, P1, then K1 from cable needle.
TW2R = slip next st onto cable needle and leave at back, K1, then P1 from cable needle.
Also see page 63.

PANEL A – worked over 7 sts.
1st row (wrong side) K5, P2.
2nd row FC, P4.
3rd row K4, P2, K1.
4th row K1, FC, P3.
5th row K3, P2, K1, P1.
6th row P1, K1, FC, P2.
7th row K2, P2, K1, P1, K1.
8th row K1, P1, K1, FC, P1.
9th row K1, P2, [K1, P1] twice.
10th row [P1, K1] twice, FC.
11th row P2, K1, [P1, K1] twice.
12th row [K1, P1] twice, BC.
13th row As 9th row.
14th row P1, K1, P1, BC, P1.
15th row As 7th row.
16th row K1, P1, BC, P2.
17th row As 5th row.
18th row P1, BC, P3.
19th row As 3rd row.
20th row BC, P4.
These 20 rows form patt.

PANEL B – worked over 10 sts.
1st row (wrong side) K1, P8, K1.
2nd row P1, C4B, C4F, P1.
3rd row As 1st row.
4th row P1, K8, P1.
5th row As 1st row.
6th row P1, C4F, C4B, P1.
7th row As 1st row.
8th row As 4th row.
These 8 rows form patt.

PANEL C – worked over 17 sts.
1st row (wrong side) K3, K into front, back, front, back, front of next st, K2, P2, K1, P2, K2, K into front, back, front, back, front of next st, K3.
2nd row P3, K5 tog tbl, P2, slip first 3 sts onto cable needle and leave at front, K2, slip first (P) st on cable needle back onto

left-hand needle, P this st, then K2 from cable needle, P2, K5 tog tbl, P3.
3rd row K6, P2, K1, P2, K6.
4th row P5, BC, P1, FC, P5.
5th row K5, P2, K3, P2, K5.
6th row P4, BC, P3, FC, P4.
7th row K4, P2, K2, K into front, back, front, back, front of next st, K2, P2, K4.
8th row P3, BC, P2, K5 tog tbl, P2, FC, P3.
9th row K3, P2, K7, P2, K3.
10th row P2, BC, P7, FC, P2.
11th row K2, P2, K2, K into front, back, front, back, front of next st, K3, K into front, back, front, back, front of next st, K2, P2, K2.
12th row P1, BC, P2, K5 tog tbl, P3, K5 tog tbl, P2, FC, P1.
13th row K1, P2, K11, P2, K1.
14th row P1, K2, P11, K2, P1.
15th row K1, P2, K3 [K into front, back, front, back, front of next st, K3) twice, P2, K1.
16th row P1, FC, P2, K5 tog tbl, P3, K5 tog tbl, P2, BC, P1.
17th row K2, P2, K9, P2, K2.
18th row P2, FC, P7, BC, P2.
19th row K3, P2, K3, K into front, back, front of next st, K3, P2, K3.
20th row P3, FC, P2, K5 tog tbl, P2, BC, P3.
21st row K4, P2, K5, P2, K4.
22nd row P4, FC, P3, BC, P4.
23rd row As 5th row.
24th row P5, FC, P1, BC, P5.
These 24 rows form patt.

PANEL D – worked over 7 sts.
1st row (wrong side) P2, K5.
2nd row P4, BC.
3rd row K1, P2, K4.
4th row P3, BC, K1.
5th row P1, K1, P2, K3.

6th row P2, BC, K1, P1.
7th row K1, P1, K1, P2, K2.
8th row P1, BC, K1, P1, K1.
9th row [P1, K1] twice, P2, K1.
10th row BC, [K1, P1] twice.
11th row [K1, P1] 3 times, P1.
12th row FC, [K1, P1] twice.
13th row As 9th row.
14th row P1, FC, P1, K1, P1.
15th row As 7th row.
16th row P2, FC, P1, K1.
17th row As 5th row.
18th row P3, FC, P1.
19th row As 3rd row.
20th row P4, FC.
These 20 rows form patt.

BACK
With 3¾ mm (No 9/US 4) needles, cast on 82 (87:97) sts.
1st row (right side) K2, [K1, P2, K2] to end.
2nd row P2, [K2, P3] to end.
3rd row K2, [TW2L, P1, K2] to end.
4th row P2, [K1, P1, K1, P2] to end.
5th row K2, [P1, TW2L, K2] to end.
6th row P2, [P1, K2, P2] to end.
7th row K2, [P1, TW2R, K2] to end.
8th row As 4th row.
9th row K2, [TW2R, P1, K2] to end.
10th row As 2nd row.
Rows 3 to 10 form rib patt. Cont in rib patt until work measures 8 (10:12) cm/3 (4:4¾) in from beg, ending with a right side row.
K 4 rows inc 3 (6:4) sts evenly across last row. 85 (93:101) sts.
Change to 4½ mm (No 7/US 6) needles.
Work in patt as follows:
1st row (wrong side) K1, [P1, K1] 2 (4:6) times, work 1st row of Panel A, *K1, P4, K1, work 1st row of Panel B, K1, P4, K1*, work 1st row of Panel C, rep from * to *, work 1st row of Panel D, K1, [P1, K1] 2 (4:6) times.
2nd row P1, [K1, P1] 2 (4:6) times, work 2nd row of Panel D, *P1, K4, P1, work 2nd row of Panel B, P1, K4, P1*, work 2nd row of Panel C, rep from * to *, work 2nd row of Panel A, P1, [K1, P1] 2 (4:6) times.
3rd row P1, [K1, P1] 2 (4:6) times, work 3rd row of Panel A, *K1, P4, K1, work 3rd row of Panel B, K1, P4, K1*, work 3rd row of Panel C, rep from * to * work 3rd row of Panel D, P1, [K1, P1] 2 (4:6) times.
4th row K1, [P1, K1] 2 (4:6) times, work 4th row of Panel D, P1, C4B, P1, work 4th row of Panel B, P1, C4B, P1, work 4th row of Panel C, P1, C4F, P1, work 4th row of Panel B, P1, C4F, P1, work 4th row of Panel A, K1, [P1, K1] 2 (4:6) times.
These 4 rows set patt. Cont in patt as set, working appropriate rows of Panels until work measures 38 (44:50) cm/15 (17¼:19¾) in from beg, ending with a wrong side row.

Shape Shoulders
Cast off 11 (13:14) sts at beg of next 2

rows and 12 (13:15) sts at beg of foll 2 rows. Leave rem 39 (41:43) sts on a holder.

FRONT

Work as given for Back until work measures 33 (38:44) cm/13 (15:17¼) in from beg, ending with a wrong side row.

Shape neck

Next row Patt 33 (36:39), turn. Work on this set of sts only. Keeping patt correct, dec one st at neck edge on every row until 23 (26:29) sts rem.
Cont without shaping for a few rows until work measures same as Back to shoulder shaping, ending at side edge.

Shape shoulder

Cast off 11 (13:14) sts at beg of next row. Work 1 row. Cast off rem 12 (13:15) sts.
With right side facing, slip centre 19 (21:23) sts onto a holder, rejoin yarn to rem sts and patt to end. Complete to match first side.

SLEEVES

With 3¾ mm (No 9/US 4) needles, cast on 32 (37:42) sts. Work in rib patt as given for Back until work measures 5 (6:6) cm/2 (2¼:2¼) in from beg, ending with a right side row. K 4 rows inc 3 (12:11) sts

evenly across last row. 35 (49:53) sts.
Change to 4½ mm (No 7/US 6) needles.
Work in patt as follows:

1st size only

1st row (wrong side) K1, P1, K2, P4, K1, work 1st row of Panel C, K1, P4, K2, P1, K1.
2nd row P1, K1, P2, K4, P1, work 2nd row of Panel C, P1, K4, P2, K1, P1.
3rd row [P1, K1] twice, P4, K1, work 3rd row of Panel C, K1, P4, [K1, P1] twice.
4th row [K1, P1] twice, C4B, P1, work 4th row of Panel C, P1, C4F, [P1, K1] twice.

2nd and 3rd sizes only

1st row (wrong side) [K1, P1] (0:1) time, work 1st row of Panel B, K1, P4, K1, work 1st row of Panel C, K1, P4, K1, work 1st row of Panel B, [P1, K1] (0:1) time.
2nd row [P1, K1] (0:1) time, work 2nd row of Panel B, P1, K4, P1, work 2nd row of Panel C, P1, K4, P1, work 2nd row of Panel B, [K1, P1] (0:1) time.
3rd row [P1, K1] (0:1) time, work 3rd row of Panel B, K1, P4, K1, work 3rd row of Panel C, K1, P4, K1, work 3rd row of Panel B, [K1, P1] (0:1) time.
4th row [K1, P1] (0:1) time, work 4th row of Panel B, P1, C4B, P1,, work 4th row of

Panel C, P1, C4F, P1, work 4th row of Panel B, [P1, K1] (0:1) time.

All sizes

These 4 rows set patt. Cont in patt as set, working appropriate rows of Panels, **at the same time**, inc one st at each end of next and every foll 2nd (2nd:3rd) row until there are 65 (77:81) sts, working inc sts into double moss st (side edge) patt.
Cont without shaping until work measures 22 (24:26) cm/8½ (9½:10¼) in from beg, ending with a wrong side row. Cast off.

NECKBAND

Join shoulder seams.
With 3¾ mm (No 9/US 4) circular needle, right side facing and beg at left shoulder seam, pick up and K 17 (21:21) sts down left front neck, K across 19 (21:23) sts at centre front, pick up and K 17 (21:21) sts up right front neck, K across 39 (41:43) sts at back neck. 92 (104:108) sts. Work in rounds of K2, P2 rib for 5 (6:7) cm/2 (2¼:2¾) in. K 5 rounds. Cast off loosely.

TO MAKE UP

Sew on sleeves, placing centre of sleeves to shoulder seams. Join side and sleeve seams.

Aran Coat with Large Collar

See Page 40

MEASUREMENTS			
To fit age	2	3	Yrs
All round at chest	68	74	cm
	26¾	29	in
Length to shoulder	42	48	cm
	16½	19	in
Sleeve seam	22	25	cm
	8¾	10	in

MATERIALS

10 (11) 50 g balls of Rowan Designer DK Wool.
1 pair each of 3¼ mm (No 10/US 3) and 4 mm (No 8/US 5) knitting needles.
Cable needle
5 (6) buttons.

TENSION

22 sts and 28 rows to 10 cm/4 in over st st on 4 mm (No 8/US 5) needles.

ABBREVIATIONS

C4B = slip next 2 sts onto cable needle and leave at back, K2, then K2 from cable needle.
C4F = slip next 2 sts onto cable needle and leave at front, K2, then K2 from cable needle.
BC = slip next st onto cable needle and leave at back, K2, then P1 from cable needle.
FC = slip next 2 sts onto cable needle and leave at front, P1, then K2 from cable needle.
Also see page 63.

These 8 rows form patt.

PANEL C – worked over 20 sts.

1st row (wrong side) K3, P2, K3, P4, K3, P2, K3.
2nd row [P2, BC] twice, [FC, P2] twice.
3rd row [K2, P2, K3, P2] twice, K2.
4th row P1, [BC, P2] twice, FC, P2, FC, P1.
5th row K1, P2, K3, P2, K4, P2, K3, P2, K1.
6th row [BC, P2] twice, pick up loop lying between sts and [K1, P1, K1, P1, K1] into it, turn, P5, turn, K5, turn, P2 tog, P1, P2 tog, turn, slip 1, K2 tog, psso, P1 then pass bobble st over first st, P1, FC, P2, FC.
7th row [P2, K3] twice, [K3, P2] twice.
8th row [FC, P2] twice, [P2, BC] twice.
9th row As 5th row.
10th row P1, [FC, P2] twice, BC, P2, BC, P1.
11th row As 3rd row.
12th row [P2, FC] twice, [BC, P2] twice.
These 12 rows form patt.

PANEL A – worked over 6 sts.

1st and foll alt row (wrong side) K1, P4, K1.
2nd row P1, K4, P1.
4th row P1, C4B, P1.
These 4 rows form patt.

PANEL B – worked over 10 sts.

1st row and every foll alt rows (wrong side) K1, P8, K1.
2nd row P1, C4B, C4F, P1.
4th row P1, K8, P1.
6th row P1, C4F, C4B, P1.
8th row As 4th row.

PANEL D – worked over 6 sts.

1st row and foll alt row (wrong side) K1, P4, K1.
2nd row P1, K4, P1.
4th row P1, C4F, P1.
These 4 rows form patt.

BACK

With 4 mm (No 8/US 5) needles, cast on 93 (101) sts.

1st row (right side) K1, [P1, K1] to end.

2nd row P1, [K1, P1] to end.

Rep these 2 rows until work measures 3 cm/1¼ in from beg, ending with a right side row and inc 15 sts evenly across last row. 108 (116) sts.

Work in patt as follows:

1st row (wrong side) K1 (5), work 1st row of Panels A, B, A, C, A, B, D, C, D, B and D, K1 (5).

2nd row P1 (5), work 2nd row of Panels D, B, D, C, D, B, A, C, A, B and A, P1 (5).

These 2 rows set patt. Cont in patt as set, working appropriate rows of Panels until work measures 42 (48) cm/16½ (19) in from beg, ending with a wrong side row.

Shape shoulders

Cast off 18 (19) sts at beg of next 2 rows and 18 (20) sts at beg of foll 2 rows. Cast off rem 36 (38) sts.

LEFT FRONT

With 4 mm (No 8/US 5) needles, cast on 43 (47) sts.

Work in rib as given for Back for 3 cm/1¼ in, ending with a right side row and inc 7 sts evenly across last row. 50 (54) sts.

Work in patt as follows:

1st row (wrong side) K1, work 1st row of Panels, D, C, D, B and D, K1 (5).

2nd row P1 (5), work 2nd row of Panels D, B, D, C and D, P1.

These 2 rows set patt. Cont in patt as set, working appropriate rows of Panels until work measures 29 (35) cm/11¼ (13¾) in from beg, ending with a wrong side row.

Shape Front

Keeping patt correct, dec one st at end (front edge) of next and 9 foll alt rows, then at same edge on every 3rd row until 36 (39) sts rem.

Cont without shaping until work measures same as Back to shoulder shaping, ending with a wrong side row.

Shape Shoulder

Cast off 18 (19) sts at beg of next row. Work 1 row. Cast off rem 18 (20) sts.

RIGHT FRONT

Work as given for Left Front, reversing all shaping and placing patt as follows:

1st row (wrong side) K1 (5), work 1st row of Panels A, B, A, C and A, K1.

2nd row P1, work 2nd row of Panels A, C, A, B and A, P1 (5).

SLEEVES

With 3¼ mm (No 10/US 3) needles, cast on 43 sts.

Work in rib as given for Back for 5 cm/2 in, ending with a wrong side row.

Next row Inc in each of next 3 sts, [rib 1, inc in each of next 3 sts] to end. 76 sts.

Change to 4 mm (No 8/US 5) needles.

Work in patt as follows:

1st row (wrong side) K1, work 1st row of Panels A, C, A, B, D, C and D, K1.

2nd row P1, work 2nd row of Panels, D, C, D, B, A, C and A, P1.

These 2 rows set patt. Cont in patt as set, working appropriate rows of Panels, **at the same time**, inc one st at each end of every foll 8th (6th) row until there are 84 (90) sts, working inc sts into reverse st st.

Cont without shaping until work measures 22 (25) cm/8¾ (10) in from beg, ending with a wrong side row. Cast off.

BUTTONHOLE BAND

With 3¼ mm (No 10/US 3) needles and right side facing, pick up and K 67 (81) sts evenly along straight edge of Right Front to beg of shaping. Beg with a 2nd row, work 3 rows in rib as given for Back.

1st buttonhole row Rib 2, [cast off 2, rib 12 sts more] 4 (5) times, cast off 2, rib to end.

2nd buttonhole row Rib to end, casting on 2 sts over those cast off in previous row. Rib 4 rows. Cast off in rib.

BUTTON BAND

Work to match Buttonhole Band, omitting buttonholes.

COLLAR

With 4 mm (No 8/US 5) needles, cast on 3 sts for left half of collar.

Next row (right side) P1, K2.

Next row Cast on 3, work 1st row of Panel D.

Next row Work 2nd row of Panel D.

Next row Cast on 3, K3 (part of 1st row of Panel C), work 3rd row of Panel D.

Next row Work 4th row of Panel D, P2, inc in next st.

Inc one st at beg (inside edge) of next row and at same edge on every row until there are 42 sts, working inc sts into Panels C, D, and B.

Cont without shaping for a few rows until work fits along shaped edge of Left Front, ending with a 1st row of Panel C.

Shape Collar

Next row Patt 8, turn.

Next row and 6 foll alt rows Slip 1, patt to end.

Next row Patt 25, turn.

Next row Patt 33, turn.

Next row Patt 42.

Next row Patt 33, turn.

Next row Patt 25, turn.

Next row Patt 8, turn.

Patt 1 row, thus ending at inside edge.

Cast on 4 sts at beg of next and 2 foll alt rows, working cast on sts into Panels D and C. 54 sts. **Patt 1 row. Leave these sts on a spare needle.

With 4 mm (No 8/US 5) needles, cast on 3 sts for right half of collar.

Next row (right side) K2, P1.

Next row K1, P2.

Next row Cast on 3, work 2nd row of Panel A.

Next row Work 3rd row of Panel A.

Next row Cast on 3, P3, (part of 2nd row of Panel C), work 4th row of Panel A.

Next row Work 1st row of Panel A, K3, inc in last st.

Work as given for left half of collar to**, but working Panel A instead of Panel D and ending with a 2nd row of Panel C before collar shaping.

Next row Patt 54, cast on 8, then patt across sts of left half of collar. 116 sts.

Cont in patt across all sts, work 16 rows.

Shape Point

Cast off 3 sts at beg of every row until 2 sts rem. K2 tog. Fasten off.

COLLAR EDGINGS

With 3¼ mm (No 10/US 3) needles and right side facing, pick up and K 59 sts along straight outside edge of left half of collar and 52 sts along shaped edge to point, turn. 111 sts.

Work in rib as given for Back for 4 rows, inc one st at beg of every row. Cast off in rib. Work other side to match.

TO MAKE UP

Join shoulder seams. Sew on sleeves, placing centre of sleeves to shoulder seams. Join side and sleeve seams. Sew collar in place, beg and ending at centre of front bands. Join row ends of collar edging at point.

Make 2 pompons and cord 10 cm long. Attach 1 pompon to each end of cord. Sew to point of collar, letting 1 pompon hang. Sew on buttons.

Tunic with Pig Motif

See Page
41

MEASUREMENTS To fit age	2–3	3–4	4–5	Years
Actual chest measurement	76	82	88	cm
	30	32¼	34¾	in
Length	44	47	50	cm
	17¼	18½	19¾	in
Sleeve seam	24	27	30	cm
	9½	10½	11¾	in

MATERIALS
10(10:11) 50 g balls of Rowan DK Handknit Cotton in Navy (MC). Small amount of same in each of Pink and Brown. Pair each of 3¼mm (No 10/US 3) and 4 mm (No 8/US 5) knitting needles.

TENSION
20 sts and 28 rows to 10 cm/4 in square over st st on 4 mm (No 8/US 5) needles.

ABBREVIATIONS
See page 63.

NOTE
Read Chart from right to left on right side rows and from left to right on wrong side rows. When working motif, use separate lengths of contrast yarn for each coloured area and twist yarns together on wrong side when changing colour to avoid holes.

BACK
With 3¼mm (No 10/US 3) needles and MC, cast on 70(76:82) sts.
1st row (right side) K2(3:2), [P2, K2] to last 0(1:0) st, K0(1:0).
2nd row P0(1:0), [P2, K2] to last 2(3:2) sts, P2(3:2).
Rep last 2 rows until work measures 4(4:5) cm/1½ (1½:2) in from beg, ending with a wrong side row.
Change to 4 mm (No 8/US 5) needles.
Next row Cast on 3 sts for top of slit, K to end.
Next row Cast on 3 sts for top of slit, P to end. 76(82:88) sts.
Cont in st st until work measures 44(47:50) cm/17¼(18½:19¾) in from beg, ending with a P row.
Shape Shoulders
Cast off 11(12:13) sts at beg of next 4 rows. Leave rem 32(34:36) sts on a holder.

POCKET LINING (make one)
With 4 mm (No 8/US 5) needles and MC, cast on 20 sts. Beg with a K row, work 18 rows in st st. Leave these sts on a holder.

FRONT
Work as given for Back until Front measures 25(27:29) cm/10(10½:11½) in from beg, ending with a P row.

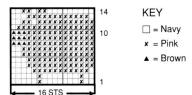

		14
		10
		1

← 16 STS →

KEY
□ = Navy
x = Pink
▲ = Brown

Next row K12(16:20)MC, K across 1st row of Chart, K48(50:52)MC.
Next row P48(50:52)MC, P across 2nd row of Chart, P12(16:20)MC.
Cont working as set until 14th row of Chart has been worked.
Cont in MC only, work 2 rows.
Place Pocket
Next row K10(14:18), slip next 20 sts onto a holder, K across sts of pocket lining, K to end.
Cont until Front measures 38(41:44) cm/15(16¼:17½) in from beg, ending with a P row.
Shape Neck
Next row K32(34:36), turn.
Work on this set of sts only. Dec one st at neck edge on every row until 22(24:26) sts rem. Cont straight until Front matches Back to shoulder shaping, ending at side edge.
Shape Shoulder
Cast off 11(12:13) sts at beg of next row.

Work 1 row. Cast off rem 11(12:13) sts. With right side facing, slip centre 12 (14:16) sts onto a holder, rejoin yarn to rem sts and K to end. Complete to match first side.

SLEEVES
With 3¼mm (No 10/US 3) needles and MC, cast on 34(38:38) sts. Work 4(5:5) cm/1½ (2:2) in in rib as given for 1st size on Back welt, ending with a 1st row.
Inc row Rib 2(3:1), inc in next st, [rib 3(5:4), inc in next st] to last 3(4:1) sts, rib 3(4:1). 42(44:46) sts.
Change to 4 mm (No 8/US 5) needles.
Beg with a K row, work in st st, inc one st at each end of 3rd row and every foll 4th row until there are 66(70:74) sts.
Cont straight for a few rows until Sleeve measures 22(25:28) cm/8¾(9¾:11) in from beg, ending with a P row.
Now work 2 cm/¾in in rib as given for 1st size on Back welt, ending with a wrong side row. Cast off in rib.

NECKBAND
Join right shoulder seam.
With 3¼mm (No 10/US 3) needles, MC and right side facing, pick up and K 21 sts down left front neck, K across centre front sts, pick up and K 21 sts up right front neck, K across back neck sts. 86(90:94) sts. Beg with a 2nd row, work 4 (5:5) cm/1½(2:2) in in rib as given for 1st size on Back welt. Cast off in rib.

POCKET TOP
With 3¼mm (No 10/US 3) needles, MC and right side facing, K across sts of pocket top inc 2 sts evenly across. 22 sts. Beg with a 2nd row, work 5 rows in rib as given for 1st size on Back welt. Cast off in rib.

SLIT EDGINGS
With 3¼mm (No 10/US 3) needles, MC and right side facing, pick up and K 8(8:12) sts from lower edge to cast on sts for top of slit at right side edge of Back. Work 4 rows in P2, K2 rib. Cast off in rib. Work left side of Back to match. Work Front slit edgings in same way.

TO MAKE UP
Join left shoulder and neckband seam. Sew on sleeves, placing centre of sleeves to shoulder seams. Join row ends of slit edgings to cast on sts for top of slits. Beginning at top of slits, join side and sleeve seams. Catch down pocket lining and sides of pocket top. Embroider pig's tail in Pink and nostrils in MC.

Navajo Jacket

See Page 42

MEASUREMENTS To fit age	2	3	Yrs
All round at chest	74	80	cm
	29	31½	in
Length to shoulder	37	40	cm
	14½	15¾	in
Sleeve seam	25	28	cm
	10	11	in

MATERIALS
4 x 50 g balls of Rowan Designer DK Wool in main colour (M).
2 balls of same in each of 2 colours (A and B)
1 ball of same in each of 3 colours (C, D and E).
1 pair each of 3¼mm (No 10/US 3) and 4 mm (No 8/US 5) knitting needles.
3 buttons.

TENSION
23 sts and 24 rows to 10 cm/4 in over patt using 4 mm (No 8/US 5) needles.

ABBREVIATIONS
See page 63.

NOTE
When working in pattern, strand yarn not in use loosely across wrong side to keep fabric elastic.

BACK
With 3¼mm (No 10/US 3) needles and M, cast on 85 (93) sts. Beg with a K row, work 7 rows in st st.
Next row K to end for hem line.
Change to 4 mm (No 8/US 5) needles.
Beg with a K row and working in st st throughout, cont in patt from chart as indicated for Back, reading K rows from right to left and P rows from left to right, until work measures 35 (38) cm/13¾(15) in from hem line, ending with a wrong side row.
Shape Neck
Next row Patt 34 (36), cast off next 17 (21) sts, patt to end. Cont on last set of sts only. Patt 1 row. Cast off 3 sts at beg of next row and foll alt row. Cast off rem 28 (30) sts. With wrong side facing, rejoin yarn to rem sts, cast off 3 sts, patt to end. Patt 1 row. Cast off 3 sts at beg of next row. Cast off rem 28 (30) sts.

RIGHT FRONT
With 3¼mm (No 10/US 3) needles and M, cast on 47 (51) sts. Beg with a K row, work 7 rows in st st.
Next row K to end for hem line.
Change to 4 mm (No 8/US 5) needles.
Beg with a K row and working in st st throughout, cont in patt from chart as indicated for Right Front until work measures 10 cm/4 in from hem line, ending with a wrong side row.
1st buttonhole row Patt 3, cast off 2, patt to end.
2nd buttonhole row Patt to last 3 sts, cast on 2, patt 3.
Patt 8 rows.
Rep last 10 rows once more then work the 2 buttonhole rows again.
Cont in patt for a few rows until work measures 19 (20) cm/7½ (8) in from hem line, ending with a wrong side row.
Shape Neck
Keeping patt correct, cast off 5 sts at beg of next row.

Dec one st at neck edge on 9 foll right side rows then on every 3rd row until 28 (30) sts rem.
Cont without shaping until work measures same as Back to cast off edge, ending at side edge. Cast off.

LEFT FRONT
Following chart as indicated for Left Front, work as given for Right Front, omitting buttonholes and reversing neck shaping.

SLEEVES
With 3¼mm (No 10/US 3) needles and M, cast on 38 (42) sts. Work 5 cm/2 in in K1, P1 rib inc 7 (3) sts evenly along last row. 45 sts.
Change to 4 mm (No 8/US 5) needles.
Work in patt as given for 2nd size on Back, **at the same time** inc one st at each end of 5th row, then on every foll 3rd row until there are 71 (75) sts, working inc sts into patt.
Cont without shaping for a few rows until work measures 25 (28) cm/10 (11) in from beg, ending with a wrong side row. Cast off.

COLLAR
Join shoulder seams.
With 4 mm (No 8/US 5) needles and B, cast on 13 (15) sts.
Beg with a P row, work 7 (5) rows in st st inc one st at each end of every K row. 19 sts.
Next row (right side) With B, K twice in first st, K 1M, [3B, 1M] to last st, with B, K twice in last st.
Next row P 1B, [3M, 1B] to end.
With M, work 3 rows in st st inc one st at each end of every K row. 25 sts.
Beg with 60th row, cont in st st and patt from chart as indicated for Collar, **at the same time**, inc one st at each end of every alt row until there are 55 (61) sts, working inc sts into patt.

Patt 1 (5) rows straight.
Shape collar
Cont in M as follows:
1st row K to last 6 (7) sts, yf, sl 1, yb, turn.
2nd row Sl 1, P to last 6 (7) sts, yb, sl 1, yf, turn.
3rd row Sl 1, K to last 12 (14) sts, yf, sl 1, yb, turn.
4th row Sl 1, P to last 12 (14) sts, yb, sl 1, yf, turn.
5th row Sl 1, K to last 18 (21) sts, yf, sl 1, yb, turn.
6th row Sl 1, P to last 18 (21) sts, yb, sl 1, yf, turn.
7th row Sl 1, K to last 24 (28) sts, yf, sl 1, yb, turn.
8th row Sl 1, P to last 24 (28) sts, yb, sl 1, yf, turn.
Work 2 rows across all sts.
Next 2 rows As 7th and 8th rows.
Next 2 rows As 5th and 6th rows.
Next 2 rows As 3rd and 4th rows.
Next 2 rows As 1st and 2nd rows.
Cont without shaping until this half of collar fits up right front neck to centre back neck. Work the other half of collar to match first half, but working decreases instead of increases. Cast off 13 (15) sts.

RIGHT FRONT FACING
With 3¼mm (No 10/US 3) needles and M, cast on 7 sts. Beg with a K row, cont in st st until work measures 7 cm/2¾in, ending with a P row.
1st buttonhole row K3, cast off 2, K to end.
2nd buttonhole row P2, cast on 2, P3.
Work 8 rows.
Rep last 10 rows once more then work the 2 buttonhole rows again. Work 2 (4) rows. Cast off.

LEFT FRONT FACING
Work as Right Front Facing, omitting buttonholes.

TO MAKE UP
Sew on sleeves, placing centre of sleeves to shoulder seams. Join side and sleeve seams. Turn hem to wrong side and slip stitch in position. Close opening at front edges.
Beg at top of hem, join facings to front edges, matching buttonholes.
With right sides together, sew one long edge of collar in place, matching patterns and sewing cast on/cast off sts of collar to top of facings and sts cast off at neck edge. Turn collar and facings to wrong side and slip stitch in position. Catch down facings to hem. Neaten buttonholes. Sew on buttons.

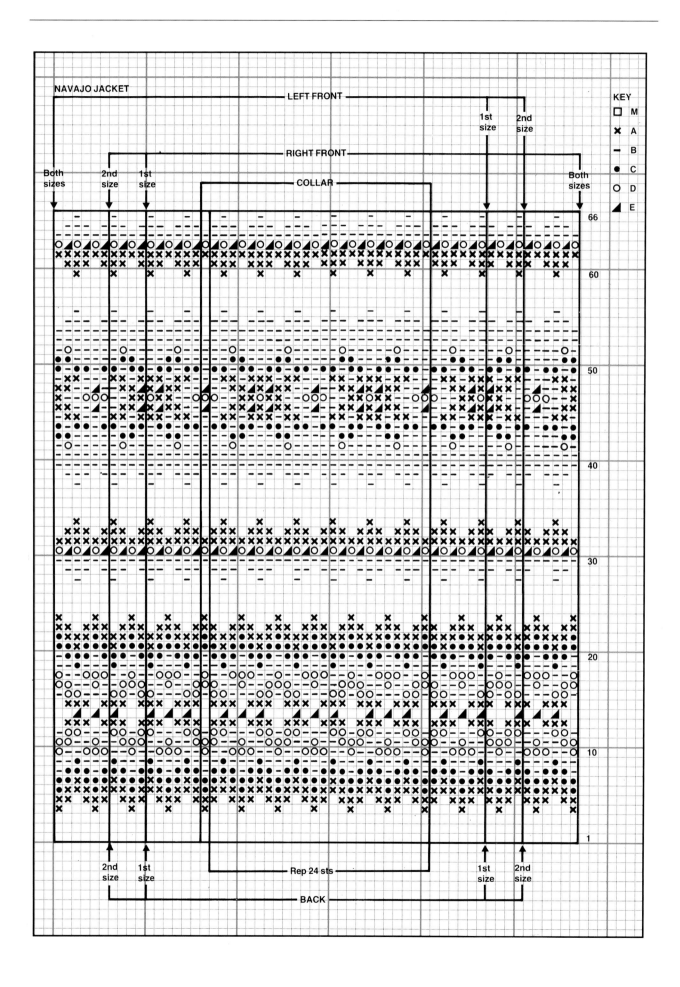

Fisherman's Rib Cardigan with Saddle Shoulders

See Page
43

MEASUREMENTS To fit age	18	24:36	Mths
All round at chest	70	74:78	cm
	27½	29:30¾	in
Length to shoulder	38	41:46	cm
	15	16:18	in
Sleeve seam (with	20	22:25	cm
cuff turned back)	8	8½:10	in

MATERIALS
5 (6:6) 100 g balls of Rowan Magpie Aran.

1 pair each of 3¾ mm (No 9/US 4) and 4½ mm (No 7/US 6) knitting needles.
6 buttons.

TENSION
20 sts and 38 rows to 10 cm/4 in over rib patt on 4½ mm (No 7/US 6) needles.

ABBREVIATIONS
K1b = knit into next st 1 row below.
Also see page 63.

BACK
With 3¾ mm (No 9/US 4) needles, cast on 69 (73:77) sts.
1st row (right side) K1, [P1, K1] to end.
2nd row P1, [K1, P1] to end.
Rep these 2 rows until work measures 3 cm/1¼ in from beg, ending with a wrong side row.
Change to 4½ mm (No 7/US 6) needles.
Work in patt as follows:
1st row (right side) Slip 1, K to end.
2nd row Slip 1, [K1b, P1] to end.
These 2 rows form rib patt**. Cont in rib patt until work measures 34 (37:42) cm/ 13½ (14½:16½) in from beg, ending with a wrong side row.
Shape shoulders
Cast off in rib 11 (11:12) sts at beg of next 2 rows and 11 (12:12) sts at beg of foll 2 rows. Leave rem 25 (27:29) sts on a holder.

POCKET LINING (make 2)
With 4½ mm (No 7/US 6) needles, cast on 14 (16:16) sts.
Work in st st for 5 cm/2 in, ending with a P row and dec one st at centre of last row. 13 (15:15) sts. Leave these sts on a holder.

LEFT FRONT
With 3¾ mm (No 9/US 4) needles, cast on 33 (35:37) sts.

Work as given for Back to **. Cont in rib patt until work measures 8 cm/3 in from beg, ending with a wrong side row.
Place Pocket
Next row Patt 13, slip next 13 (15:15) sts onto a holder, patt across sts of one pocket lining, patt to end.
Cont in patt until work measures 19 (22:25) cm/7½ (8¾:10) in from beg, ending with a wrong side row.
Front Shaping
Keeping patt correct, dec one st at end (front edge) of next and at the same edge on every foll 5th (4th:4th) row until 22 (23:24) sts rem.
Cont without shaping until work measures same as Back to shoulder shaping, ending with a wrong side row.
Shape Shoulder
Cast off in rib 11 (11:12) sts at beg of next row. Patt 1 row. Cast off rem 11 (12:12) sts.

RIGHT FRONT
Work as given for Left Front, reversing all shaping and placing pocket as follows:
Next row Patt 7 (7:9), slip next 13 (15:15) sts onto a holder, patt across sts of one pocket lining, patt to end.

SLEEVES
With 3¾ mm (No 9/US 4) needles, cast on

35 (37:39) sts.
Work as given for Back to **.
Cont in rib patt, inc one st at each end of 7th and every foll 3rd (3rd:4th) row until there are 65 (69:73) sts, working inc sts into patt. Cont without shaping until work measures 23 (25:28) cm/9 (10:11) in from beg, ending with a wrong side row.
Shape Saddle
Cast off 24 (26:28) sts at beg of next 2 rows.
Mark each end of last row.
Cont without shaping on rem 17 sts for saddle for 11 (11½:12) cm/4¼ (4½:4¾) in, ending with a wrong side row. Mark each end of last row. Leave these sts on a holder.

FRONT BAND
Sew on sleeves, sewing saddles between markers to cast off sts of Back and Fronts.
With 3¾ mm (No 9/US 4) needles and right side facing, pick up and K 45 (50:57) sts evenly along straight edge of Right Front, 40 (40:44) sts up shaped edge, rib across right saddle, back neck and left saddle, pick up and K 40 (40:44) sts down shaped edge of Left Front, then 45 (50:57) sts down straight edge of Left Front. 229 (241:265) sts. Beg with a 2nd row, work 2 rows in rib as given for Back.
1st buttonhole row: Rib to last 45 (50:55) sts, [cast off 2, rib 5 (6:7) sts more] 5 times, cast off 2, rib to end.
2nd buttonhole row: Rib to end, casting on 2 sts over those cast off in previous row. Rib 3 rows. Cast off in rib.

POCKET TOPS
With 3¾ mm (No 9/US 4) needles and right side facing, rib across sts of one pocket top. Rib 6 rows. Cast off in rib.

TO MAKE UP
Join side and sleeve seams. Catch down pocket linings and sides of pocket edgings. Sew on buttons.

Fisherman's Rib Sweater with Saddle Shoulders

See Page 44

MEASUREMENTS

To fit age	12	18:24	Mths
All round at chest	65	69:73	cm
	25½	27:28¾	in
Length to shoulder	35	38:41	cm
	13¾	15:16	in
Sleeve seam	21	23:25	cm
	8¼	9:10	in

MATERIALS
4 (5:5) 100 g balls of Rowan Magpie Aran.
1 pair each of 3¾ mm (No 9/US 4) and 4½ mm (No 7/US 6) knitting needles.
Set of four 3¾ mm (No 9/US 4) double pointed knitting needles.

TENSION
20 sts and 38 rows to 10 cm/4 in over rib patt on 4½ mm (No 7/US 6) needles.

ABBREVIATIONS
K1b = knit into next st 1 row below.
Also see page 63.

BACK & FRONT ALIKE
With 3¾ mm (No 9/US 4) needles, cast on 65 (69:73) sts.
1st row (right side) K1, [P1, K1] to end.
2nd row P1, [K1, P1] to end.
Rep these 2 rows until work measures 4 cm/1½ in from beg, ending with a wrong side row.
Change to 4½ mm (No 7/US 6) needles.
Work in patt as follows:
1st row (right side) Slip 1, K to end.
2nd row Slip 1, [K1b, P1] to end.
These 2 rows form rib patt. Cont in rib patt until work measures 31 (34:37) cm/12¼ (13½:14½) in from beg, ending with a wrong side row.
Shape Shoulders
Cast off in rib 20 (21:22) sts at beg of next 2 rows. Leave rem 25 (27:29) sts on a holder.

SLEEVES
With 3¾ mm (No 9/US 4) needles, cast on 35 (37:39) sts. Work in rib as given for Back for 4 cm/1½ in, ending with a wrong side row.
Change to 4½ mm (No 7/US 6) needles.
Work in rib patt as given for Back, **at the same time,** inc one st at each end of 5th and every foll 4th row until there are 57 (63:67) sts, working inc sts into rib patt.
Cont without shaping until work measures 21 (23:25) cm/8¼ (9:10) in from beg, ending with a wrong side row.
Shape Saddle
Cast off in rib 20 (23:25) sts at beg of next 2 rows. Mark each end of last row.
Cont without shaping on rem 17 sts for saddle for 10.5 (11:11½) cm/4 (4¼:4½) in, ending with a wrong side row. Mark each end of last row. Leave these sts on a holder.

NECKBAND
Sew on sleeves, sewing saddles between markers to cast off sts of Back and Front.
With set of four 3¾ mm (No 9/US 4) needles, right side facing and beg at left back saddle, work in rib across left saddle, front neck, right saddle and back neck. 84 (88:92) sts. Work in rounds and rib for 6 cm/2¼ in. Cast off loosely in rib.

TO MAKE UP
Join side and sleeve seams.

Hearts and Hens Sweater

See Page 45

MEASUREMENTS

To fit age	18–24	24–36	Months
Actual chest measurement	75	81	cm
	29½	32	in
Length	38	41	cm
	15	16	in
Sleeve seam	22	24	cm
	8½	9½	in

MATERIALS
5(6) 50 g balls of Rowan DK Handknit Cotton in Light Blue (MC).
1(1) 50 g ball of same in each of Pink, Red, Cream, Dark Blue and Brown.
Pair each of 3¼ mm (No 10/US 3) and 4 mm (No 8/US 5) knitting needles.

TENSION
20 sts and 28 rows to 10 cm/4 in square over st st on 4 mm (No 8/US 5) needles.

ABBREVIATIONS
See page 63.

NOTE
Read Chart from right to left on right side rows and from left to right on wrong side rows. Use separate lengths or small balls of yarn for each coloured area and twist yarns together on wrong side when changing colour to avoid holes.

BACK
With 3¼ mm (No 10/US 3) needles and MC, cast on 74(78) sts.
1st row (right side) K2, [P2, K2] to end.
2nd row P2, [K2, P2] to end.
Rep last 2 rows until work measures 3(4) cm/1¼(1½) in from beg, ending with a 2nd row and inc 1(3) sts evenly across last row. 75(81) sts.
Change to 4 mm (No 8/US 5) needles.
Beg with a K row, work in st st and patt from Chart until 100th(104th) row of Chart has been worked.
Cont in MC only.
Shape Shoulders
Cast off 12(13) sts at beg of next 4 rows.
Leave rem 27(29) sts on a holder.

FRONT
Work as given for Back until 84th row of Chart has been worked.
Shape Neck
Next row Patt 30(32), turn.
Work on this set of sts only. Keeping patt correct, dec one st at neck edge on every

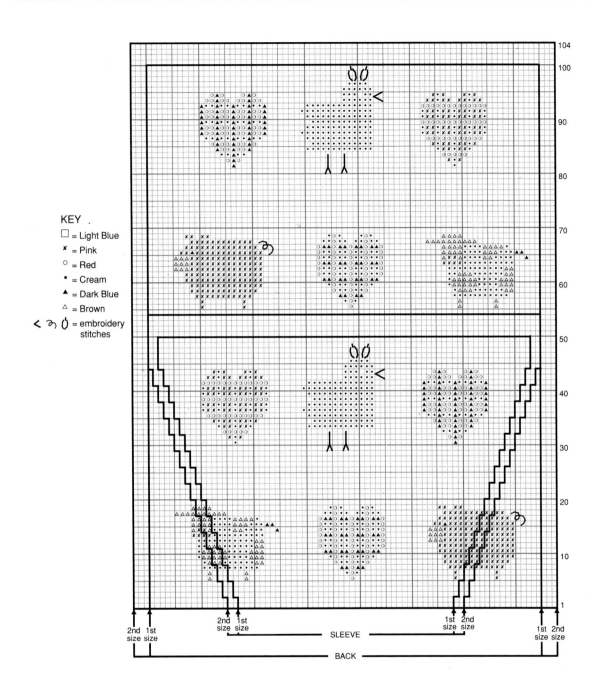

KEY .

☐ = Light Blue

✗ = Pink

○ = Red

• = Cream

▲ = Dark Blue

△ = Brown

< ∾ ◊ = embroidery stitches

104
100
90
80
70
60
50
40
30
20
10
1

2nd 1st
size size

2nd 1st
size size

1st 2nd
size size

1st 2nd
size size

SLEEVE

BACK

row until 24(26) sts rem. Cont straight until 100th(104th) row of Chart has been worked.
Cont in MC only.

Shape Shoulder
Cast off 12(13) sts at beg of next row. Work 1 row. Cast off rem 12(13) sts. With right side facing, slip centre 15(17) sts onto a holder, rejoin yarn to rem sts and patt to end. Complete to match first side, reversing shoulder shaping.

SLEEVES
With 3¼-mm (No 10/US 3) needles and MC, cast on 34(38) sts.
Work 4(5) cm/1½(2) in in rib as given for Back welt, ending with a 1st row.

Inc row Rib 2(3), inc in next st, [rib 4, inc in next st] 6 times, rib 1(4). 41(45) sts. Change to 4 mm (No 8/US 5) needles. Beg with a K row, work in st st and patt from Chart, inc one st at each end of every 3rd row until there are 71(75) sts, omitting pig and cow motifs. Patt 5(9) rows straight. Cast off.

NECKBAND
Join right shoulder seam.
With 3¼-mm (No 10/US 3) needles, MC and right side facing, pick up and K 19 (21) sts down left front neck, K across centre front sts dec one st, pick up and K 19(21) sts up right front neck, K across back neck sts dec one st. 78(86) sts. Beg

with a 2nd row, work 9 rows in rib as given for Back welt. Beg with a K row, work 4 rows in st st. Cast off.

TO MAKE UP
Join left shoulder and neckband seam, reversing seam on last 4 rows of neckband. Allow the top of neckband to roll back. Sew on sleeves, placing centre of sleeves to shoulder seams. Join side and sleeve seams. Embroider pigs' tails with Pink and nostrils with Dark Blue. With Red, work 2 lazy daisy stitches (see diagram page 54) on hens heads for comb. Embroider beak, legs and feet on each hen with Red and straight stitch (see diagram page 90).

Sampler Sweater

See Page
46

MEASUREMENTS

To fit age	3–4	5–6	Years
Actual chest measurement	84	89	**cm**
	33	35	**in**
Length to shoulder	45	49	**cm**
	17¾	19¼	**in**
Sleeve seam	26	29	**cm**
	10¼	11½	**in**

MATERIALS
8(9) 50 g balls of Rowan Designer DK Wool in Dark Blue (MC).
1(1) 50 g ball of same in each of Cream (A) and Red (B).
Pair each of 3¼ mm (No 10/US 3) and 4 mm (No 8/US 5) knitting needles.

TENSION
23 sts and 33 rows to 10 cm/4 in square over patt on 4 mm (No 8/US 5) needles.

ABBREVIATIONS
MB = make bobble, K into front, back, front and back of next st, turn, P4, turn, K4, turn, [K2 tog] twice, turn, K2 tog. Also see page 63.

NOTE
Read Charts from right to left on right side rows and from left to right on wrong side rows. Use separate lengths of A and B yarn for each motif and twist yarns together on wrong side when changing colour to avoid holes. If preferred the motifs may be Swiss Darned when knitting is complete.

BOBBLE PATTERN – worked over 17 sts.
1st row (right side) K17.
2nd row and every alt row P17.
3rd row K8, MB, K8.
5th row K17.
7th row K5, MB, K5, MB, K5.
9th row K17.
11th row K2, [MB, K5] twice, MB, K2.
13th row K17.
15th row As 7th row.
17th row K17.
19th row As 3rd row.
20th row P17.
These 20 rows form Bobble patt.

BACK
With 3¼ mm (No 10/US 3) needles and MC, cast on 97(103) sts. K 13(15) rows. Change to 4 mm (No 8/US 5) needles. Work in patt as follows:
1st row (right side) K2(3)MC, K across 1st row of Chart 1, * with MC, K2(3), work 1st row of Bobble patt, K2(3)*; K across 1st row of Chart 2, rep from * to *, K across 1st row of Chart 3, K2(3)MC.
2nd row K2(3)MC, P across 2nd row of Chart 3, * with MC, K2(3), work 2nd row of Bobble patt, K2(3)*; P across 2nd row of Chart 2, rep from * to *, P across 2nd row of Chart 1, K2(3)MC.
3rd to 20th rows Rep last 2 rows 9 times but working 3rd to 20th rows of Bobble patt and Charts.
21st to 24th(26th) rows With MC, K.
25th(27th) row * With MC, K2(3), work 1st row of Bobble patt, k2(3)*; K across 1st row of Chart 4, rep from * to *, K across 1st row of Chart 5, rep from * to *.
26th(28th) row * With MC, K2(3), work 2nd row of Bobble patt, K2(3)*; P across 2nd row of Chart 5, rep from * to *, P across 2nd row of Chart 4, rep from * to *.
27th(29th) to 44th(46th) rows Work as 3rd to 20th rows.
45th(47th) to 48th(52nd) rows With MC, K.
49th(53rd) to 72nd(78th) rows Work as 1st to 24th(26th) rows but working from Chart 6 instead of Chart 1, Chart 7 instead of Chart 2 and Chart 1 instead of Chart 3.
73rd(79th) to 96th(104th) rows Work as

25th(27th) to 48th(52nd) rows but working from Chart 3 instead of Chart 4 and Chart 4 instead of Chart 5.
97th(105th) to 120th(130th) rows Work as 1st to 24th(26th) rows but working from Chart 2 instead of Chart 1, Chart 5 instead of Chart 2 and Chart 6 instead of Chart 3.
121st(131st) to 140th(150th) rows Work as 25th(27th) to 44th(46th) rows but working from Chart 7 instead of Chart 4 and Chart 1 instead of Chart 5.
With MC, K 2(4) rows. Cast off.

FRONT
Work as Back until Front measures 16(18) rows less than Back to cast off edge, ending with a wrong side row.
Shape Neck
Next row Patt 43(45) sts and turn. Work on this set of sts only. Keeping patt correct, dec one st at neck edge on next 11 rows. Patt 4(6) rows straight. Cast off rem 32(34) sts.
With right side facing, rejoin yarn to rem sts, cast off centre 11(13) sts, patt to end. Complete to match first side.

SLEEVES
With 3¼ mm (No 10/US 3) needles and MC, cast on 43(45) sts.
1st row (right side) K1, [P1, K1] to end.
2nd row P1, [K1, P1] to end.
Rep last 2 rows until work measures 4(5) cm/1½ (2) in from beg, ending with a right side row.
Inc row Rib 1(3), [inc in next st, rib 3, inc in next st, rib 2] to end. 55(57) sts.
Change to 4 mm (No 8/US 5) needles.
Work in patt as follows:
1st row K across 1st row of Chart 1, with MC, K2(3), work 1st row of Bobble patt, K2(3), K across 1st row of Chart 2.
2nd row P across 2nd row of Chart 2, with MC, K2(3), work 2nd row of Bobble patt, K2(3), P across 2nd row of Chart 1.
These 2 rows set position of patt. Cont in

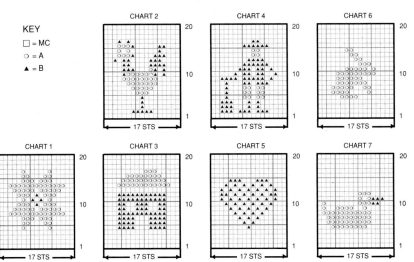

KEY
□ = MC
○ = A
▲ = B

CHART 2   CHART 4   CHART 6
CHART 1   CHART 3   CHART 5   CHART 7

17 STS

patt as set, **at the same time,** inc one st at each end of 3rd row and every foll 4th row until there are 85(89) sts, working inc sts into patt to match Back. Patt 11(13) rows straight. Cast off.

COLLAR

With 3¼ mm (No 10/US 3) needles and

MC, cast on 86(90) sts.
Work 8(9) cm/3(3½) in in garter st (every row K). Cast off loosely.

TO MAKE UP

Work Swiss Darning (see diagram page 111) if necessary. With B, embroider each cockerel's beak. Join shoulder seams.

Sew on sleeves, placing centre of sleeves to shoulder seams. Beginning at top of welt, join side and sleeve seams. Sew cast on edge of collar to neck edge, beginning and ending at centre front.

Milk-Maid Sweater

See Page
47

MEASUREMENTS

To fit age	3–4	Yrs
Actual chest measurement	92	**cm**
	36¼	**in**
Length	42	**cm**
	16½	**in**
Sleeve seam	33	**cm**
	13	**in**

MATERIALS

9x50 g balls of Rowan DK Handknit Cotton in Cream (MC).
1x50 g ball of same in each of Brown, Pink, Green, Yellow, Light Blue and Dark Blue.
Pair each of 3¼ mm (No 10/US 3) and 4 mm (No 8/US 5) knitting needles.
Set of four 3¼ mm (No 10/US 3) double pointed knitting needles.

TENSION

20 sts and 28 rows to 10 cm/4 in square over st st on 4 mm (No 8/US 5) needles.

ABBREVIATIONS

See page 63.

NOTE

Read Charts from right to left on right side rows and from left to right on wrong side rows. When working motifs, use separate lengths of contrast yarns for each coloured area and twist yarns together on wrong side when changing colour to avoid holes.

BACK

With 3¼ mm (No 10/US 3) needles and MC, cast on 86 sts.
Work 5 cm /2 in in K1, P1 rib.
Inc row Rib 10, inc in next st, [rib 12, inc in next st] to last 10 sts, rib 10. 92 sts.
Change to 4 mm (No 8/US 5) needles.
Work in patt as follows:
1st row (right side) K1MC, K across 1st row of Chart 1, K2MC, K across 1st row of Chart 2, K2MC, K across 1st row of Chart 3, K2MC, K across 1st row of Chart 4, K1MC.
2nd row K1MC, P across 2nd row of Chart 4, K2MC, P across 2nd row of Chart 3, K2MC, P across 2nd row of Chart 2, K2MC, P across 2nd row of Chart 1, K1MC.
3rd to 24th rows Rep last 2 rows 11 times more but working 3rd to 24th rows of Charts.
25th to 28th rows With MC, K.
29th row K1MC, K across 1st row of Chart 5, K2MC, K across 1st row of Chart 6, K2MC, K across 1st row of Chart 1, K2MC, K across 1st row of Chart 2, K1MC.
30th row K1MC, P across 2nd row of Chart 2, K2MC, P across 2nd row of Chart 1, K2MC, P across 2nd row of Chart 6, K2MC, P across 2nd row of Chart 5, K1MC.
31st to 56th rows Work 3rd to 28th rows.
57th row K1MC, K across 1st row of Chart 3, K2MC, K across 1st row of Chart 4, K2MC, K across 1st row of Chart 5, K2MC, K across 1st row of Chart 6, K1MC.
58th row K1MC, P across 2nd row of Chart 6, K2MC, P across 2nd row of Chart 5, K2MC, P across 2nd row of Chart 4, K2MC, P across 2nd row of Chart 3, K1MC.
59th to 84th rows Work 3rd to 28th rows.
85th to 112th rows Work 1st to 28th rows.
Shape Shoulders
Next row With MC, cast off 29 sts, K to last 29 sts, cast off last 29 sts.
Leave rem 34 sts on a holder.

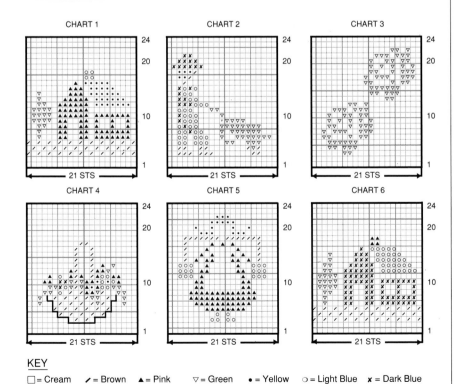

CHART 1   CHART 2   CHART 3
CHART 4   CHART 5   CHART 6
21 STS

KEY

□ = Cream   ╱ = Brown   ▲ = Pink   ▽ = Green   ● = Yellow   ○ = Light Blue   ✗ = Dark Blue

━━ = Embroidery outlines

FRONT

Work as given for Back until Front measures 20 rows less than Back to shoulder shaping, ending with a wrong side row.

Shape Neck

Next row Patt 38, turn.

Work on this set of sts only. Keeping patt correct, cast off 3 sts at beg of next row. Dec one st at neck edge on every row until 29 sts rem.

Cont straight until Front matches Back to shoulder shaping, ending with a wrong side row. Cast off.

With right side facing, slip centre 16 sts onto a holder, rejoin yarn to rem sts and patt to end. Patt 1 row. Complete to match first side.

SLEEVES

With 3¼ mm (No 10/US 3) needles and MC, cast on 46 sts.

Work 5 cm/2 in in K1, P1 rib.

Inc row Rib 1, [inc in next st, rib 4] to end. 55 sts.

Change to 4 mm (No 8/US 5) needles. Work in patt as follows:

1st row (right side) K17MC, K across 1st row of Chart 1, K17MC.

2nd row P15MC, K2MC, P across 2nd row of Chart 1, K2MC, P15MC.

Work a further 22 rows as set, inc one st at each end of 2nd row and 4 foll 5th rows, working inc sts in MC. With MC, K 4 rows, inc one st at each end of last row. 67 sts.

29th row K across 1st row of Chart 2, K2MC, K across 1st row of Chart 3, K2MC, K across 1st row of Chart 4.

30th row P across 2nd row of Chart 4, K2MC, P across 2nd row of Chart 3, K2MC, P across 2nd row of Chart 2.

Work a further 22 rows as set, inc one st at each end of 2nd row and 4 foll 5th rows, working first 2 inc sts into MC and garter st (every row K) and last 3 inc sts in MC and st st. With MC, K 4 rows, inc one st at each end of last row. 79 sts.

57th row K6MC, K across 1st row of Chart 5, K2MC, K across 1st row of Chart 6, K2MC, K across 1st row of Chart 1, K6MC.

58th row P4MC, K2MC, P across 2nd row of Chart 1, K2MC, P across 2nd row of Chart 6, K2MC, P across 2nd row of Chart 5, K2MC, P4MC.

Work a further 22 rows as set. With MC, K 4 rows. Cast off.

COLLAR

Join shoulder seams.

With right side facing, slip first 8 sts from centre front holder onto a safety pin, join MC yarn and using set of four 3¼ mm (No 10/US 3) double pointed needles, K rem 8 sts, pick up and K 16 sts up right front neck, K back neck sts, pick up and K 16 sts down left front neck, then K8 from safety pin. 82 sts. Work 5 rounds in K1, P1 rib. Turn and work backwards and forwards as follows:

Next row K2, rib to last 2 sts, K2.

Next row K2, m1, rib to last 2 sts, m1, K2.

Rep last 2 rows 8 times more, then work first of the 2 rows again.

Cast off loosely in rib.

TO MAKE UP

Sew on sleeves, placing centre of sleeves to shoulder seams. Join side and sleeve seams. With Brown, outline base of each basket and embroider face features on each girl.

Alphabet Sweater

See Page 48

MEASUREMENTS

To fit age	4–6	Yrs
Actual chest measurement	83	cm
	32½	in
Length	48	cm
	19	in
Sleeve seam	28	cm
	11	in

MATERIALS

750 g balls of Rowan Designer DK Wool in Cream (MC).

150 g ball of same in each of Rust, Dark Blue, Green, Brown, Grey, Navy, Red, Light Blue and Beige.

Pair each of 3¼ mm (No 10/US 3) and 4 mm (No 8/US 5) knitting needles.

BACK

With 3¼ mm (No 10/US 3) needles and MC, cast on 100 sts. K 13 rows.

Change to 4 mm (No 8/US 5) needles. Beg with a K row, work in st st and patt from Chart 1 until 25th row of Chart 1 has been worked. Cont in st st and patt from Chart 2 until 97th row of Chart 2 has been worked.

Cont in st st and MC only until work measures 48 cm/19 in from beg, ending with a P row.

TENSION

24 sts and 32 rows to 10 cm/4 in square over st st on 4 mm (No 8/US 5) needles.

ABBREVIATIONS

See page 63.

NOTE

Read Charts from right to left on right side rows and from left to right on wrong side rows. When working in pattern from Chart 1, strand yarn not in use loosely across wrong side to keep fabric elastic. When working in pattern from Chart 2, use separate small balls or lengths of contrast yarn for each coloured area and twist yarns together on wrong side when changing colour to avoid holes.

Shape Shoulders

Cast off 34 sts at beg of next 2 rows. Cast off rem 32 sts.

FRONT

Work as given for Back until 85th row of Chart 2 has been worked.

Shape Neck

Next row Patt 44, turn.

Work on this set of sts only. Cont working in patt from Chart 2, dec one st at neck edge on every row until 34 sts rem. Patt 1 row. Cont in st st and MC only until Front matches Back to shoulder shaping, ending at side edge. Cast off.

With right side facing, rejoin yarn to rem sts, cast off centre 12 sts, patt to end. Complete to match first side.

SLEEVES

With 3¼ mm (No 10/US 3) needles and MC, cast on 44 sts. Work 4 cm/1¼ in in K1, P1 rib.

Inc row Rib 5, [inc in next st, rib 2] to last 3 sts, rib 3. 56 sts.

Change to 4 mm (No 8/US 5) needles. Beg with a K row, work in st st and patt from Chart 2 until 72nd row of Chart 2 has been worked, **at the same time**, inc one st at each end of 3rd row and every foll 4th row until there are 86 sts, working inc sts into patt. Cast off.

COLLAR

With 3¼ mm (No 10/US 3) needles and MC, cast on 86 sts. Work 8 cm/3 in in garter st (every row K). Cast off loosely.

TO MAKE UP

Join shoulder seams. Sew on sleeves, placing centre of sleeves to shoulder seams. Beg at top of welt, join side seams then sleeve seams. Sew cast on edge of collar to neck edge, beginning and ending at centre front, then join collar together for first 2 cm/¾ in. With Navy, embroider cockerels' beaks.

CHART 1

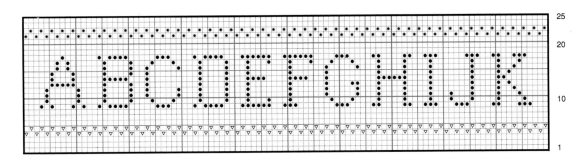

CHART 2

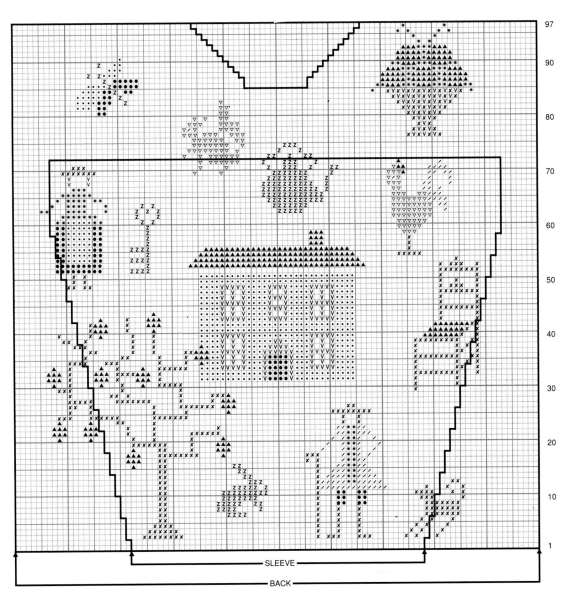

SLEEVE

BACK

KEY

☐ = Cream   ● = Dark Blue   x = Brown   ⟋ = Navy   • = Light blue

▽ = Rust   ✳ = Green   z = Grey   ▲ = Red   v = Beige

Striped "Wee Willie Winkie" Hat and Socks

See Page
49

MEASUREMENTS
To fit age
3 (6:9) months

MATERIALS
Hat 1 x 50 g ball of Rowan 4 ply Cotton
in each of Black (A) and Cream (B).
Set of four in each of 2¾mm (No 12/US
1) and 3¼ mm (No 10/US 3) double-
pointed knitting needles.
Socks Small amount of Rowan 4 ply
Cotton in each of Black (A) and Cream
(B).
Set of four in each of 2¾mm (No 12/US 1)
and 3 mm (No 11/US 2) double-pointed
knitting needles.

TENSION
28 sts and 36 rows to 10 cm/4 in square
over st st on 3¼mm (No 10/US 3)
needles.
30 sts and 38 rows to 10 cm/4 in square
over st st on 3 mm (No 11/US 2)
needles.

ABBREVIATIONS
See page 63.

Hat

With set of four 2¾mm (No 12/US 1)
needles and A, cast on 104 (114:122) sts.
Place marker after last st to indicate end
of rounds. Taking care not to twist the
work, cont in rounds of K1, P1 rib for 3
cm/1¼in.
Dec round *Rib 4 (3:1), [work 2 tog, rib 2
(2:3), work 2 tog, rib 2 (3:3)] 6 times; rep
from * once. 90 (90:98) sts.
Change to set of four 3¼mm (No 10/US 3)
needles.
Working in rounds of st st (every round K)
and stripe patt of 4 rounds B and 2
rounds A throughout, cont until work
measures 14 (16:18) cm/5½ (6¼:7) in from
beg, dec 2 sts evenly across last round
on **2nd** and **3rd** sizes only. 80 (88:96) sts.
Shape Top
Dec round [K 18 (20:22), K2 tog] 4 times.
Work 3 rounds.
Dec round [K 17 (19:21), K2 tog] 4 times.
Work 3 rounds.
Dec round [K 16 (18:20), K2 tog] 4 times.
Cont in this way, dec 4 sts as set on every
4th round until 8 sts rem.
Dec round [K2 tog] 4 times.
Break off yarn, thread end through rem
sts, pull up and secure. Join seam. With
A, make a large pompon and attach
to top.

Socks

With set of four 2¾mm (No 12/US 1)
needles and A, cast on 30 (36:40) sts.
Place marker after last st to indicate end
of rounds. Taking care not to twist the
work, cont in rounds of K1, P1 rib for 8
rounds.
Change to set of four 3 mm (No 11/US 2)
needles.
Working in rounds of st st (every round K)
and stripe patt of 4 rounds B and 2 rounds
A throughout, patt 18 (24:30) rounds.
Break off yarns.
Shape Heel
Slip last 7 (9:10) sts of last round and first
8 (9:10) sts of next round onto one needle
for heel, divide rem 15 (18:20) instep sts
onto two needles.
With right side facing rejoin B yarn to 15
(18:20) heel sts. Beg with a K row and
working in st st and stripe patt of 4 rows B
and 2 rows A, work 14 (16:16) rows.
Cont in B only.
Next row K9 (10:12), K2 tog tbl, K1, turn.
Next row Sl 1 purlwise, P4 (3:5), P2 tog,
P1, turn.
Next row Sl 1 knitwise, K5 (4:6), K2 tog tbl,
K1, turn.
Next row Sl 1 purlwise, P6 (5:7), P2 tog,
P1, turn.
2nd and 3rd sizes only

Next row Sl 1 knitwise, K (6:8), K2 tog tbl,
K1, turn.
Next row Sl 1 purlwise, P (7:9), P2 tog, P1,
turn.
All sizes
Next row Sl 1 knitwise, K7 (8:10), K2 tog
tbl, turn.
Next row Sl 1 purlwise, P7 (8:10), P2 tog.
9 (10:12) sts.
Break off yarn.
Shape Instep
Next round Slip first 4 (5:6) heel sts onto a
safety pin, rejoin B yarn to rem heel sts,
K5 (5:6), pick up and K8 (9:9) sts along
side edge of heel, K15 (18:20) instep sts,
pick up and K8 (9:9) sts along other side
edge of heel, K4 (5:6) sts from safety pin.
40 (46:50) sts.
Keeping stripe patt correct, work as
follows:
Dec round K11 (12:13), K2 tog, K15
(18:20), K2 tog tbl, K10 (12:13).
K 1 round.
Dec round K10 (11:12), K2 tog, K15
(18:20), K2 tog tbl, K9 (11:12).
K 1 round.
Dec round K9 (10:11), K2 tog, K15
(18:20), K2 tog tbl, K8 (10:11).
Cont in this way, dec 2 sts as set on every
alt round until 30 (34:38) sts rem. Patt 10
(14:18) rounds straight.
Shape Toes
Dec round [K5 (6:7), K2 tog, K2, K2 tog
tbl, K4 (5:6)] twice.
K 1 round.
Dec round [K4 (5:6), K2 tog, K2, K2 tog
tbl, K3 (4:5)] twice.
K 1 round.
Dec round [K3 (4:5), K2 tog, K2, K2 tog
tbl, K2 (3:4)] twice.
Cont in this way, dec 4 sts as set on every
alt round until 14 sts rem.
K 1 round.
Dec round [K1, K2 tog, K2, K2 tog tbl]
twice.
Dec round Sl 1, K2, sl 1, K2 tog, psso, K2,
sl 1, K2 tog the 2 slipped sts from beg of
round, psso.
Break off yarn, thread end through rem
sts, pull up and secure.

Teddy Bear

See Page
49

MEASUREMENTS
Approximately 16 cm/6½ in high.

MATERIALS
1 x 50 g ball of Rowan Designer DK
Wool in main colour (MC).
Oddment of Black for embroidery.
Pair of 3¼-mm (No 10/US 3) knitting
needles.
Small amount of wadding.

ABBREVIATIONS
See page 63.

BODY
Begin at lower edge.
With 3¼-mm (No 10/US 3) needles and
MC, cast on 14 sts.
Inc row K1, [K twice in next st] 12 times,
K1, 26 sts.
Beg with a P row, work 3 rows in st st.
Inc row K7, m1, K11, m1, K8.
Work 5 rows in st st.
Inc row K7, m1, K13, m1, K8.
Work 6 rows in st st.
Dec row P7, P2 tog, P13, P2 tog, P6.
Work 2 rows in st st.
Dec row [K2 tog] to end.
Dec row [P2 tog] to end. 7 sts.
Break off yarn, thread end through rem
sts, pull up and secure.

LEGS (make 2)
Begin at sole.

With 3¼-mm (No 10/US 3) needles and
MC, cast on 10 sts.
Inc row K1, [K twice in next st] 8 times,
K1, 18 sts.
Beg with a P row, work 3 rows in st st.
Dec row K4, K2 tog, [K3 tog] twice, K2
tog, K4.
Work 9 rows in st st, inc one st at each
end of 2nd row. 14 sts.
Dec row [K2 tog] to end. 7 sts.
P 1 row. Break off yarn, thread end
through rem sts, pull up and secure.

ARMS (make 2)
Begin at top.
With 3¼-mm (No 10/US 3) needles and
MC, cast on 7 sts.
Inc row K1, [K twice in next st] 5 times,
K1, 12 sts.
Beg with a P row, work 9 rows in st st.
Dec row K3, [K2 tog] 3 times, K3.
Work 3 rows in st st.
Dec row K1, [K2 tog] to end. 5 sts.
Break off yarn, thread end through rem
sts, pull up and secure.

HEAD
Begin at centre back.
With 3¼-mm (No 10/US 3) needles and
MC, cast on 12 sts. K 1 row.
Inc row P1, [P twice in next st] 10 times, P
1. 22 sts.
Beg with a K row, work 4 rows in st st.
Inc row K6, m1, K1, m1, K8, m1, K1, m1, K6.
Work 3 rows in st st.
Inc row K7, m1, K1, m1, K10, m1, K1, m1, K7.

P 1 row.
Dec row K1, [K2 tog] to last st, K1.
P 1 row.
Dec row K2 tog, K3, [K3 tog] twice, K3,
K2 tog.
P 1 row.
Dec row [K2 tog] to end. 5 sts.
Break off yarn, thread end through rem
sts, pull up and secure.

EARS (make 2)
With 3¼-mm (No 10/US 3) needles and
MC, cast on 8 sts.
Cont in st st, work 2 rows. Dec one st at
each end of next 2 rows. Inc one st at each
end of next 2 rows. Work 2 rows. Cast off.

TO MAKE UP
Join back seam of body and legs,
underarm seam of arms and bottom
seam of head, leaving cast on edges
free. Stuff, then run a gathering thread
round cast on edges, pull up and secure.
With sewing needle, attach yarn to inner
edge of top of one leg, then pass needle
through body at side approximately 1
cm/½ in from base, catch inner edge of
top of other leg, then pass needle
through body again in same place and
catch inner edge of first leg again in
same place, pull yarn tightly to depress
legs and fasten off securely. Attach arms
to top of body in same way. Fold ears in
half widthwise and join seam all round.
Sew ears in position. With Black,
embroider face, then sew head to body.

Teddy Bear Hood, Mittens and Bootees

See Page
50

MEASUREMENTS
Hood
To fit age 3–6 (6–9) months

Mittens and bootees
To fit age 3–9 months

MATERIALS
Hood 1 x 50 g ball of Rowan Designer
DK Wool in main colour (MC).
Small amount of same in contrast
colour (A). 1 button.
Small amount of wadding.
Mittens and Bootees 1 x 50 g ball of

Rowan Designer DK Wool in main
colour (MC).
Small amount of same in contrast
colour (A).
Pair each of 3¼-mm (No 10/US 3) and 4
mm (No 8/US 5) knitting needles.

TENSION
22 sts and 28 rows to 10 cm/4 in square
over st st on 4 mm (No 8/US 5) needles.

ABBREVIATIONS
See page 63.

Hood

MAIN PART
With 3¼-mm (No 10/US 3) needles and
MC, cast on 63 (67) sts.
1st row (right side) P1, [K1, P1] to end.
2nd row K1, [P1, K1] to end.
Rib a further 5 rows.
Next row Rib 5 and slip these sts onto
safety pin, rib 5 (4), inc in next st, [rib 6
(7), inc in next st] to last 10 (9) sts, rib 5
(4), slip last 5 sts onto safety pin. 60 (64)
sts. Change to 4 mm (No 8/US 5) needles.
Beg with a K row, cont in st st until work
measures 14 (16) cm/5½ (6) in from beg,
ending with a P row.

Shape Top

Next row K39 (41), K2 tog tbl, turn.
Next row Sl 1 purlwise, P18, P2 tog, turn.
Next row Sl 1 purlwise, K18, K2 tog tbl, turn.
Rep last 2 rows until all sts are decreased on each side of centre sts, ending with a P row. Leave rem 20 sts on a holder.

EDGING

With 3¼ mm (No 10/US 3) needles, right side facing and MC, rib across 5 sts from safety pin, pick up and K 29 (32) sts up right side of hood, K across centre 20 sts, dec one st, pick up and K 29 (32) sts down left side of hood, then rib 5 sts from safety pin. 87 (93) sts.
Work 7 rows in rib. Cast off in rib.

BUTTONHOLE BAND

With 3¼ mm (No 10/US 3) needles, right side facing and MC, pick up and K 12 sts evenly along right side of hood rib and rib edging. Work 3 rows in K1, P1 rib.
1st buttonhole row Rib 5, cast off in rib 2 sts, rib to end.
2nd buttonhole row Rib 5, cast on 2, rib to end.
Rib 4 rows. Cast off in rib.

BUTTON BAND

Work to match Buttonhole Band omitting buttonhole.

EARS (make 4)

With 4 mm (No 8/US 5) needles and MC, cast on 16 sts. Work 8 rows in st st. Cont in st st, dec one st at each end of next

and 2 foll alt rows. 10 sts.
P 1 row. Cast off.

EAR LININGS (make 2)

With 4 mm (No 8/US 5) needles and A, cast on 12 sts. Work in garter st (every row K) for 6 rows. Cont in garter st, dec one st at each end of next and foll alt row. 8 sts. Cast off.

TO MAKE UP

With right sides of paired ear pieces together, join seam all round, leaving cast on edges open. Turn to right side. Insert wadding and close opening. Sew ear linings in place. Sew ears to hood as shown on photograph. Sew on button.

Mittens

With 4 mm (No 8/US 5) needles and MC, cast on 34 sts. K 10 rows for cuff. Work 6 rows in K1, P1 rib. Beg with a K row, cont in st st until work measures 10 cm/4 in from beg, ending with a P row.
Next row K1, [K2 tog tbl, K12, K2 tog] twice, K1.
P 1 row.
Next row K1, [K2 tog tbl, K10, K2 tog] twice, K1.
P 1 row. Cast off. Join seam, reversing seam on cuff. Turn back cuff.
With 4 mm (No 8/US 5) needles and A, cast on 10 sts for palm pad. Cont in garter st (every row K), work 2 rows. Inc one st at each end of next row. K 15 rows. Dec one st at each end of next row. K 2 rows. Cast off.

Sew pad in place.
Make one more.

Bootees

UPPER PART

With 4 mm (No 8/US 5) needles and MC, cast on 57 sts.
Beg with a K row, work 6 rows in st st.
Dec row K20, K2 tog, K13, K2 tog tbl, K20.
P 1 row.
Dec row K19, K2 tog, K13, K2 tog tbl, K19.
P 1 row.
Dec row K18, K2 tog, K13, K2 tog tbl, K18.
Cont in this way, dec 2 sts as set on every alt row until 39 sts rem.
P 1 row.
Next row K1, [P1, K1] to end.
Next row P1, [K1, P1] to end.
K 10 rows for cuff. Cast off knitwise.

SOLE

With 4 mm (No 8/US 5) needles and A, cast on 13 sts. K 40 rows. Cast off knitwise.

TO MAKE UP

Join back seam of bootee, reversing seam on cuff. Sew in sole. With MC, make a cord approximately 36 cm/14¼ in long and thread through sts just below rib. Turn back cuff.
Make one more.

Crown Hat

See Page 53

MEASUREMENTS

To fit age 6–9 (12–24) months

MATERIALS

1 x 50 g ball of Rowan Cotton Glace in each of 2 colours (A and B).
Pair each of 3¾ mm (No 9/US 4) and 4 mm (No 8/US 5) knitting needles.

TENSION

22 sts and 28 rows to 10 cm/4 in square over st st on 4 mm (No 8/US 5) needles.

ABBREVIATIONS

See page 63.

MAIN PART

With 4 mm (No 8/US 5) needles and A, cast on 80 (96) sts.
Beg with a K row, work 9 (10) cm/3½ (4) in in st st, ending with a P row and dec 2 sts evenly across last row on **1st** size only. 78 (96) sts.
Shape Top
Dec row [K11 (14), K2 tog] to end.
P 1 row.

Dec row [K10 (13), K2 tog] to end.
P 1 row.
Dec row [K9 (12), K2 tog] to end.
Cont in this way, dec 6 sts as set on every alt row until 12 sts rem.
Break off yarn, thread end through rem sts, pull up and secure.

BRIM

With 3¾ mm (No 9/US 4) needles, wrong

side facing and B, pick up and K84 (102) sts along cast on edge of main part. K 15 (21) rows.
Work points as follows:
**Next row (right side) K14 (17), turn.
Work on this set of sts only. K 1 row.
Next row K1, K2 tog, K to last 3 sts, K2 tog, K1.
K 1 row.
Rep last 2 rows 3 (5) times more.
Next row K1, [K2 tog] 2 (1) times, K1 (2).
K 1 row.
Next row K1, K2 tog, K1.
Cast off rem 3 sts.
With right side facing, rejoin yarn to rem sts and rep from ** until all sts are worked off.

TO MAKE UP

Join seam, reversing seam on brim. Turn back brim and catch down each point.

Mouse Hat and Bootees

See Page
51

MEASUREMENTS
Hat and bootees
To fit age 6–12 months

MATERIALS
Hat 1 x 50 g ball of Rowan Designer DK
Wool in main colour (MC).
Small amount of same in each of 2
contrast colours (A and B).
Pair of 4 mm (No 8/US 5) knitting
needles.
Small amount of wadding.
1 button.
Bootees 1 x 50 g ball of any 4 ply in
main colour (MC).

Small amount of same in each of 2
contrast colours (A and B).
Pair each of 2¾mm (No 12/US 1) and 3¼
mm (No 10/US 3) knitting needles.
Small amount of wadding.
TENSION
22 sts and 28 rows to 10 cm/4 in square
over st st on 4 mm (No 8/US 5) needles
using DK yarn.
28 sts and 36 rows to 10 cm/4 in square
over st st on 3¼mm (No 10/US 3)
needles using 4 ply yarn.

ABBREVIATIONS
See page 63.

Hat

MAIN PART
With 4 mm (No 8/US 5) needles and MC,.
cast on 105 sts. K 4 rows.
1st row (right side) K1, m1, K17, sl 1, K1,
psso, K1, K2 tog, K17, m1, K1, m1, K9, sl 1,
K1, psso, K1, K2 tog, K9, m1, K1, m1, K17,
sl 1, K1, psso, K1, K2 tog, K17, m1, K1.
2nd row P.
Rep last 2 rows 11 times more.
Shape Top
1st dec row K1, K2 tog, K15, sl 1, K1,
psso, K1, K2 tog, [K27, sl 1, K1, psso, K1,
K2 tog] twice, K15, sl 1, K1, psso, K1.
P 1 row.
2nd dec row K16, sl 1, K1, psso, K1, K2
tog, [K25, sl 1, K1, psso, K1, K2 tog]
twice, K16.
P 1 row.
3rd dec row K1, K2 tog, K12, sl 1, K1,
psso, K1, K2 tog, [K23, sl 1, K1, psso, K1,
K2 tog] twice, K12, sl 1, K1, psso, K1.
4th dec row P13, P2 tog, P1, P2 tog tbl,
[P21, P2 tog, P1, P2 tog tbl] twice, P13.
5th dec row K12, sl 1, K1, psso, K1, K2
tog, [K19, sl 1, K1, psso, K1, K2 tog]
twice, K12.
6th dec row P11, P2 tog, P1, P2 tog tbl,
[P17, P2 tog, P1, P2 tog tbl] twice, P11.
7th dec row K1, K2, tog, K7, sl 1, K1,
psso, K1, K2 tog, [K15, sl 1, K1, psso, K1,
K2 tog] twice, K7, sl 1, K1, psso, K1.
8th dec row P8, P2 tog, P1, P2 tog tbl,
[P13, P2 tog, P1, P2 tog tbl] twice, P8.
9th dec row K1, K2 tog, K4, sl 1, K1, psso,
K1, K2 tog, [K11, sl 1, K1, psso, K1, K2
tog] twice, K4, sl 1, K1, psso, K1.
10th dec row P5, P2 tog, P1, P2 tog tbl,
[P9, P2 tog, P1, P2 tog tbl] twice, P5.
11th dec row K4, sl 1, K1, psso, K1, K2
tog, [K7, sl 1, K1, psso, K1, K2 tog] twice,
K4.
12th dec row P3, P2 tog, P1, P2 tog tbl,
[P5, P2 tog, P1, P2 tog tbl] twice, P3.
13th dec row K2, sl 1, K1, psso, K1, K2
tog, [K3, sl 1, K1, psso, K1, K2 tog] twice,
K2.

14th dec row P1, [P2 tog, P1, P2 tog tbl,
P1] 3 times. 13 sts.
Break off yarn, thread end through rem
sts, pull up and secure.

STRAP
With 4 mm (No 8/US 5) needles and MC,
cast on 5 sts. Work in garter st (every row
K) for 11 cm/4½ in.
Buttonhole row K1, K2 tog, yf, K2.
K 4 rows. Cast off.

EARS (make 4)
With 4 mm (No 8/US 5) needles and MC,
cast on 16 sts. Work 8 rows in st st. Cont
in st st, dec one st at each end of next
and 2 foll alt rows. 10 sts.
P 1 row. Cast off.

EAR LININGS (make 2)
With 4 mm (No 8/US 5) needles and A,
cast on 12 sts. Work in garter st for 6
rows. Cont in garter st, dec one st at each
end of next and foll alt row. 8 sts. Cast off.

TO MAKE UP
Join seam of main part. Attach cast on
edge of strap to wrong side of one ear
point and sew button to other on main
part. With right sides of paired ear pieces
together, join seam all round, leaving cast
on edges open.
Turn to right side, stuff lightly and close
opening. Sew ear linings in place. Sew
ears to main part as shown on
photograph.
With 4 mm (No 8/US 5) needles and B,
cast on 3 sts for nose.
Next row [K1, P1] in first st, [K1, P1, K1] in
next st, [K1, P1] in last st.
K 5 rows.
Next row K2 tog, K3 tog, K2 tog.
Next row K3 tog and fasten off.
Work a running st around edge, draw up
to form bobble and secure. Attach to front
point on main part. With B and back st,
embroider whiskers.

Bootees

With 2¾mm (No 12/US 1) needles and
MC, cast on 53 sts. K 11 rows.
1st row (right side) K1, [P1, K1] to end.
2nd row P1, [K1, P1] to end.
Rep last 2 rows 3 times more.
Eyelet hole row Rib 3, [P2 tog, yrn, rib 3,
K2 tog, yf, rib 3] to end.
Rib 5 rows.
Shape instep
Next row K33, turn.
Next row K 13, turn.
K 22 rows on these 13 sts only. Break off
yarn. Leave these sts on a holder.
With right side facing, rejoin yarn to base
of instep, pick up and K 12 sts evenly
along side edge of instep, K 13 sts from
holder, then pick up and K 12 sts evenly
along other side edge of instep, K rem sts.
77 sts. K 17 rows. Beg with a K row, work
9 rows in st st.
Next row [P next st tog with corresponding
st 9 rows below] to end.
K 13 rows for sole. Cast off.

EARS (make 4)
With 3¼mm (No 10/US 3) needles and
MC, cast on 16 sts.
Work 8 rows in st st. Cont in st st, dec one
st at each end of next and 2 foll alt rows.
10 sts. Work 1 row. Cast off.

EAR LININGS (make 2)
With 3¼mm (No 10/US 3) needles and A,
cast on 12 sts. Work in garter st (every
row K) for 6 rows. Cont in garter st, dec
one st at each end of next and foll alt row.
8 sts. Cast off.
Nose
With 3¼mm (No 10/US 3) needles and B,
cast on 3 sts.
Next row [K1, P1] in first st, [K1, P1, K1] in
next st, [K1, P1] in last st.
Beg with a P row, work 5 rows in st st.
Next row K2 tog, K3 tog, K2 tog.
Next row P3 tog and fasten off.

TO MAKE UP
Join seam of bootee, reversing seam on
cuff. Join sole seam, folding knitting to
form mitred corners. With right sides of
paired ear pieces together, join seam all
round, leaving cast on edges open. Turn
to right side, stuff lightly and close
opening. Sew ear linings in place. Attach
to bootee. Work a running stitch all round
nose, draw up to form bobble and secure.
Attach to bootee. With B and back stitch,
embroider whiskers. Make a cord
approximately 40 cm/15¾ in long and
thread through eyelet holes. Turn back
cuff. Make one more.

Multi-coloured Hat and Socks

See Page
52

MEASUREMENTS
Hat and socks
To fit age 3–6 (6–9 months)

MATERIALS
Small amount of Rowan Cotton Glace in each of Green (A), Lilac (B), Orange (C), Rust (D), Turquoise (E), Pink (F), Red (G), Purple (H) and Blue (J).
Pair each of 3¼-mm (No 10/US 3) and 3¾ mm (No 9/US 4) knitting needles.

TENSION
24 sts and 30 rows to 10 cm/4 in square over st st on 3¾-mm (No 9/US 4) needles.

ABBREVIATIONS
See page 63.

NOTE
Read Chart from right to left on K rows and from left to right on P rows. When working in pattern, strand yarn not in use loosely across wrong side to keep fabric elastic.

Hat

With 3¼-mm (No 10/US 3) needles and A, cast on 105 (117) sts.
1st row (right side) K1, [P1, K1] to end.
2nd row P1, [K1, P1] to end.
Rep last 2 rows twice more.
Change to 3¾-mm (No 9/US 4) needles.
Beg with a K row and working in st st throughout, work in patt as follows:

2nd size only
Work 2 rows in J and 2 rows in H.
Both sizes
Work 2 rows in B.
Next row 1B, [2C, 2B] to end.
Next row [2B, 2C] to last st, 1B.
Next row 1D, [2E, 2D] to end.
Next row [2D, 2E] to last st, 1D.
Work 2 rows in F and 1 row in G.
Next row 2 (3)G, [1E, 4G] to last 3 (4) sts, 1E, 2 (3)G.

Next row 2 (3)G, [2E, 3G] to last 3 (4) sts, 2E, 1 (2)G.
Next row 0 (1)G, [3E, 2G] to last 0 (1) st, 0 (1)E.
Next row 1 (2)E, [1G, 4E] to last 4 (5) sts, 1G, 3 (4)E.
Work 1 row in E, 2 rows in H, 2 rows in A and 1 row in J.
Next row 4J, [1F, 5J] to last 5 sts, 1F, 4J.
Next row 3J, [3F, 3J] to end.
Next row 1F, [1J, 5F] to last 2 sts, 1J, 1F.
Work 1 row in F, 2 rows in G, 1 row in E, dec one st at centre of last row on 1st size only. 104 (117) sts.
Shape Top
Dec row With E, [K2 tog, K6 (7)] to end.
Work 1 row in B.
Dec row With B, [K2 tog, K5 (6)] to end.
Work 1 row in D.
Dec row With D, [K2 tog, K4 (5)] to end.
Work 1 row in C.
Dec row With C, [K2 tog, K3 (4)] to end.
Work 1 row in H.
Dec row With H, [K2 tog, K2 (3)] to end.
Work 1 row in A.
Dec row With A, [K2, K1(2)] to end.
2nd size only
Work 1 row in B.

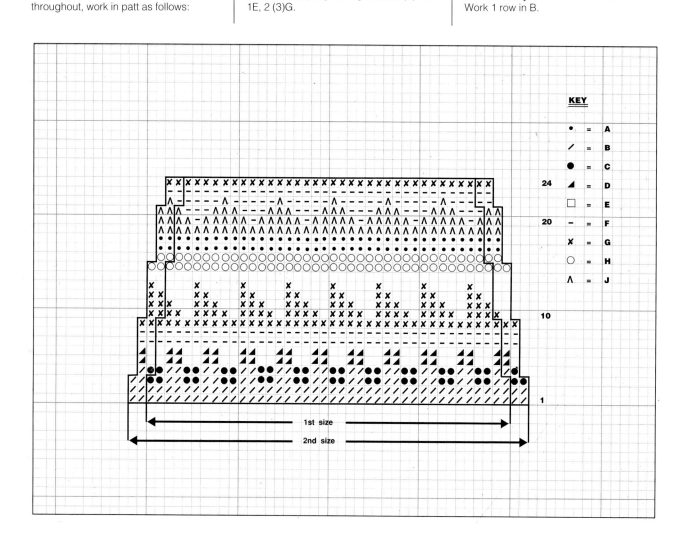

KEY

•	=	A
/	=	B
●	=	C
◢	=	D
□	=	E
–	=	F
x	=	G
○	=	H
∧	=	J

24

20

10

1

1st size
2nd size

Dec row With B, [K2 tog, K (1)] to end.
Both sizes
Dec row With A (B), [P2 tog] to end.
13 sts.
Break off yarn, thread end through rem sts, pull up and secure. Join seam.

Socks

With 3¼mm (No 10/US 3) needles and A, cast on 40 (44) sts.
Work 6 rows in K1, P1 rib.
Change to 3¾mm (No 9/US 4) needles.
Beg with a K row and working in st st throughout, work in patt as follows:
2nd size only
Work 2 rows in J and 2 rows in H.
Both sizes
Work 1st to 24th rows of Chart, dec one st at each end of 3rd and 3 foll 6th rows. 32 (36) sts.
Dec row With G, K3, [K2 tog, K6 (7)] 3 times, K2 tog, K3 (4), 28 (32) sts.
Shape Heel
Next row With A, P8 (9), turn.
Work 9 rows in st st on these 8 (9) sts only.

Dec row P2 (3), P2 tog, P1, turn.
Next row Sl 1, K3 (4).
Dec row P3 (4), P2 tog, P1, turn.
Next row Sl 1, K4 (5).
Dec row P4 (5), P2 tog.
Leave rem 5 (6) sts on a holder.
With wrong side facing, slip centre 12 (14) sts onto a holder, rejoin A yarn to rem 8 (9) sts, P to end. Work 8 rows in st st on these 8 (9) sts only.
Dec row K2 (3), K2 tog tbl, K1, turn.
Next row Sl 1, P3 (4).
Dec row K3 (4), K2 tog tbl, K1, turn.
Next row Sl 1, P4 (5).
Dec row K4 (5), K2 tog tbl, turn.
Next row Sl 1, P4 (5).
Shape Instep
Change to E.
Next row K5 (6), pick up and K8 sts evenly along inside edge of heel, K12 (14) sts from holder, pick up and K8 sts evenly along inside edge of heel and K5 (6) sts from holder, 38 (42) sts. P 1 row.
Dec row K11 (12), K2 tog, K12 (14), K2 tog tbl, K11 (12).
P 1 row.
Dec row K10 (11), K2 tog, K12 (14), K2 tog tbl, K10 (11).

P 1 row.
Dec row K9 (10), K2 tog, K12 (14), K2 tog tbl, K9 (10).
P 1 row.
Dec row K8 (9), K2 tog, K12 (14), K2 tog tbl, K8 (9), 30 (34) sts.
Work 11 (15) rows straight. Change to A and work 2 rows.
Shape Toes
Dec row K1, [K2 tog tbl, K5 (6)] 4 times, K1.
P 1 row.
Dec row K1, [K2 tog tbl, K4 (5)] 4 times, K1.
P 1 row.
Dec row K1, [K2 tog tbl, K3 (4)] 4 times, K1.
P 1 row.
Dec row K1, [K2 tog tbl, K2 (3)] 4 times, K1.
2nd size only
P 1 row.
Dec row K1, [K2 tog tbl, K(2)] 4 times, K1.
Both sizes
Dec row [P2 tog] to end. 7 sts.
Break off yarn, thread end through rem sts, pull up and secure. Join seam.
Make one more.

Nursery Hat and Shoes

See Page 54

MEASUREMENTS
Hat and shoes
To fit age 6–12 months

MATERIALS
Hat 1 x 50 g ball of Rowan Designer DK Wool in Cream (M).
Small amount of same in each of Blue (A), Green (B), Pink, Yellow, Red, Grey and Black.
Shoes 1 x 50 g ball of Rowan Designer DK Wool in Cream (M).
Small amount of same in each of Blue (A), Green (B), Pink and Yellow.
Pair each of 3¾mm (No 9/US 4) and 4 mm (No 8/US 5) knitting needles.

TENSION
22 sts and 28 rows to 10 cm/4 in square over st st on 4 mm (No 8/US 5) needles.

ABBREVIATIONS
See page 63.

NOTE
Read Charts from right to left on K rows and from left to right on P rows unless otherwise stated. When working motifs, use separate lengths of yarn for each coloured area and twist yarns together on wrong side at joins to avoid holes.

Hat

With 4 mm (No 8/US 5) needles and M, cast on 91 sts.
1st row (right side) K1, [P1, K1] to end.
2nd row P1, [K1, P1] to end.
K 1 row.
Stranding yarn not in use loosely across wrong side over no more than 4 sts at a time, work brim patt as follows:
1st row (wrong side) P3M, 1A, [6M, 1B, 6M, 1A] to last 3 sts, 3M.
2nd row K2M, 3A, [4M, 3B, 4M, 3A] to last

2 sts, 2M.
3rd row P1M, 5A, [2M, 5B, 2M, 5A] to last st, 1M.
4th row K7A, [7B, 7A] to end.
With M, work a further 2 rows in st st.
Beg with a K row (thus reversing fabric), work 8 rows in st st.
Cont in st st and patt from Chart 1 until 30th row of Chart 1 has been worked.
Shape Top
Cont working from Chart 1, dec one st at each end of next and 6 foll alt rows. Work 1 row. Cast off 2 sts at beg of every row

until 1 st rem. Fasten off. Join seam, reversing seam on brim. Turn back brim.

Shoes

With 3¾mm (No 9/US 4) needles and M, cast on 42 sts.
K 4 rows. Beg with a K row, work 2 rows in st st.
Stranding yarn not in use loosely across wrong side over no more than 4 sts at a time, work cuff patt as follows:
1st row (right side) [K7A, 7B] to end.
2nd row [P1M, 5B, 2M, 5A, 1M] to end.
3rd row [K2M, 3A, 4M, 3B, 2M] to end.
4th row [P3M, 1B, 6M, 1A, 3M] to end.
Cont in M, K 3 rows, then work 10 rows in K1, P1 rib, inc 1 st at centre of last row. 43 sts.
Beg with a K row (thus reversing fabric), work 4 rows in st st.
Shape Instep
Next row K28, turn.
Next row P13, turn.
Work on these 13 sts only. Cont in st st, work 1st to 14th rows of Chart 2. With M, work 2 rows in st st. Break off yarn and leave these sts on a holder.
With right side facing, rejoin M at base of instep, pick up and K10 sts evenly along side edge of instep, K across 13 sts on holder, pick up and K10 sts evenly along other side

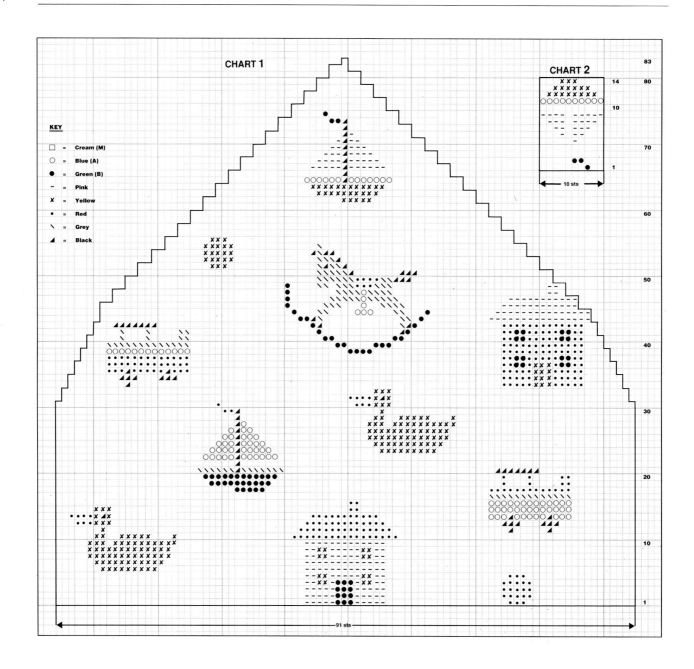

CHART 1

KEY

□	=	Cream (M)
○	=	Blue (A)
●	=	Green (B)
–	=	Pink
X	=	Yellow
•	=	Red
\	=	Grey
◢	=	Black

CHART 2

10 sts

91 sts

edge of instep, K rem 15 sts. 63 sts.
K 8 rows.
Next row [K next st tog with
corresponding st 7 rows below] to end.
Beg with a K row, work 2 rows in st st.
Now work patt as follows
1st row K3M, [1A, 6M, 1B, 6M] to last 4
sts, 1A, 3M.
2nd row P2M, 3A, [4M, 3B, 4M, 3A] to last
2 sts, 2M.
3rd row K1M, [5A, 2M, 5B, 2M] to last 6
sts, 5A, 1M.
4th row P7A, [7B, 7A] to end.
With M, work 2 rows in st st. Break off
yarn.
Shape Sole

With right side facing, slip first 25 sts onto
right hand needle, rejoin M and work as
follows:
Next row K12, K2 tog, turn.
Next row Sl 1, K11, K2 tog tbl, turn.
Next row, Sl 1, K11, K2 tog, turn.
Rep last 2 rows 10 times more, then work
first of the 2 rows again.
Next row Sl 1, K4, sl 1, K2 tog, psso, K4,
K2 tog, turn.
Next row Sl 1, K9, K2 tog tbl, turn.
Next row Sl 1, K9, K2 tog, turn.
Rep last 2 rows once more, then work first
of the 2 rows again.
Next row Sl 1, K3, sl 1, K2 tog, psso, K3,
K2 tog, turn.

Next row Sl 1, K7, K2 tog tbl, turn.
Next row Sl 1, K7, K2 tog, turn.
Rep last 2 rows 4 times more.
Next row Sl 1, K3, K2 tog, K2, K2 tog tbl.
Place rem 4 sts at each side of sole on
one needle, pointing in the same direction
as needle with sole sts. With right sides of
sole and upper sts together, cast off
together rem 8 sts.
Join seam, reversing seam on cuff. Turn
back cuff.
Make one more, reversing cuff patt by
using A instead of B and B instead of A
and Chart 2 position by reading K rows
from left to right and P rows from right
to left.

Inca Hat and Socks

See Page
55

MEASUREMENTS
Hat
To fit age 6–12 (18–24) months
Socks
To fit age 6–12 months

MATERIALS
1 x 50 g ball of Rowan Designer DK
Wool in Pink (A).
Small amount of same in each of Green
(B), Yellow (C), Blue (D), Navy (E),
Cream (F), Red (G) and White (H).
Pair of 4 mm (No 8/US 5) knitting needles.
One 3¾mm (No 9/US 4) circular needle
for hat.

Pair of 3¼mm (No 10/US 3) knitting
needles for socks.

TENSION
22 sts and 28 rows to 10 cm/4 in square
over st st on 4 mm (No 8/US 5) needles.

ABBREVIATIONS
See page 63.

NOTE
Read Chart from right to left on K rows
and from left to right on P rows. When
working in pattern, strand yarn not in use
loosely across wrong side over no more
than 4 sts at a time to keep fabric elastic.

Hat

EAR FLAPS (make 2)
With 4 mm (No 8/US 5) needles and E, cast
on 6 (8) sts.
Beg with a K row and working in st st
throughout, work 2 rows E, 2 rows D, 2
rows B, **at the same time**, inc one st at
each end of every row. 18(20) sts.
Work 2 rows C, 2 rows H, 2 rows G and 2
rows A.
Now work 2 rows E, 2 rows D and 2 rows B,
at the same time, dec one st at each end of
first and 2 foll alt rows. 12 (14) sts. Work 2
rows C.
Work 2 rows H and 2 rows G, inc one st at
each end of first and foll alt row. 16 (18)
sts. Leave these sts on a holder.

MAIN PART
With 4 mm (No 8/US 5) needles and A, cast
on 10 (12) sts, K across 16 (18) sts of one
ear flap, cast on 39 (43) sts, K across 16
(18) sts of other ear flap, cast on 10 (12)
sts. 91 (103) sts.
Cont in st st, work 1 row A, 2 rows E, 2
rows D, 2 rows B, 2 rows C, 2 rows H and 2
rows G.
Inc row With A, K1 (3), [m1, K15 (10)] to
end. 97 (113) sts.
Work 1 row A.
Now work 1st to 15th rows of Chart. Work 2
rows A.
Shape Top
Dec row With G, P2 (3), [P2 tog, P3] to end.
Work 1 row G and 2 rows H.
Dec row With C, P2 (3), [P2 tog, P2] to end.
Work 1 row C and 2 (4) rows B.
Dec row With B, P2 (0), [P2 tog, P1] to end.
Work 3 rows B. Cont in D only.
Dec row [P2 tog] to end.
Work 1 row.
Dec row P0 (1), [P2 tog] to end. 10 (12) sts.
Work 4 rows. Break off yarn, thread end
through rem sts, pull up and secure.

LOWER EDGING
With 3¼mm (No 9/US 4) circular needle,
right side facing and H, pick up and K1 st
for each cast on st along cast on edges
and 44 (46) sts around each ear flap. 147
(159) sts. Work backwards and forwards,
K 2 rows. Cast off knitwise. Join seam.

Socks

With 3¼mm (No 10/US 3) needles and D,
cast on 35 sts.
1st row (right side) K1, [P1, K1] to end.
2nd row P1, [K1, P1] to end.
Rep last 2 rows once more.
Change to 4 mm (No 8/US 5) needles.
Beg with a K row and working in st st
throughout, work 2 rows B, 2 rows C, 2
rows H, 2 rows G and 2 rows A, inc 6 sts
evenly across last row. 41 sts.
Work patt from Chart as follows:
1st row Work edge st of 15th row of Chart,

rep the 16 sts twice, work first 7 sts of the
16 sts, then work edge st again.
2nd row Work edge st of 14th row of
Chart, work last 7 sts of the 16 sts, rep the
16 sts twice, then work edge st again.
Cont working from Chart as set, work 13th
to 1st rows.
Work 2 rows A, dec 7 sts evenly across
last row. 34 sts. Work 2 rows G.
Shape Heel
Next row With D, P9, turn.
Cont in D on these 9 sts only, work 7
rows.
Dec row P3, P2 tog, turn.
Next row and foll alt row Sl 1, K to end.
Dec row P4, P2 tog, turn.
Dec row P5, P2 tog.
Leave rem 6 sts on a holder.
With wrong side facing, slip centre 16 sts
onto a holder, rejoin D to rem 9 sts. P to
end. Cont in D on these 9 sts only, work 6
rows.
Dec row K3, K2 tog tbl, turn.
Next row and foll alt row Sl 1, P to end.
Dec row K4, K2 tog tbl, turn.
Dec row K5, K2 tog tbl, turn.
Next row Sl 1, P to end.
Shape Instep
Next row With H, K6, pick up and K8 sts
along inside edge of heel, K16 sts from
holder, pick up and K8 sts along inside
edge of heel, K6 sts from holder. 44 sts.
Work 1 row H.
Dec row With C, K12, K2 tog, K16, K2 tog
tbl, K 12.
Work 1 row C.
Dec row With B, K11, K2 tog, K16, K2 tog
tbl, K11.
Work 1 row B.
Dec row With D, K10, K2 tog, K16, K2 tog
tbl, K10.
Work 1 row D.
Dec row With E, K9, K2 tog, K16, K2 tog

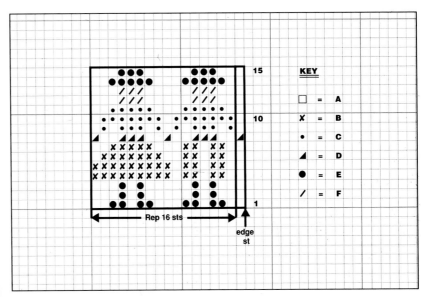

tbl, K9. 36 sts.
Work 1 row E, 2 rows A, 2 rows G, 2 rows H and 2 rows C. Cont in B only work 2 rows.

Shape Toes
Dec row [Sl 1, K1, psso, K7] 4 times.

Work 1 row.
Dec row [Sl 1, K1, psso, K6] 4 times.
Work 1 row.
Dec row [Sl 1, K1, psso, K5] 4 times.
Cont in this way, dec 4 sts as set on every alt row until 12 sts rem.

Work 1 row.
Dec row [K2 tog] to end.
Break off yarn, thread end through rem sts, pull up and secure. Join seam. Make one more.

Ladybird Hat and Slippers

See Page
56

MEASUREMENTS
Hat and Slippers
To fit age 6–12 months

MATERIALS
Hat 1 x 50 g ball of Rowan Designer DK Wool in Red (MC).
Small amount of same in Black (A).
2 pipe cleaners.
Slippers 1 x 50 g ball of Rowan Designer DK Wool in Red (MC).
Small amount of same in Black (A).
2 buttons.
Pair each of 3¼mm (No 10/US 3) and 4 mm (No 8/US 5) knitting needles.

TENSION
22 sts and 28 rows to 10 cm/4 in square over st st on 4 mm (No 8/US 5) needles.

ABBREVIATIONS
See page 63.

Hat

MAIN PART
Work as given for Main Part of Mouse Hat (see page 131).

SPOTS (make 5)
With 4 mm (No 8/US 5) needles and A, cast on 8 sts. Work in garter st (every row K) inc one st at each end of 3rd and 2 foll alt rows. K 8 rows. Dec one st at each end of next and 2 foll alt rows. K 2 rows. Cast off knitwise.

FEELERS (make 2)
With 4 mm (No 8/US 5) needles and A, cast on 9 sts. Work 10 cm/4 in in st st. Cast off.

TO MAKE UP
Join back seam of main part. Sew on spots. Fold feelers lengthwise and join seam. Insert pipe cleaners and close up ends. Attach to front point of main part.

Slippers

With 3¼mm (No 10/US 3) needles and MC, cast on 18 sts.
Work in garter st (every row K) throughout, inc one st at each end of every alt row until there are 32 sts. Dec one st at each end of next and every alt row until 18 sts rem.
Next row Cast on 7 sts for heel, K to end. 25 sts.
Inc one st at end of 6 foll alt rows. 31 sts. K 1 row.
Next row Cast off knitwise 17 sts (mark 9th st of these sts), K to last st, inc in last st. K 12 rows.
Next row K2 tog, K to end, turn and cast on 17 sts (mark 9th st of these sts). 31 sts. Dec one st at beg of 6 foll alt rows. 25 sts. K 1 row. Cast off knitwise.
Join back heel seam.
With 3¼mm (No 10/US 3) needles, A and right side facing, pick up and K9 sts from marker to back seam and 9 sts from back seam to next marker. 18 sts.
Next row Cast on 14 sts, K to end, turn and cast on 14 sts.
K 2 rows.
1st buttonhole row K2, cast off 3, K to end.
2nd buttonhole row K to last 2 sts, cast on 3, K2.
K 2 rows. Cast off knitwise.

TO MAKE UP
Fold slipper along row just below cast on sts for heel and, with right sides together, join seam all round, easing in fullness at toes and sewing the 7 cast on sts and last 7 sts of cast off edge to sole. Turn to right side. With 4 mm (No 8/US 5) needles and A, cast on 6 sts for spot. Work in garter st, inc one st at each end of 2 foll alt rows. K2 rows.
Dec one st at each end of next and foll alt row. K 1 row. Cast off knitwise.
Make 2 more spots. Sew on spots and button.
Make one more, reversing buttonhole rows.

Reindeer Hat, Scarf, Mittens and Socks

See Page
57

MEASUREMENTS
Hat, Scarf, Mittens and Socks
To fit age 6–12 months

MATERIALS
4 x 50 g balls of Rowan Designer DK
Wool in Black (M) and 2 x 50 g balls in
Cream (A).
Small amount of same in Red (C).
Pair of 4 mm (No 8/US 5) knitting
needles. Medium-size crochet hook.

TENSION
24 sts and 25 rows to 10 cm/4 in
square over Fair Isle pattern on 4 mm
(No 8/US 5) needles.

ABBREVIATIONS
See page 63.

NOTE
Read Charts from right to left on K
rows and from left to right on P rows
unless otherwise stated. When working
in pattern, strand yarn not in use
loosely across wrong side over no
more than 5 sts at a time to keep fabric
elastic.

Hat

With 4 mm (No 8/US 5) needles and M,
cast on 97 sts.
1st row K1, [P1, K1] to end.
2nd row P1, [K1, P1] to end.
Beg with a K row and 1st row of Chart 1,
work 9 rows in st st and patt from Chart 1
for brim. With M, P 2 rows.
Beg with a K row and 1st row of Chart 1,
work 55 rows in st st and patt from Chart
1. Cont in M only, P 1 row.
Shape Top
Dec row K1, [K2 tog, K6] 12 times.
P 1 row.
Dec row K1, [K2 tog, K5] 12 times.
P 1 row.
Dec row K1, [K2 tog, K4] 12 times.
Cont in this way, dec 12 sts as set on
every alt row until 25 sts rem, ending with
a P row.
Dec row K1, [K2 tog] 12 times. 13 sts.
Break off yarn, thread end through rem
sts, pull up and secure. Join seam,
reversing seam on brim. With C, make a
large pompon and attach to top. Turn
back brim.

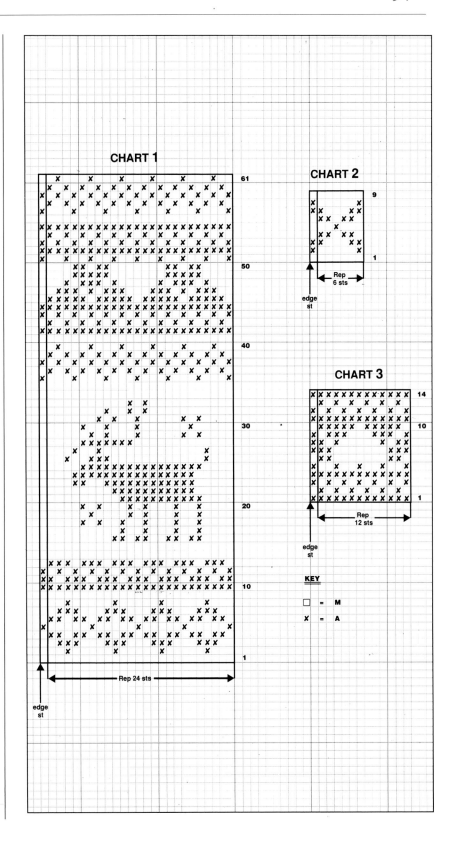

CHART 1

CHART 2

CHART 3

Rep 6 sts

edge st

Rep 12 sts

edge st

Rep 24 sts

edge st

KEY

□ = M

X = A

Scarf

With 4 mm (No 8/US 5) needles and M, cast on 49 sts. Beg with a K row, work 8 rows in st st. Cont in st st and patt from Chart 1, work 1st to 61st rows, then 1st to 35th rows. Turn Chart 1 upside down. Now reading Chart 1 from left to right on K rows and from right to left on P rows and working rows in reverse order, work 35th to 1st rows, then 61st to 1st rows. With M only, work 8 rows in st st. Cast off. Fold scarf in half lengthwise and join long seam. Gather short ends, draw up and secure. With C, make 2 pompons and attach to each end.

Mittens

With 4 mm (No 8/US 5) needles and M, cast on 37 sts.
1st row K1, [P1, K1] to end.
2nd row P1, [K1, P1] to end.
Beg with a K row and 1st row of Chart 2, work 9 rows in st st and patt from Chart 2 for cuff.
Cont in M, P 1 row, then rep 1st and 2nd rows 6 times.
Beg with a P row, work 4 rows in st st.
Cont in st st and patt from Chart 3, work 1st to 14th rows. Cont in M only, P 1 row.
Dec row K2, [K2 tog tbl, K12, K2 tog, K1] twice, K1.
P 1 row.
Dec row K2, [K2 tog tbl, K10, K2 tog, K1] twice, K1.
P 1 row.

Cast off. Make one more.
Join side seams, reversing seams on cuffs.
With crochet hook and using C yarn double, make a chain cord approximately 80 cm/31½ in long. Make 2 pompons with C and sew to each end of cord.
Attach cord to each mitten as shown on photograph. Turn back cuffs.

Socks

With 4 mm (No 8/US 5) needles and M, cast on 37 sts.
1st row K1, [P1, K1] to end.
2nd row P1, [K1, P1] to end.
Beg with a K row and 1st row of Chart 2, work 9 rows in st st and patt from Chart 2 for cuff.
Cont in M only, P1 row, then rep 1st and 2nd rows 6 times, P 1 row. Beg with a K row and 1st row of Chart 3, work 14 rows in st st and patt from Chart 3. Cont in M only, K 1 row, dec 3 sts evenly across last row. 34 sts.
Shape Heel
Next row P9, turn.
Work 7 rows in st st on these 9 sts only.
Dec row P3, P2 tog, turn.
Next row Sl 1, K3.
Dec row P4, P2 tog, turn.
Next row Sl 1, K4.
Dec row P5, P2 tog.
Leave rem 6 sts on a holder.
With wrong side facing, slip centre 16 sts onto a holder, rejoin yarns to rem 9 sts, P to end. Work 6 rows in st st on these 9 sts only.

Dec row K3, K2 tog tbl, turn.
Next row Sl 1, P3.
Dec row K4, K2 tog tbl, turn.
Next row Sl 1, P4.
Dec row K5, K2 tog tbl, turn.
Next row Sl 1, P5.
Shape Instep
Next row K6, pick up and K8 sts along inside edge of heel, K 16 sts from holder, pick up and K8 sts along inside edge of heel, K6 sts from holder. 44 sts.
P 1 row.
Dec row K12, K2 tog, K16, K2 tog tbl, K12.
P 1 row.
Dec row K11, K2 tog, K16, K2 tog tbl, K11.
P 1 row.
Dec row K10, K2 tog, K16, K2 tog tbl, K10.
Cont in this way, dec 2 sts as set on every alt row until 34 sts rem.
Work 15 rows straight.
Shape Toes
Dec row K1, [sl 1, K1, psso, K6] 4 times, K1.
P 1 row.
Dec row K1, [sl 1, K1, psso, K5] 4 times, K1.
P 1 row.
Dec row K1, [sl 1, K1, psso, K4] 4 times, K1.
Cont in this way, dec 4 sts as set on every alt row until 14 sts rem.
Dec row [P2 tog] 7 times.
Break off yarn, thread end through rem sts, pull up and secure. Join seam, reversing seam on cuff. Turn back cuff. Make one more.

Jester Hat and Gloves

See Page
58

MEASUREMENTS
Jester hat and gloves
To fit age 1–2 (3–4) years

MATERIALS
Hat 1 x 50 g ball of Rowan True 4 ply Botany in each of 3 colours (A, B and C).
Gloves Small amount of Rowan True 4 ply Botany in each of 3 colours (A, B and C).
Pair each of 2¾mm (No 12/US 1) and 3¼ mm (No 10/US 3) knitting needles.

TENSION
28 sts and 36 rows to 10 cm/4 in square over st st on 3¼mm (No 10/US 3) needles.

ABBREVIATIONS
See page 63.

NOTE
When working in pattern, use separate ball for each coloured area and twist yarns together on wrong side at joins to avoid holes.

Rep last 2 rows until work measures 18 (20) cm/7 (8) in from beg, ending with a wrong side row.
Shape Points
Next row With B, K58 (62), turn.
Work in B on this set of sts only. Cont in st st, dec one st at each end of 4th row, then on 2 foll 8th rows.
Now dec one st at each end of every foll 4th row until 28 (30) sts rem, then on every foll alt row until 4 sts rem, ending with a P row. Break off yarn, thread end through rem sts, pull up and secure.
With right side facing, return to rem sts. Work in C on rem sts, K to end. Complete to match first side.
Join back seam to beginning of point shapings, then join seam of each point. With A, make 2 pompons and attach one to end of each point.

Hat

With 2¾mm (No 12/US 1) needles and A, cast on 116 (124) sts.
Work 8 cm/3 in K1, P1 rib.

Change to 3¼mm (No 10/US 3) needles.
Work in patt as follows:
1st row (right side) With B, K58 (62), with C, K58 (62).
2nd row With C, P58 (62), with B, P58 (62).

Gloves

RIGHT HAND

With 2¾mm (No 12/US 1) needles and A, cast on 36 (40) sts.
Work 20 rows in K1, P1 rib, inc 5 (6) sts evenly across last row. 41 (46) sts.
Change to 3¼mm (No 10/US 3) needles and B.
Beg with a K row, work 10 (12) rows in st st. **

Shape for Thumb

Next row K17 (19)B, 9(10)C, turn. Cont in C only.
Next row Cast on 2 sts, P11 (12), turn and cast on 2 sts.
Work 12 (14) rows in st st on these 13 (14) sts only.
Next row K1 (0), [K2 tog] to end.
Next row P1, [P2 tog] to end. 4 sts.
Break off yarn, thread end through rem sts, pull up and secure. Join seam.
With right side facing and B, pick up and K3 sts from base of thumb, then K last 15 (17) sts. 35 (39) sts.
*** Work a further 9 (11) rows in st st across all sts.

Divide for Fingers

Join in C.
Next row K23 (25), turn.
Next row Cast on 1 st, P11 (12), turn and cast on 1 st.
Work 16 (18) rows in st st on these 12 (13) sts only for first finger.
Next row K0 (1), [K2 tog] to end.
Next row P0 (1), [P2 tog] to end. 3 (4) sts.
Break off yarn, thread end through rem sts, pull up and secure. Join seam.
With right side facing rejoin yarn to base of first finger, pick up and K2 sts from base of first finger, K4, turn.
Next row Cast on 1 st, P11 (12), turn and cast on 1 st.
Work 18 (20) rows in st st on these 12 (13) sts only for second finger.
Complete as given for first finger.
With right side facing rejoin yarn to base of second finger, pick up and K2 sts from base of second finger, K4 (5), turn.
Next row Cast on 1 st, P11 (12), turn and cast on 1 st.
Work 16 (18) rows in st st on these 12 (13) sts only for third finger.
Complete as given for first finger.

With right side facing rejoin yarn to base of third finger, pick up and K2 sts from base of third finger, K4 (5). Work 13 (15) rows in st st on rem 11 (12) sts for fourth finger.
Next row K1 (0), [K2 tog] to end.
Next row [P2 tog] to end. 3 sts.
Break off yarn, thread end through rem sts, pull up and secure. Join finger and side seam.

LEFT HAND

Work as given for Right Hand to **.
Shape for thumb
Next row K15 (17)B, 9 (10)C, turn. Cont in C only.
Next row Cast on 2 sts, P11 (12), turn and cast on 2 sts.
Work 12 (14) rows in st st on these 13 (14) sts only.
Next row K1 (0), [K2 tog] to end.
Next row P1, [P2 tog] to end. 4 sts.
Break off yarn, thread end through rem sts, pull up and secure. Join seam. With right side facing and B, pick up and K3 sts from base of thumb, then K last 17 (19) sts. 35 (39) sts. Complete as given for Right Hand from *** to end.

Crochet Bonnet

See Page *59*

MEASUREMENTS

To fit age 1–2 years

MATERIALS

1 x 50 g ball of Rowan Handknit Cotton.
3.50 mm crochet hook.

TENSION

20 sts and 15 rows to 10 cm/4 in square over pattern on 3.50 mm hook.

ABBREVIATIONS

Ch = chain; dc = double crochet; ss = slip stitch; tr = treble.
Also see page 63.

TO MAKE

With 3.50 mm hook, make 4 ch, ss in first ch to form ring.
1st round Work 6 dc into ring, ss in first dc.
2nd round 2 dc in first dc, [1 dc in next dc, 2 dc in next dc] twice, 1 dc in last dc, ss in first dc.
3rd round 2 dc in first dc, [1 dc in next dc, 2 dc in next dc] 4 times, ss in first dc.
4th round 2 dc in first dc, [2 dc in next dc, 1 dc in next dc, 2 dc in next dc] 4 times, 2 dc in last dc, ss in first dc, 24 sts.
5th round 3 ch (counts as tr in first dc), 1

tr in last dc of last round, [miss next dc, 1 tr in next dc, 1 tr in missed dc] to end, ss in top of 3 ch.
6th round 2 dc in top of 3 ch, [2 dc in next tr, 1 dc in next tr. 2 dc in next tr] 7 times, 2 dc in next tr, 1 dc in last tr, ss in first dc. 40 sts.
7th round As 5th round.
8th round 2 dc in top of 3 ch, [2 dc in next tr, 1 dc in each of next 2 tr, 2 dc in next tr] 9 times, 2 dc in next tr, 1 dc in each of last 2 tr, ss in first dc. 60 sts.
9th round As 5th round.
10th round 2 dc in top of 3 ch, [2 dc in next tr, 1 dc in each of next 3 tr, 2 dc in

next tr] 11 times, 2 dc in next tr, 1 dc in each of last 3 tr, ss in first dc. 84 sts.
11th round As 5th round.
12th round 1 dc in top of 3 ch, [1 dc in next tr] to end, ss in first dc.
13th round 1 dc in back loop of first dc, [1 dc in back loop of next dc] to end, ss in first dc, turn.
1st row (wrong side) 3 ch (counts as tr in first dc), [miss next dc, 1 tr in next dc, 1 tr in missed dc] 36 times, 1 tr in next dc, turn. 74 sts.
2nd row 1 dc in first tr, [1 dc in next tr] 72 times, 1 dc in top of 3 ch, turn.
Rep these 2 rows 4 times more, do not turn after last row.
Ties and edgings round Make 51 ch for tie, turn, 1 dc in 2nd ch from hook, [1 dc in next ch] 49 times, now work 35 dc along lower edge of bonnet, make 51 ch for tie, turn, 1 dc in 2nd ch from hook, [1 dc in next ch] 49 times, 1 dc in first dc, [3 ch, ss in 3rd ch from hook (picot made), miss next dc, 1 dc in next dc] to end, ss in last dc. Fasten off.

Lace-trimmed Hat

See Page
59

MEASUREMENTS
To fit age 1 (2–3: 4–5) years

MATERIALS
2 x 50 g balls of any Cotton DK.
Pair of 3¾mm (No 9/US 4) knitting needles.

TENSION
24 sts and 30 rows to 10 cm/4 in square over st st on 3¾mm (No 9/US 4) needles.

ABBREVIATIONS
See page 63.

MAIN PART
With 3¾mm (No 9/US 4) needles cast on 94 (104:114) sts.
Beg with a K row, work 9 (10:11) cm/3½ (4:4½) in in st st, ending with a P row and dec 3 (4:5) sts evenly across last row. 91 (100:109) sts.
Shape top
Dec row K1, [K2 tog, K8 (9:10)] to end.
P 1 row.
Dec row K1, [K2 tog, K7 (8:9)] to end.
P 1 row.
Dec row K1, [K2 tog, K6 (7:8)] to end.
Cont in this way, dec 9 sts as set on every alt row until 19 sts rem.
P 1 row.
Dec row K1, [K2 tog] to end.
Break off yarn, thread end through rem sts, pull up and secure.

BRIM
With 3¾mm (No 9/US 4) needles and right side facing, pick up and K92 (106:113) sts evenly along cast on edge of main part.
Beg with a P row, cont in st st, work 1 row.
Inc row K1, [m1, K6 (7:8), m1, K7 (8:8)] 7 times.
Work 2 rows straight.

Inc row [P8 (9:9), m1, P7 (8:9), m1] 7 times, P1.
Work 2 rows straight.
Inc row K1, [m1, K8 (9:10), m1, K9 (10:10)] 7 times.
Work 2 rows straight.
Inc row [P10 (11:11), m1, P9 (10:11), m1] 7 times, P1. 148 (162:169) sts.
K 1 row. Cast off purlwise.

EDGING
With 3¾mm (No 9/US 4) needles cast on 4 sts.
1st row (wrong side) K2, yf, K2.
2nd row and 2 foll alt rows K.
3rd row K3, yf, K2.
5th row K2, yf, K2 tog, yf, K2.
7th row K3, yf, K2 tog, yf, K2.
8th row Cast off 4, K to end.
These 8 rows form patt. Cont in patt until edging fits around brim, ending with 8th row. Cast off. Sew edging to brim. Join seam.

Aran Scarf and Fingerless Gloves

See Page
61

MATERIALS
Scarf 3 x 50 g balls of Rowan True 4 ply Botany.
One 3¼mm (No 10/US 3) circular knitting needle.
Pair each of 2¾mm (No 12/US 1) and 3¼ mm (No 10/US 3) knitting needles.
Cable needle.
Gloves 1 x 50 g ball of Rowan True 4 ply Botany.
Pair each of 2¾mm (No 12/US 1) and 3 mm (No 11/US 2) knitting needles.

MEASUREMENTS
Aran scarf and fingerless gloves
To fit age 3 years

TENSION
38 sts and 40 rows to 10 cm/4 in square over pattern on 3¼mm (No 10/US 3) needles.
30 sts and 38 rows to 10 cm/4 in square over st st on 3 mm (No 11/US 2) needles.

ABBREVIATIONS
C4B = slip next 2 sts onto cable needle and leave at back, K2, then K2 from cable needle.
C4F = slip next 2 sts onto cable needle and leave at front, K2, then K2 from cable needle.
Cr3L = slip next 2 sts onto cable needle and leave at front, P1, then K2 from cable needle.
Cr3R = slip next st onto cable needle and leave at back, K2, then P1 from cable needle
Also see page 63.

Scarf

PANEL A – worked over 20 sts.
1st row (right side) [P2, Cr3R] twice, [Cr3L, P2] twice.
2nd row K2, P2, K3, P2, K2, P2, K3, P2, K2.
3rd row P1, [Cr3R, P2] twice, Cr3L, P2, Cr3L, P1.
4th row K1, P2, K3, P2, K4, P2, K3, P2, K1.
5th row [Cr3R, P2] twice, pick up loop lying between st just worked and next st and work [K1, P1, K1] all into the back of it, turn, P3, turn, K3, turn, P3, turn, P3 tog, P1 then pass bobble st over first st, P1, Cr3L, P2, Cr3L.

6th row [P2, K3] twice, [K3, P2] twice.
7th row [Cr3L, P2] twice, [P2, Cr3R] twice.
8th row As 4th row.
9th row P1, [Cr3L, P2] twice, Cr3R, P2, Cr3R, P1.
10th row As 2nd row.
11th row [P2, Cr3L] twice, [Cr3R, P2] twice.
12th row [K3, P2] twice, [P2, K3] twice.
These 12 rows form patt.

PANEL B – worked over 6 sts.
1st row (right side) P1, K4, P1.
2nd row K1, P4, K1.
3rd row P1, C4F, P1.
4th row As 2nd row.
These 4 rows form patt.

PANEL C – worked over 10 sts.
1st row (right side) P1, K8, P1.
2nd row and 2 foll alt rows K1, P8, K1.
3rd row P1, C4B, C4F, P1.
5th row As 1st row.
7th row P1, C4F, C4B, P1.
8th row As 2nd row.
These 8 rows form patt.

PANEL D – worked over 6 sts.
1st row (right side) P1, K4, P1.
2nd row K1, P4, K1.

3rd row P1, C4B, P1.
4th row As 2nd row.
These 4 rows form patt.

FIRST SIDE

With 3¼-mm (No 10/US 3) needles cast on 21 sts.
1st row (wrong side) K1, work 12th row of Panel A.
2nd row Cast on 6 sts, work 3rd row of Panel D, work 1st row of Panel A, P1.
3rd row K1, work 2nd row of Panel A, work 4th row of Panel D.
4th row Cast on 10 sts, work 1st row of Panel C, work 1st row of Panel D, patt to last st, P1.
5th row K1, patt 20, work 2nd row of Panel D and Panel C.
6th row Cast on 6 sts, work 3rd row of Panel B, patt to last 3 sts, work 3 tog.
7th row Work 2 tog, patt to last 6 sts, work 4th row of Panel B.
8th row Cast on 20 sts, work 7th row of Panel A, work 1st row of Panel B, patt to last 2 sts, work 2 tog.
9th row Work 2 tog, patt to last 26 sts, work 2nd row of Panel B and 8th row of Panel A.
Cont in this way, casting on 6 sts for Panel D at beg of next row, 10 sts for Panel C at beg of foll alt row, 6 sts for Panel B at beg of foll alt row, then 20 sts for Panel A at beg of foll alt row, at the same time, dec one st at end of next row and at same edge on foll 2 rows, then 2 sts at same edge on next row and one st at same edge on foll 3 rows until there are 160 sts, ending with a wrong side row and 5th set of 6 cast on sts for Panel D. Leave these sts on a spare needle.

SECOND SIDE

With 3¼-mm (No 10/US 3) needles cast on 21 sts.
1st row (right side) P1, work 1st row of Panel A.
2nd row Cast on 6 sts, work 4th row of Panel B and 2nd row of Panel A, K1.
3rd row P1, patt 20, work 1st row of Panel B.
4th row Cast on 10 sts, work 2nd row of Panel C and Panel B, patt to last st, K1.
5th row Work 3 tog, patt to last 10 sts, work 3rd row of Panel C.
6th row Cast on 6 sts, work 4th row of Panel D and Panel C, patt to last 2 sts, work 2 tog.

7th row Work 2 tog, patt to last 6 sts, work 1st row of Panel D.
8th row Cast on 20 sts, work 8th row of Panel A and 2nd row of Panel D, patt to last 2 sts, work 2 tog.
Cont in this way, dec one st at beg of next row and at same edge on 2 foll rows, then 2 sts at same edge on next row and one st at same edge on foll 3 rows, at the same time, casting on 6 sts for Panel B at beg of foll alt row, 10 sts for Panel C at beg of foll alt row, 6 sts for Panel D at beg of foll alt row, then 20 sts for Panel A at beg of foll alt row until there are 160 sts, ending with a wrong side row and 5th set of 6 cast on sts for Panel B.
Change to 3¼-mm (No 10/US 3) circular needle. Work backwards and forwards.
Next row Work 2 tog, patt to end, cast on 10 sts for Panel C, patt across first side to last 2 sts, work 2 tog, 328 sts.
Cont in patt, dec one st at each end of next 3 rows, 2 sts at each end of next row, then one st at each end of foll 3 rows until 2 sts rem.
Work 2 tog and fasten off.

EDGINGS

With 2¾-mm (No 12/US 1) needles and right side facing, pick up and K194 sts evenly along one short edge. Work 6 rows in K1, P1 rib, inc one st at each end of every alt row. Cast off in rib.
Work other short edge in same way.
With 2¾-mm (No 12/US 1) needles and right side facing, pick up and K306 sts evenly along long edge omitting edgings. Work 6 rows in K1, P1 rib, inc one st at each end of every alt row. Cast off in rib.

TO MAKE UP

Mitre all corners. Make 3 pompons and attach one to each corner.

Fingerless Gloves

With 2¾-mm (No 12/US 1) needles cast on 39 sts.
1st row (right side) K1, [P1, K1] to end.
2nd row P1, [K1, P1] to end.
Rep last 2 rows until work measures 4 cm/1½ in from beg, ending with a 2nd row.
Change to 3 mm (No 11/US 2) needles.
Beg with a K row, cont in st st, work 4 rows.

Shape for Thumb

Inc row K19, m1, K1, m1, K19.
P 1 row.
Inc row K19, m1, K3, m1, K19.
P 1 row.
Inc row K19, m1, K5, m1, K19.
Cont in this way, inc 2 sts as set on every alt row until there are 49 sts.
P 1 row.
Next row K30, turn.
Next row Cast on 2, P13, turn and cast on 2 sts.
Work on these 15 sts only.
** Change to 2¾-mm (No 12/US 1) needles. Rep 1st and 2nd rows twice. Cast off in rib. Join seam. **
With right side facing, rejoin yarn to base of thumb and with 3 mm (No 11/US 2) needles, pick up and K3 sts from base of thumb, K rem sts. 41 sts.
Work 11 rows.

Shape for Fingers

Next row K26, turn.
Next row Cast on 1 st, P12, turn and cast on 1 st.
Work on these 13 sts only for first finger as given for thumb from ** to **.
With right side facing, rejoin yarn to base of first finger and with 3 mm (No 11/US 2) needles, pick up and K2 sts from base of first finger, K5, turn.
Next row Cast on 1 st, P13, turn and cast on 1 st.
Work on these 14 sts only for second finger.
Change to 2¾-mm (No 12/US 1) needles and work 4 rows in K1, P1 rib.
Cast off in rib. Join seam.
With right side facing, rejoin yarn to base of second finger and with 3 mm (No 11/US 2) needles, pick up and K2 sts from base of second finger, K5, turn.
Next row Cast on 1 st, P6, P2 tog, P5, turn and cast on 1 st.
Work on these 13 sts only for third finger as given for thumb from ** to **.
With right side facing, rejoin yarn to base of third finger and with 3 mm (No 11/US 2) needles, pick up and K2 sts from base of third finger, K5, turn, P12.
Work on these 12 sts for fourth finger.
Change to 2¾-mm (No 12/US 1) needles and work 4 rows in K1, P1 rib. Cast off in rib. Join finger and side seam.
Make one more.

African-style Hat

See Page 60

MEASUREMENTS
To fit age 1–2 years

MATERIALS
1 x 50 g ball of Rowan Handknit Cotton in Black (M).
Small amount of same in each of Jade (A) and Brick (B).
Pair of 3¾mm (No 9/US 5) knitting needles. Medium-size crochet hook.

TENSION
22 sts and 28 rows to 10 cm/4 in square over st st on 3¾mm (No 9/US 5) needles.

ABBREVIATIONS
Ch = chain; dc = double crochet.
Also see page 63.

NOTE
Read Chart from right to left on K rows and from left to right on P rows. When working in pattern, strand M and A yarns when not in use loosely across wrong side over no more than 4 sts at a time to keep fabric elastic; use separate lengths of B yarn for each motif and twist yarns together on wrong side at joins to avoid holes.

MAIN PART
With 3¾mm (No 9/US 5) needles and M, cast on 109 sts.
Beg with a K row, work 2 rows in st st.
Cont in st st and patt from Chart until 17th row of Chart has been worked. Cont in M only, P 1 row.

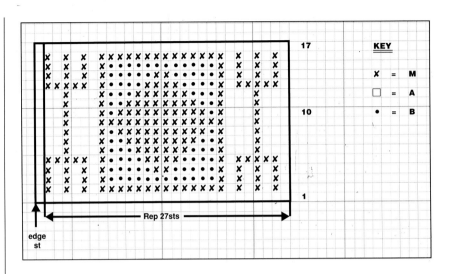

KEY

X = M

☐ = A

• = B

Rep 27sts

edge st

Dec row [K8, K2 tog] to last 9 sts, K9. 99 sts
Cast off purlwise.

CROWN
With 3¾mm (No 9/US 5) needles and M, cast on 99 sts. K 1 row. P 1 row.
Dec row [K9, K2 tog] to end.
P 1 row.
Dec row [K8, K2 tog] to end.
P 1 row.
Dec row [K7, K2 tog] to end.
Cont in this way, dec 9 sts as set on every alt row until 18 sts rem. P1 row.
Dec row [K2 tog] to end.
Break off yarn, thread end through rem sts, pull up and secure.

TO MAKE UP
Work crochet edging along cast on (lower) edge of main part as follows:
With crochet hook, right side facing and M, work 1 row of dc. DO NOT TURN. Now work 1 row of backward dc (dc worked from left to right). Fasten off. Work crochet edging along top edge of main part. Join seam of main part and crown. Sew crown in place, just below crochet edging. Make stalk as follows: With crochet hook and M, make 5 ch.
1st row 1 dc in 2nd ch from hook, 1 dc in each of next 3 ch, turn.
2nd row 1 ch, miss first dc, 1 dc in each of next 3 dc, turn.
Rep 2nd row once. Fasten off.
Fold stalk in half lengthwise and join seam all round. Attach to top of crown.

Fair Isle Beret and Gloves

See Page 62

MEASUREMENTS
Fair Isle beret and gloves
To fit age 5–7 years

MATERIALS
2 x 50 g balls of Rowan Designer DK Wool in Natural (MC).
Small amount of same in each of Light Blue (A), Dark Blue (B), Light Yellow (C), Dark Yellow (D), Navy (E), Red (F) and Pink (G).
Pair each of 3¼mm (No 10/US 3), 3¾mm (No 9/US 4) and 4 mm (No 8/US 5) knitting needles.

TENSION
22 sts and 28 rows to 10 cm/4 in square over st st on 4 mm (No 8/US 5) needles.

ABBREVIATIONS
See page 63.

NOTE
Read Chart from right to left on K rows and from left to right on P rows. When working in pattern, strand yarn not in use loosely across wrong side over no more than 4 sts at a time to keep fabric elastic.

Beret

With 3¼mm (No 10/US 3) needles and MC, cast on 92 sts. Work 7 rows in K1, P1 rib.
Inc row Rib 6, [m1, rib 2] to last 4 sts, rib 4. 133 sts.
Change to 4 mm (No 8/US 5) needles.
Beg with a K row and working in st st throughout work 2 rows.
Next row 1MC, [1E, 1MC] to end.
Next row 1E, [1MC, 1E] to end.
Work 1 row MC.
Inc row With MC, P3, [m1, P5] to end. 159 sts.
Work patt as follows:

142

1st row 2MC, [1F, 1MC, 1F, 5MC] to last 5 sts, 1F, 1MC, 1F, 2MC.
2nd row 1MC, [2F, 1MC, 2F, 3MC] to last 6 sts, 2F, 1MC, 2F, 1MC.
3rd row 3MC, [1G, 3MC] to end.
4th row As 2nd row.
5th row As 1st row.
Work 1 row MC.
Inc row With MC, K1, m1, K4, m1, [K7, m1] to last 7 sts, K6, m1, K1. 183 sts.
Now work 1st to 19th rows of Chart.
Shape Top
Dec row With A, K1, * [K2 tog] 3 times, K1, [K2 tog] 4 times, [K1, K2 tog] twice, [K2 tog] twice, K1; rep from * to end. 106 sts.
Next row With A, P to last 2 sts, P2 tog.
Next row 1A, [1E, 1A] to end.
Next row 1E, [1MC, 1E] to end.
Work 2 rows MC.
Dec row With MC, K1, K2 tog, *[K1F, 1MC] twice, with MC, [K2 tog] 4 times; rep from * to last 6 sts, K1F, 1MC, 1F, with MC, K2 tog, K1, 71 sts.
Now work 2nd to 5th rows of patt, then work 1 row MC.
Dec row With MC, K1, *[K2 tog, K1] twice, K2 tog; rep from * to last 6 sts, [K2 tog, K1] twice. 45 sts.
Next row 1E, [1MC, 1E] to end.
Next row 1A, [1E, 1A] to end.
Work 3 rows A.
Dec row With A, K1, [K2 tog] to end.
P 1 row A.
Dec row With A, K1, [K2 tog] to end. 12 sts.
Break off yarn, thread end through rem sts, pull up and secure. Join seam.

Gloves

RIGHT HAND
With 3¼-mm (No 10/US 3) needles and MC, cast on 36 sts.
Work 4 cm/1½ in in K1, P1 rib.
Inc row Rib 2, [inc in next st, rib 5] to last 4 sts, inc in next st, rib 3. 42 sts.
Change to 4 mm (No 8/US 5) needles.
Beg with a K row and working in st st throughout, work 2 rows.
Work patt from Chart as follows:
1st row (right side) Work 4th to 24th sts of

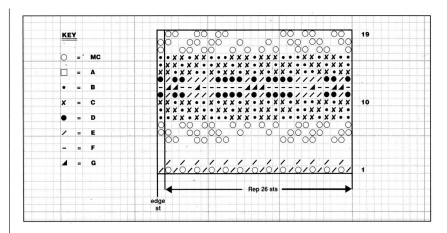

the 26 sts of 1st row of Chart twice.
2nd row Work 24th to 4th sts of the 26 sts of 2nd row of Chart twice.
Cont working from Chart as set, work a further 10 rows.**
Shape for Thumb
Next row Patt 22, with MC, K7, turn.
Change to 3¾-mm (No 9/US 4) needles.
Next row With MC, P7, turn and cast on 6 sts.
*** Work in MC on these 13 sts only for 14 rows.
Dec row K1, [K2 tog] to end.
P1 row. Break off yarn, thread end through rem sts, pull up and secure.
Join seam.
With right side facing, 4 mm (No 8/US 5) needles and colours as required by patt, pick up and K7 sts from base of thumb, patt to end. 42 sts.
Work a further 6 rows in patt, then work 1 row A.
Dec row With A, [K4, K2 tog, K5, K2 tog] 3 times, K3. 36 sts.
Next row [P1E, 1A] to end.
Next row [K1E, 1MC] to end.
Change to 3¾-mm (No 9/US 4) needles.
Cont in MC only, work 1 row.
Shape for Fingers
Next row K23, turn.
Next row Cast on 1 st, P11, turn and cast on 1 st.
Work 16 rows on these 12 sts only for first finger.
Dec row [K2 tog] to end.

P 1 row. Break off yarn, thread end through rem sts, pull up and secure.
Join seam.
With right side facing, rejoin yarn to base of first finger, pick up and K2 sts from base of first finger, K5, turn.
Next row Cast on 1 st, P13, turn and cast on 1 st.
Work 18 rows on these 14 sts only for second finger. Complete as given for first finger.
With right side facing, rejoin yarn to base of second finger, pick up and K2 sts from base of second finger, K4, turn.
Next row Cast on 1 st, P11, turn and cast on 1 st.
Work 16 rows on these 12 sts only for third finger. Complete as given for first finger.
With right side facing, rejoin yarn to base of third finger, pick up and K3 sts from base of third finger, K rem 4 sts. Work 11 rows on rem 11 sts for fourth finger.
Dec row K1, [K2 tog] to end.
P 1 row. Break off yarn, thread end through rem sts, pull up and secure.
Join finger and side seam.

LEFT HAND
Work as given for Right Hand to **.
Shape for Thumb
Next row Patt 13, with MC, K7, turn.
Change to 3¾-mm (No 9/US 4) needles.
Next row With MC, cast on 6 sts, P13, turn.
Complete as given for Right Hand from *** to end.

Yarn Source Guide

Rowan Yarn Addresses
Rowan Yarns are widely available in yarn shops. For details of stockists and mail order sources of Rowan Yarns, please write or contact the distributors listed below.
For advice on how to use a substitute yarn, see page 63.

UNITED KINGDOM
Rowan Yarns,
Green Lane Mill, Holmfirth,
West Yorkshire, England
HD7 1RW
Tel: (01484) 681 881

USA
Westminster Trading Corporation,
5 Northern Boulevard, Amherst,
NH 03031
Tel: (603) 886 5041/5043

AUSTRALIA
Rowan (Australia),
191 Canterbury Road,
Canterbury, Victoria 3126
Tel: (03) 830 1609

BELGIUM
Hedera,
Pleinstraat 68,
3001 Leuven
Tel: (016) 23 21 89

CANADA
Diamond Yarn,
9697 St Laurent, Montreal,
Quebec, H3L 2NI
Tel: (514) 388 6188

155 Martin Ross, Unit 3,
Toronto, Ontario M3J 2L9
Tel: (416) 736 6111

DENMARK
Ruzicka,
Hydesbyvej 27,
DK 4990 Saskoing
Tel: (8) 54 70 78 04

FRANCE
Elle Tricote,
52 Rue Principale,
67300 Schiltigheim
Tel: (33) 88 62 65 31

GERMANY
Wolle + Design,
Wolfshover Strasse 76,
52428 Julich Stetternich
Tel: (49) 2461 54735

HOLLAND
de Afstap,
Oude Leliestraat 12,
1015 Amsterdam
Tel: (020) 623 1445

HONG KONG
East Unity Company Ltd,
RM 902, Block A, Kailey Industrial Centre,
12 Fung Yip Street, Chai Wan
Tel: (852) 2869 7110

ICELAND
Stockurinn,
Kjorgardi, Laugavegi 59,
ICE-101 Reykjavik
Tel: (01) 551 82 58

ITALY
Victoriana,
Via Fratelli Pioli 14,
Rivoli, Torino
Tel: (011) 95 32 142

JAPAN
Diakeito Co Ltd,
2-3-11 Senba-Higashi, Minoh City,
Osaka 562
Tel: (0727) 27 6604

NORWAY
Eureka,
PO Box 357, N-1401 Ski
Tel: (64) 86 55 70

SWEDEN
Wincent,
Sveavagen 94,113 58 Stockholm
Tel: (08) 673 70 60

Yarn, kits, ready-to-wear garments, books and toys
are available from Debbie Bliss's shop:

Debbie Bliss,
365 St. John Street,
London, EC1.